Crazy History Facts Book

CRAFTED BY SKRIUWER

Copyright © 2025 by Skriuwer.

All rights reserved. No part of this book may be used or reproduced in any form whatsoever without written permission except in the case of brief quotations in critical articles or reviews.

At **Skriuwer**, we're more than just a team—we're a global community of people who love books. In Frisian, "Skriuwer" means "writer," and that's at the heart of what we do: creating and sharing books with readers worldwide. Wherever you are in the world, **Skriuwer** is here to inspire learning.

Frisian is one of the oldest languages in Europe, closely related to English and Dutch, and is spoken by about **500,000 people** in the province of **Friesland** (Fryslân), located in the northern Netherlands. It's the second official language of the Netherlands, but like many minority languages, Frisian faces the challenge of survival in a modern, globalized world.

We're using the money we earn to promote the Frisian language.

For more information, contact : **kontakt@skriuwer.com** (www.skriuwer.com)

Disclaimer:
The images in this book are creative reinterpretations of historical scenes. While every effort was made to accurately capture the essence of the periods depicted, some illustrations may include artistic embellishments or approximations. They are intended to evoke the atmosphere and spirit of the times rather than serve as precise historical records.

TABLE OF CONTENTS

CHAPTER 1: STRANGE BEGINNINGS: ODD FACTS ABOUT EARLY CIVILIZATIONS

- *Earliest city-states and bizarre rituals in Mesopotamia*
- *Mysterious Indus Valley planning and hidden scripts*
- *Surprising burial customs and ancestor veneration*

CHAPTER 2: THE MYSTERIOUS MIDDLE KINGDOM: WEIRD TALES FROM ANCIENT CHINA

- *Oracle bones, dynastic power, and human sacrifices*
- *The "Mandate of Heaven" and odd imperial rituals*
- *Terracotta Army and Qin Shi Huang's quest for immortality*

CHAPTER 3: ECCENTRIC EMPIRES: PECULIAR CUSTOMS IN MESOPOTAMIA & PERSIA

- *Babylonian laws, fierce Assyrians, and magical lion hunts*
- *Persian royal roads, satraps, and bizarre funeral rites*
- *Zoroastrian fire temples and the Immortals' elite guard*

CHAPTER 4: MARVELOUS MYTHS: ODD TRADITIONS FROM ANCIENT GREECE

- *Oracle of Delphi, sacred games, and strange festivals*
- *Wild gods, monstrous creatures, and heroic epics*
- *Spartan discipline and the Athenian democracy's quirks*

CHAPTER 5: ROMAN ODDITIES: STRANGE STORIES FROM THE ETERNAL CITY

- *Sacred chickens, gladiator games, and emperor cults*
- *Scandalous feasts, vomitoriums, and bizarre punishments*
- *Foreign gods, architecture marvels, and curious beliefs*

CHAPTER 6: EERIE EGYPT: HIDDEN SECRETS AND BIZARRE RITUALS

- *Mummification processes, canopic jars, and pharaoh tombs*
- *Animal cults, giant pyramids, and the strange gods*
- *Architectural wonders like obelisks and labyrinthine temples*

CHAPTER 7: BARBARIAN NATIONS: SURPRISING FACTS ABOUT EUROPE'S EARLY TRIBES

- *Celtic head-hunting, druidic lore, and women warriors*
- *Germanic comitatus, trial by ordeal, and migration legends*
- *Mix of tribal customs and early contact with Rome*

CHAPTER 8: MEDIEVAL CURIOSITIES: KNIGHTS, CASTLES, AND STRANGE EVENTS

- *Feudal oaths, jousts, and code of chivalry extremes*
- *Witch trials, relic manias, and bizarre medical practices*
- *Symposia, festivals, and odd punishments*

CHAPTER 9: DARK TIMES: WEIRD LEGENDS & UNUSUAL BELIEFS

- *Medieval superstition, dancing plagues, and doomsday fears*
- *Mythical beasts, fairies, and the cult of relics*
- *Flagellants, witch hunts, and hidden Christian sects*

CHAPTER 10: RENAISSANCE WONDERS: ODD DETAILS OF A CHANGING WORLD

- *Rebirth of art, da Vinci's strange machines, and alchemy*
- *Courtly intrigues, patronage, and eccentric inventions*
- *Astrology, exploration, and the first hints of modern science*

CHAPTER 11: AGE OF EXPLORATION: STRANGE JOURNEYS & SHOCKING DISCOVERIES

- *Columbus's mix-up, myths of monstrous races, and lost gold*
- *Magellan's fatal circumnavigation and Pacific encounters*
- *Cannibal rumors, sea creatures, and cross-cultural confusion*

CHAPTER 12: CONQUESTS & COLONIES: CURIOUS EVENTS FROM GROWING EMPIRES

- *Encomiendas, missionary zeal, and colonial competition*
- *African coastal empires, odd trade alliances, and forced labor*
- *Settlement patterns, rebellions, and early global networks*

CHAPTER 13: ODD KINGDOMS: STRANGE TALES FROM AFRICAN EMPIRES

- *Ghana, Mali, and Songhai with gold wealth and lavish courts*
- *Benin bronzes, Ethiopia's Ark legend, and Zimbabwe's stone complexes*
- *Spirit mediums, Luba memory boards, and unusual succession rules*

CHAPTER 14: WILD WORLDS IN THE AMERICAS: SURPRISING FACTS OF AZTECS, MAYA, AND MORE

- *Maya calendars, Aztec sacrifices, and Inca mummies*
- *Mound builders, cliff dwellings, and lost city myths*
- *Ballgames, bloodletting, and elaborate empire structures*

CHAPTER 15: ANCIENT INDIA'S WONDERS: STRANGE CUSTOMS & BELIEFS

- *Indus Valley enigma, Vedic rituals, and epic tales*
- *Maurya and Gupta empires with iron pillars and zero concept*
- *Sadhus' ascetic extremes, temple erotica, and odd medicine*

CHAPTER 16: SHOGUNS & SAMURAI: FASCINATING FEUDAL JAPAN

- *Bushido code, seppuku rites, and ninja espionage*
- *Tea ceremony, isolationism, and masked feudal intrigues*
- *Geisha arts, sumo spectacles, and the downfall of the shogunate*

CHAPTER 17: ROYAL SCANDALS: HIDDEN SECRETS OF KINGS AND QUEENS

- *Cleopatra's tangled marriages, Byzantine plots, and poison rumors*
- *European court intrigues, mother-son feuds, and bizarre executions*
- *Empress Wu's rise, Ottoman harems, and African queen conundrums*

CHAPTER 18: PIRATE LEGENDS: ODD FACTS FROM THE HIGH SEAS

- *Democratic pirate codes, treasure myths, and secret havens*
- *Female pirates, flamboyant flags, and terrifying reputations*
- *Collisions with navies, merciless trials, and flamboyant last stands*

CHAPTER 19: THE START OF INDUSTRIAL CHANGE: CRAZY INVENTIONS & SURPRISING ADVANCES

- *Steam engines, spinning machines, and factory life shocks*
- *Luddite rebellions, canal mania, and iron bridges*
- *Railway fears, balloon mania, and medical quirks*

CHAPTER 20: NINETEENTH CENTURY SHIFTS: STRANGE EVENTS BEFORE MODERN TIMES

- *Political upheavals, odd wars, and global colonial grabs*
- *Darwin's evolution debate, spiritual séances, and utopian communes*
- *Railroads worldwide, last empires forming, and steps into modernity*

CHAPTER 1

Strange Beginnings: Odd Facts About Early Civilizations

In this chapter, we will travel far back in time to the earliest civilizations. These were the first groups of people to form complex societies with cities, kings, priests, and many special customs. People often think that these ancient societies were dull or very simple, but the truth is that they were filled with strange rules, mysterious rituals, and odd inventions. Here, we will explore some of these early societies, such as the Sumerians, Babylonians, and others in the region called Mesopotamia. We will also learn about the Indus Valley civilization and the early peoples around the Nile River and other parts of the world. There are many bizarre facts waiting for us as we step into the world of ancient times.

1. Ancient Mesopotamia: Land Between Rivers

Mesopotamia means "land between rivers." This region lay between the Tigris and Euphrates Rivers in what is now the Middle East. Today, this place might not seem very green, but long ago, it was the birthplace of some of the first city-states and kingdoms. The Sumerians were among the first people to settle here, building cities like Uruk and Ur. They made impressive temples called ziggurats, which were tall, tower-like structures built in steps. Priests would stand on top to talk to their gods.

But let's begin with a really weird fact: some of the earliest written records from Sumer were not about great heroes or kings. Instead, they were about beer. Yes, beer! The Sumerians loved to brew and drink beer. They even had poems and hymns praising Ninkasi, the goddess of brewing. It might sound odd to us, but beer was safer to drink than river water, which often carried diseases. It was also a key part of their diet.

The Sumerians also had some very strict laws about daily life. One set of rules, known as the Code of Ur-Nammu, is one of the oldest legal codes in the world. It had punishments for different crimes, including some that sound strange to us. For example, if a person accused someone else of witchcraft, the suspect might have to jump in the river. If the suspect drowned, they were found guilty, but if they floated, they were innocent. This method might remind us of later witch trials in other parts of the world, but the Sumerians did it first.

Another unusual Sumerian practice had to do with how people paid for goods. Instead of using coins for everything, they often used barley as money. Imagine going to a shop and paying with handfuls of grain instead of coins or paper bills. It must have been hard to carry around.

2. Babylonians and Their Crazy Observations

After the Sumerians, the Babylonians rose to power in Mesopotamia. Their most famous king was Hammurabi, known for his set of laws called the Code of Hammurabi. People are sometimes surprised to see that many parts of these laws had to do with property, money, and even medical costs. For instance, if a doctor saved your life, there was a set fee. But if the doctor messed up, he could have his hands cut off. That is a very harsh punishment!

The Babylonians also watched the sky. They kept detailed records of the movements of stars and planets. Some of their beliefs about these heavenly bodies were quite strange. They thought the positions of planets could predict when a king would die or if the harvest would fail. They wrote these predictions on clay tablets. Some historians say this was an early form of astrology. Although many of these ideas seem odd to us today, they were serious business back then. If the stars warned of danger, priests might tell a king to hide or perform a certain ritual to please the gods.

Babylonian temples also served as places to study math. In fact, the Babylonians used a base-60 number system. That is why we still have 60 minutes in an hour and 360 degrees in a circle. It might not be "crazy," but it is surprising that something so old remains part of our daily life. We often take it for granted, never thinking about how it began.

---

3. Assyrians: Fierce Warriors with Odd Customs

The Assyrians were known for being fierce warriors who built a mighty empire in Mesopotamia. But aside from war, they had some strange customs. One of the strangest had to do with how they treated lions. Lions once roamed parts of this region, and the Assyrian kings loved to show off their bravery by hunting them. They would invite important guests to watch these lion hunts, which were more like staged battles. The lions were sometimes kept in cages and then released for the king to kill. This might seem cruel to us now, but to the Assyrians, it was a big show of power.

Another strange practice was the way they carved magical symbols onto their walls. The Assyrians believed in protective spirits and demons. They thought certain symbols or statues placed at city gates could scare away evil forces. In some palaces, archaeologists have found hidden figurines of strange creatures with human heads and animal bodies. These figures were buried under doorways or inside walls. Imagine living in a giant palace that had hidden statues to keep away ghosts and evil spirits. That might have been quite spooky!

---

4. The Indus Valley Civilization: Mystery and Surprise

While Mesopotamia was thriving, the Indus Valley civilization was also growing in what is now Pakistan and northwest India. Cities like Harappa and Mohenjo-daro were large and well planned. They had straight streets and advanced drainage systems. This civilization is still full of mysteries because we have not fully deciphered their writing. We see symbols on seals and pottery, but we do not know for sure what they mean.

One of the strange facts about the Indus people is that they built what might have been the first public bath or swimming pool in the ancient world. Archaeologists call it the Great Bath. It was a huge pool built with baked bricks and a drainage system. It seems they took cleanliness and bathing seriously. This might suggest some form of religious ritual involving water, or it might have been just for ordinary use. We are not sure.

Even more mysterious is that the Indus cities do not seem to have grand palaces or big temples like we see in Mesopotamia or Egypt. This has led some researchers to guess that they might have had a more equal society without huge class differences. But nobody knows for sure because we cannot read their writing. It is quite amazing how such a large civilization left behind so few clues we can understand. This puzzle makes the Indus Valley civilization both fascinating and strange.

---

5. Early Farming Communities and Surprising Jobs

Long before big cities, people lived in small farming villages. They grew crops like wheat, barley, and later rice. But they also had some unusual jobs and roles. For example, in many Neolithic (New Stone Age) settlements, certain people became experts in tool-making. They would shape stone blades, arrowheads, and other tools with great care. Others might have focused on making pottery. As time went on, some communities had special craftworkers who made only jewelry or wove cloth.

One strange fact about early farming communities is that they sometimes built houses one on top of another. In a place called Çatalhöyük (in modern-day Turkey), people built their homes so closely that they entered from the roof instead of a door on the ground level. They even buried their dead under the floors of their houses. Imagine living in a house where your ancestors' bones might be right under your bedroom floor. This might seem scary to us, but for them, it could have been a way to keep family close.

Another odd custom was the use of plaster to shape the skulls of the dead. Archaeologists have found skulls covered in plaster, with shells used for eyes. This practice is often linked to the idea of honoring ancestors. We are not sure if it was to keep them in the community or to show respect, but either way, it is quite an eerie find.

---

6. Strange Beliefs About the Afterlife

Many ancient cultures had beliefs about life after death, and they often used complex burial customs. For instance, in ancient Jericho, as mentioned, some people kept skulls of their ancestors and displayed them. Other cultures placed food, tools, or personal belongings in tombs. They believed the dead would need these items in the next world. The strangest part is sometimes these items included real animals or even servants to serve the dead person in the afterlife.

In some places, like in ancient China (though that is for the next chapter), servants and animals might be buried with important people. But similar customs popped up in different early societies. It shows how widespread the belief in an afterlife was, even if the details were different. These beliefs might look odd to us now, but it was a key part of how ancient people understood life and death.

---

7. Ancient Tools and Crazy Inventions

It might surprise some to learn about the clever inventions ancient people made. We have already mentioned beer, advanced drains, and the base-60 number system. But there are many more. The earliest known wheels were invented in Mesopotamia. The potter's wheel may have come first, then the wheel for carts. This changed how goods and people moved across land.

Another early invention was the plow for farming. At first, people used sticks to poke holes in the ground, but over time, they attached stronger blades to frames so animals could pull them. This made it easier to grow crops and feed more people.

We should also remember the earliest calendars. Ancient farmers needed to know when to plant or harvest, so they watched the seasons and stars. The Sumerian and Egyptian calendars were especially important. They marked out days and months based on the sun, moon, or a mix of both. Though they were not always perfectly accurate, these calendars helped people organize large groups to work together. It might seem simple to us now, but it was a giant leap for people back then.

---

8. Bizarre Rituals and Festivities

People in the earliest civilizations often held festivals to honor their gods. Some of these festivals were joyful, with dancing, singing, and feasting. Others had more unusual elements. For example, in parts of Mesopotamia, there was a New Year festival where the king might be ritually humiliated. A priest could slap the king's face to make him cry, which was believed to show that the king was humble before the gods. To us, this might look like a bizarre way of celebrating, but to them, it was part of a ceremony to bring luck and blessings for the year ahead.

Then there was the concept of sacred prostitution in some temples, though historians still argue about how common it was. Some sources suggest that women would offer themselves in a temple to please a goddess, and men would pay money to the temple. This would seem extremely odd in many societies now, but in the ancient world, certain temples were believed to represent fertility and the power of creation. These ideas might shock us, but they were part of the culture back then.

9. Animal Worship and Strange Creatures

Many early civilizations respected or even worshipped animals. In Mesopotamia, gods and goddesses were often shown with animal-like features or animals by their side. The bull was a popular symbol of power. You might see carvings of winged bulls with human heads, called lamassu, placed at city gates as guardians.

It is also interesting how people created mythical creatures by mixing different animals. The Sumerians and Babylonians believed in creatures like the lion-dragon or the bull-lion. These creatures appeared on royal seals and palace walls, perhaps to show the king's might or to scare away evil. We might see these images as part of an old fantasy story, but for them, it was part of religion and state power.

---

10. Daily Life: Food, Clothing, and Family

In early civilizations, the day-to-day life could be surprising. For instance, in Mesopotamia, clothing was made from wool or flax. Wealthy people might wear more colorful outfits, dyed with natural pigments. Ordinary folks wore simple clothes. They often ate barley porridge, bread, onions, and fruits. Meat was a luxury, except for fish, which was more common along rivers.

Families could be large, and children were expected to help out at home or in the fields. Women sometimes ran businesses, especially if they were widowed or if their husbands traveled. These societies might sound old-fashioned to us, but in some ways, they had freedoms or practices we might not expect.

---

11. The Odd Rise and Fall of Kingdoms

Another crazy fact about these early civilizations is how quickly they could fall apart after reaching greatness. Sumerian city-states fought each other often. One city might become very powerful, then lose control to another. At times, outside groups, like the Akkadians, came in, took over, and started their own empire. Centuries later, the Babylonian Empire rose, then the Assyrian Empire took power. After the Assyrians, the Neo-Babylonian Empire appeared. This cycle of rise and fall was like a repeating pattern, sometimes caused by war, other times by drought or economic problems.

It is also strange how new rulers would sometimes adopt the gods and traditions of the people they conquered. Instead of trying to force their own ways on everyone, they just blended customs. This mixing made the region's culture rich, but it also added many unusual beliefs and stories.

12. Climate Shifts and Unexpected Changes

In many ancient places, climate changes altered the course of history. When rivers changed their path or rains became less frequent, entire cities could be abandoned. Some historians think the Indus Valley civilization might have faded in part because the monsoon patterns shifted, making farming harder. Others say invasions or disease might have played a role. Regardless, it is surprising to see how large cities could become ghost towns, left for the desert sands to cover over time.

In Mesopotamia, salt buildup in the soil from irrigation could harm farmland. As the ground became salty, crops would not grow as well. This might have pushed people to move or fight for better land. So, while humans built amazing cities, they also fought against nature's challenges. Sometimes, these challenges were too big to handle, leading to the collapse of entire ways of life.

13. Early Sailors and Strange Sea Journeys

Though we often think about the land, some of these early civilizations also built boats and traveled by sea or rivers. The Sumerians used reed boats, which might look too simple to cross large bodies of water. But they did sail on them along the rivers and possibly across the Persian Gulf. Trade was important. They needed to get metals, wood, and precious stones from other regions, so they had to travel. Some stories suggest that people in the Indus Valley might have sailed to Mesopotamia to trade goods like cotton, beads, and spices. It is fascinating to imagine these early merchants risking their lives on wooden or reed vessels to cross unknown seas.

---

14. Arts, Music, and Strange Instruments

Many of us forget that early civilizations also had music, dance, and art. In Mesopotamia, they played stringed instruments like the lyre or harp, and also some simple wind and percussion instruments. One odd fact is that archaeologists discovered an ancient gold and lapis lazuli lyre in the Royal Tombs of Ur. This lyre has a bull's head on it. It is both beautiful and a bit strange to see an instrument decorated with the face of a bull. It shows how important animals were to their beliefs.

People also painted or carved scenes of daily life, battles, and gods on seals or stone reliefs. The style might look stiff to us, but it was their way of telling stories. Sometimes, a single seal could show gods with horns, humans carrying gifts, and mythical beasts all in one scene. It can be fun to imagine how these pictures were explained to children in that time.

---

15. Writing Systems: From Pictures to Cuneiform

One of the craziest inventions of early civilizations was writing. The Sumerians started with small pictures to show objects. Over time, these pictures became wedge-shaped marks we call cuneiform. Scribes would press a reed stylus into soft clay tablets to create these marks. It might look like random lines to us, but it was a detailed system for recording numbers, goods, laws, and even stories.

Another interesting detail is that scribes were sometimes among the most respected people in society because writing was hard to learn. They studied in special schools, learning many signs and practicing for years. Reading and writing might be common skills now, but in those days, it was a special art reserved for a few. That gave scribes power, since kings and merchants depended on them to keep records of taxes, trade, and laws.

16. Gilgamesh: The World's Oldest Epic

Before we move on from Mesopotamia, we should mention "The Epic of Gilgamesh," often considered the oldest surviving story. It tells of Gilgamesh, a king (or demigod) of Uruk, and his friend Enkidu, a wild man created by the gods. They go on adventures, fight monsters, and even search for immortality. This story has surprising parts, like a great flood that destroys the world—long before stories of a great flood appeared in other texts. Another strange element is how Gilgamesh rejects a goddess named Ishtar, who then sends the Bull of Heaven to punish him. The story mixes gods and humans in a way that might feel wild to us now. Yet it shows how people saw their place in the world, always linked with the gods.

This epic also reveals the fear of death that many people shared. Gilgamesh becomes desperate when he loses his friend Enkidu. He tries to find a way to live forever but fails. The lesson seems to be that death is part of being human, and even kings must accept it. This is a deep message hidden in an old, mythic tale.

17. Stone Circles and Megalithic Mysteries

Moving away from Mesopotamia for a moment, we can find strange early structures in other parts of the world. For instance, in Europe, people built stone circles and large stone tombs. Stonehenge in England is famous, but it is not the only one. Many cultures around the world seemed to have the idea of placing huge rocks in circles or other shapes, perhaps for religious or astronomical reasons. These megalithic monuments still puzzle scientists. Some say they might have been places to watch the sun and moon. Others think they were used for ceremonies or even healing rituals. It is hard to say why so many people across different lands built these giant stone structures, but it is certainly a weird phenomenon.

18. Ötzi the Iceman: A Strange Glimpse into the Past

In the Alps between Italy and Austria, hikers found a frozen mummy known as Ötzi. He lived around 5,300 years ago, making him one of the oldest preserved bodies ever discovered. The strange part is how well his clothing, tools, and even his last meal were preserved by the ice. He wore a cloak made of woven grass, a coat, leggings of goat hide, and shoes stuffed with grass to keep his feet warm. He also carried a copper axe, which was a valuable tool at the time.

Scientists learned he had tattoos on his body, mostly simple lines and crosses. These might have been a form of therapy for pain, like acupuncture marks. It is surprising to find evidence that people used such treatments so long ago. His last meal included grains and meat. Even the pollen in his stomach showed where he might have walked in his final days. Ötzi's story is a tiny window into life during the Copper Age, showing us that these ancient people had more advanced skills than we might guess.

---

19. Strange Diseases and Early Medicine

Without modern medicine, ancient people relied on herbs, prayers, and guesswork to heal diseases. In Mesopotamia, sickness was often blamed on evil spirits or angry gods. Priests might perform rituals to drive away the demons. However, they also used natural remedies, like mixing plants and oils to treat wounds. It is strange how they combined magic spells with real herbal knowledge. Some tablets describe treatments that worked, while others seem more like superstition.

Similarly, in the Indus Valley, people had a good sense of hygiene with their advanced drainage. This might have helped prevent some illnesses. But across many early societies, childbirth was dangerous, wounds could easily get infected, and life was short for many people. Perhaps that is why religion and superstition played such a large role in health and daily life.

20. The Legacy of Strange Beginnings

When we look back at these earliest civilizations, we might be amazed by their weird and wonderful achievements. They invented writing, built huge cities, developed complex religions, and created laws that still echo through time. They had festivals that seem bizarre to us, used barley as money, and built roads for trade. Yet, in many ways, they were not so different from us. They wanted to understand the world, take care of their families, and find answers to life's big questions. They simply went about it in ways that might look odd to our modern eyes.

These strange beginnings laid the foundation for later cultures. The idea of writing and record-keeping would spread. The concept of laws and structured government would evolve. Religious and mythic stories would carry on or inspire new tales. Even that base-60 system of counting is still with us. Though we might see some customs as crazy, they were part of humanity's first steps toward building societies. Without them, the world would be quite different today.

CHAPTER 2

The Mysterious Middle Kingdom: Weird Tales from Ancient China

---

In this chapter, we explore Ancient China, often called the "Middle Kingdom" by its own people. Ancient China was filled with dynasties, powerful emperors, and many unusual customs. From strange food practices to odd rituals and beliefs, we will see that Chinese history is full of surprising facts. We will look at early dynasties like the Xia, Shang, and Zhou. We will also peer into some later periods to discover more weird details, stopping well before modern times. Let us step into this vast land and see what secrets and surprises it holds.

---

1. Early Legends: Yu the Great and the Xia Dynasty

Ancient Chinese legends talk about a king named Yu the Great who controlled floods. The story goes that there was a great flood that threatened all the lands. The people were suffering, and the waters would not recede. Yu found a way to dig channels and build dikes, guiding the waters into the sea. He worked so hard that he supposedly passed by his own home three times without going in, showing how dedicated he was.

Some historians debate whether Yu was real or only a legend. But the Xia Dynasty is often considered the first dynasty in China, said to be founded by Yu. Written records are sparse, so it is hard to confirm facts. However, it is odd how so many cultures have stories of a great flood. Whether it was a real event or a myth, the story of Yu the Great shows us how important flood control and water management were to ancient Chinese people.

---

2. The Shang Dynasty: Oracle Bones and Surprising Sacrifices

The Shang Dynasty left behind some strange artifacts called oracle bones. These were turtle shells or animal bones that priests would carve questions on, such as "Will the harvest be good?" or "Should the king go to war?" Then they would heat the bones until they cracked. The pattern of the cracks was believed to show the answer from the spirits or ancestors. These oracle bones are how we know the earliest form of Chinese writing. It is fascinating to see that writing might have begun as a way to talk to the spirit world.

Another odd fact about the Shang Dynasty is the extent of human sacrifices. In some royal tombs, archaeologists have found the remains of hundreds of people buried along with the king. These might have been prisoners of war, servants, or others who were sacrificed to serve the king in the afterlife. It is gruesome, but it was a real custom of the time. Sacrifices also extended to animals like horses and dogs. This might seem especially strange to modern eyes, but in the Shang worldview, the afterlife mirrored real life. The king would need servants and animals in the next world, so they were buried together.

---

3. The Zhou Dynasty: Mandate of Heaven and Strange Rituals

After the Shang came the Zhou Dynasty. One big idea that started under the Zhou was the "Mandate of Heaven." This meant that a ruler's power was given by Heaven, and if a ruler became unjust or cruel, Heaven could take that power away. This idea was used by many future dynasties to justify taking over. If an emperor lost a war or had natural disasters happen, people might say he had lost the Mandate of Heaven.

But the Zhou also had some bizarre customs. One was the tradition of burying important officials near the king, though perhaps not as extreme as the Shang. Some texts mention that the Zhou kings performed rituals on top of tall platforms or towers, where they would pray to the gods of the sky. These ceremonies were highly secret. People believed that if done correctly, these rituals would keep balance between Heaven and Earth. If done poorly, disasters could happen.

The Zhou also practiced divination, like the Shang, but used different methods. Some used the "Book of Changes" or "I Ching," which involves throwing yarrow sticks or coins to get a pattern, which is then interpreted. While many today see the "I Ching" as a philosophical text, the Zhou saw it as a way to predict events and find guidance. It might look like superstition to us, but it was serious business then.

---

4. Confucius and Weird Situations He Faced

Confucius was a famous teacher and thinker who lived during the late Zhou period, a time of chaos and war called the Spring and Autumn period, and later the Warring States period. He believed in respecting elders, showing loyalty, and acting with virtue. But his life was not easy. He wandered from one kingdom to another, hoping to find a ruler who would follow his teachings. It is said that at one point, Confucius and his followers ran out of supplies, nearly starving. Yet people claim he remained calm and continued to teach about virtue and proper conduct.

While Confucius's teachings might not seem "crazy," the circumstances in which he taught were quite wild. Different states were constantly fighting. Plots and betrayals were common. Confucius tried to bring moral order in the midst of chaos. He even faced strange accusations, like worshipping ghosts improperly or not honoring certain customs. To us, these might seem minor, but for him, it was a big deal to be accused of disrespecting the ancestral spirits.

---

5. The Warring States: Odd Weapons and Tactics

During the Warring States period, states like Qin, Chu, and Zhao fought for control. It was a brutal time with constant warfare. But they also came up with strange weapons and tactics. One odd fact is that the state of Qin developed a powerful crossbow that could shoot arrows with deadly force. Some states used chariots, but over time, infantry armies grew bigger, and cunning strategies became more important than just raw strength.

Another interesting twist is how philosophers like Sun Tzu wrote books about war, especially "The Art of War." This book talks about tricking the enemy and winning without fighting if possible. It might seem strange that in a time of endless battles, some thinkers wanted to reduce bloodshed by using intelligence. But it makes sense if you want to save resources.

6. Qin Shi Huang: The Emperor Who Wanted to Live Forever

Eventually, the state of Qin conquered the others, and Qin Shi Huang became the first emperor of a united China. He is known for ordering the building of parts of the Great Wall, but he also had many strange habits. One of the strangest is his obsession with living forever. He sent out servants to find elixirs that would grant immortality. Some stories say he traveled to distant islands to find wizards or magicians who claimed they had the secret to eternal life.

Sadly for him, many of these elixirs contained mercury, which is poisonous. So instead of living forever, he probably harmed his health. The emperor's search for immortality also led him to build a massive tomb guarded by the famous Terracotta Army. This army of clay soldiers stands ready to protect him in the afterlife. It is so large that archaeologists are still uncovering parts of it. The strange thing is that historical records suggest the tomb might contain rivers of mercury, which was believed to represent flowing water in the afterlife. This toxic belief might still keep us from fully exploring the tomb, because of the potential hazards inside.

7. The Terracotta Army: A Clay Mystery

Discovered in 1974 by farmers digging a well, the Terracotta Army is one of the most impressive finds in history. Thousands of life-sized clay soldiers stand in battle formation. Each has unique facial features and hairstyles. They also have weapons, chariots, and horses made of clay. The detail is remarkable, from their armor to their shoes.

What is weird is the scale of this project. It must have taken an enormous workforce. Some archaeologists believe the workers were not allowed to leave once they started, to keep the tomb's layout secret. Many might have died during the process. It sounds harsh, but such was the power of Qin Shi Huang. It is eerie to imagine these thousands of silent clay figures, buried with the Emperor for over two thousand years, waiting for him to command them in the afterlife.

8. The Han Dynasty: Strange Inventions and Silk Road Oddities

After the short-lived Qin Dynasty fell, the Han Dynasty rose. This was a time of relative stability and growth. Many weird and amazing inventions came from this period. Paper was invented, which might be one of the most important discoveries ever. There was also the seismograph, invented by Zhang Heng, which used bronze dragons that dropped balls into bronze toads when an earthquake happened.

The Silk Road also flourished during the Han Dynasty. This was a network of trade routes connecting China with the Middle East and Europe. Strange products traveled along these roads. Chinese silk was highly prized by Romans, while China received glassware, horses, and even rare foods. Imagine a merchant carrying exotic goods across deserts and mountains, facing bandits and harsh weather. The Silk Road was a place of adventure and risk, filled with tall tales of monstrous creatures and magical lands. Some rumors said that people in the far West had giant noses or three heads. These stories might sound silly, but they show how mysterious distant lands were to ancient travelers.

9. Empress Lü and the Palace Intrigues

After the Han Dynasty's founder, Liu Bang, died, his wife Empress Lü gained power. She is remembered for her cruel treatment of rivals. One famous story says she had the mother of a rival boiled to death and turned into "human soup." Another says she cut off the arms and legs of her enemies and threw them in a latrine. While some details might be exaggerated, it is clear that palace politics could be gruesome.

Ancient China's royal courts were often full of plots, betrayals, and twisted punishments. Emperors had many wives and concubines, leading to jealous fights for power among their families. Some might whisper false rumors to the emperor, leading to an official's disgrace or execution. It might be shocking, but these dark tales were part of life at the highest levels of power.

10. Banquets and Bizarre Foods

Food in ancient China had many regional varieties. People enjoyed grains like millet, wheat, and rice, depending on where they lived. They also ate pork, chicken, fish, and vegetables. But the Chinese court, especially during lavish feasts, sometimes served dishes that might surprise us. For instance, they might have served delicacies like bear paws, monkey brains, or even unusual sea creatures. These foods were considered rare and fancy, a show of wealth and status.

Drinking was also common, with wine made from fermented grains. Some emperors were known to host drunken banquets where they forced guests to keep drinking until they passed out. Others believed wine could help them see spirits or connect with higher realms. Combining food and drink with the belief in ancestor worship led to special offerings placed on altars for the ancestors to "enjoy."

---

11. Weird Medical Beliefs: Needles and Potions

Traditional Chinese medicine developed over many centuries. By the Han period, texts like the "Huangdi Neijing" or "Yellow Emperor's Inner Canon" discussed concepts like qi (the body's vital energy) and acupuncture points. The idea of sticking needles in the body to balance energy might seem strange if you have never heard of it before. But it became a standard practice in ancient China.

Another odd medical practice was the search for "alchemy" to create elixirs. This was partly tied to Taoist beliefs about immortality. Alchemists experimented with mercury, cinnabar, and other materials, hoping to find a substance that would grant eternal life. Sadly, some of these potions were poisonous. Yet, the lure of living forever was strong, so emperors and nobles often funded these experiments.

---

12. The Strange Case of Emperor Wu and Magicians

Emperor Wu of Han was one of the most powerful rulers of the Han Dynasty. He expanded the empire and developed the Silk Road. But he also fell for stories of magicians who claimed they could contact the spirit world or find the secret to immortality. He spent large sums of money on rituals and journeys to find these magical islands where immortals were said to live.

One account says that Emperor Wu believed a magician who claimed to need special items or huge funds to complete a ritual. After taking the money, the magician vanished. Emperor Wu was so angry when he learned it was a trick that he blamed and punished others at court. It shows how superstition and greed could mix in the highest circles, leading to some odd and dramatic events.

---

13. Eunuchs and Court Intrigue

Eunuchs were men who had been castrated, often at a young age, so they could serve in the royal palace without posing a threat to the emperor's wives or concubines. Over time, some eunuchs gained enormous power, whispering advice to emperors or controlling access to them. This led to bizarre situations where eunuchs could decide who met with the emperor, or even speak on his behalf.

It might seem strange that a ruler would trust a eunuch more than other officials, but the idea was that eunuchs had no family ties or heirs. Therefore, they were seen as loyal only to the emperor. In practice, many eunuchs formed alliances and schemed for their own benefit. Some became very wealthy. This system caused tension in many dynasties, leading to rebellions or palace power struggles.

---

14. The Four Beauties and Their Strange Tales

Chinese history and legend talk about the "Four Beauties," women so beautiful that kingdoms fell or rose because of them. Each has a unique story. One of them, Daji, was said to be a wicked consort of the last Shang king. She is blamed for encouraging the king to torture people and do weird things like fill a pond with wine and hang raw meat in the forest for drunken orgies. This might be partly myth, but it suggests how a single person's influence could be seen as the cause of a dynasty's downfall.

Another beauty, Xi Shi, was offered by the state of Yue to the king of Wu. Her goal was to distract him and cause his downfall. Some tales say her beauty was so great that fish forgot how to swim. While these stories are obviously filled with exaggeration, they show how people believed a single woman's charm could change the course of history. It is both romantic and strange to think that entire states could be manipulated by such means.

---

15. Inventing Strange Things: Kites, Umbrellas, and More

The Chinese are credited with many inventions, some of which might seem normal to us now but were odd or amazing back then. Kites, for example, were originally used for military purposes, to send messages or measure distances. Imagine an army general flying a kite to see how far the enemy camp was. Or using the sound of a special kite string to frighten enemy soldiers at night. It might look like a child's toy to us now, but it was once a strategic tool.

Umbrellas also have a long history in China. Some say the first umbrellas were made from paper or silk stretched over bamboo frames. They were a symbol of rank and authority. An emperor or noble might have many servants carrying parasols to shield him from the sun or rain. Seeing a line of attendants carrying big, colorful umbrellas for one person would look quite odd to us today, but it was a sign of prestige.

---

16. Legalism and Harsh Laws

While Confucius taught virtue, another school of thought, called Legalism, believed in strict laws and punishments. During the Qin Dynasty, Legalist ideas dominated. People could be punished or even executed for small crimes, like failing to report a neighbor's wrongdoing. This created a society where fear kept order.

Later dynasties also sometimes used harsh measures. For example, cutting off a person's nose or feet was an ancient punishment. Another strange punishment was a form of exile to distant regions. Some criminals were forced to wear wooden collars or cangues that made it hard to move. These punishments seem cruel now, but in ancient China, rulers believed that strong punishments were needed to maintain control over large populations.

17. The Grand Canal and Other Giant Projects

The building of large structures and projects was another aspect of ancient China that could be considered crazy. Aside from the Great Wall, emperors also built huge canals to connect rivers and improve trade routes. The Grand Canal, for instance, eventually stretched over a thousand miles, linking northern and southern China. It took enormous labor, and many workers died from exhaustion or disease. The canal was important for moving grains and troops, but the scale of it was monumental.

We might also mention the building of big palaces. Some emperors constructed giant palace complexes with artificial lakes, mountains, and elaborate gardens. Empress Wu Zetian, later in the Tang Dynasty (a bit beyond the scope of this chapter), had huge statues of herself placed around. While these achievements show power and wealth, they also show how rulers sometimes pushed their people to extremes for personal glory.

18. Strange Court Etiquette and Customs

The Chinese court had many rules for how officials and even family members should behave in front of the emperor. Bowing or kneeling was common, and certain officials had to perform a kowtow—a series of bows until their forehead touched the floor. Some emperors insisted that visitors not look them in the eye. This might sound strange, but it was a way to show respect for the "Son of Heaven."

There were also rules about what colors could be worn at court. Yellow became a color reserved for the emperor, symbolizing the center of everything. Officials risked punishment if they wore the wrong color or style. Such strict customs might seem odd, but they helped maintain the emperor's image as a semi-divine ruler.

19. Superstitions and Omens

Ancient China was full of superstitions. Comets, eclipses, and natural disasters were seen as signs that Heaven was upset. If a solar eclipse happened, people might blame the emperor for losing the Mandate of Heaven. Emperors would sometimes issue proclamations, taking responsibility for the event and promising to be better rulers. They might reduce taxes or punish corrupt officials to show they were sincere.

There were also local superstitions about ghosts and spirits. People believed that restless spirits could haunt the living. To keep ghosts away, families might burn incense or paper money as offerings. During the Ghost Festival, people set out food for hungry ghosts who roam the earth. These customs are still practiced in some form today, but in ancient times, the fear of ghosts was even stronger.

20. The End of an Era and Lasting Oddities

As centuries passed, Chinese dynasties rose and fell. Each era had its own strange stories, from powerful dowager empresses to child emperors who played with gold toys. But one thing remained clear: ancient China was a place of deep tradition, spiritual beliefs, and sometimes frightening power struggles. People balanced Confucian ideas about proper conduct with more mysterious practices like oracle bones, alchemy, and the worship of countless gods and ancestors.

All these weird and wonderful tales shaped Chinese civilization. Many traditions continued into later ages, evolving over time. Even though we are stopping our look at ancient China before modern times, the influence of these early customs and beliefs can still be felt in Chinese culture today. We have only scratched the surface of the strange history of the Middle Kingdom, but it is enough to show just how full of surprises it was.

CHAPTER 3

Eccentric Empires: Peculiar Customs in Mesopotamia and Persia

In this chapter, we will look at later empires that rose in the region of Mesopotamia, as well as the mighty Persian Empire. Although we visited early Mesopotamian civilizations before, we will now focus on more recent powers in that same area—like the Neo-Babylonian Empire—and then move east into ancient Persia. We will find new, strange facts about leaders, customs, and beliefs that shaped these powerful kingdoms. These lands were home to legendary wonders, fierce armies, and peculiar traditions that might surprise us today.

1. Introduction to the Later Mesopotamian Empires

After the days of early city-states like Sumer and Akkad, Mesopotamia continued to change hands. Assyrians, Babylonians, and other groups fought to control this fertile land between the Tigris and Euphrates Rivers. By the time we reach the Neo-Babylonian Empire (also called the Chaldean Empire), we see a mix of old traditions and new styles of rule. They worshipped ancient gods but built newer, grander structures. They created fresh legends that blended with older stories.

The Neo-Babylonian period is famous for King Nebuchadnezzar II, who conquered Jerusalem and took captives back to Babylon. This empire did not last very long before the rise of Persia, but it left behind tales of amazing buildings, unusual ceremonies, and strict kings. It is in this setting that we find some of the most curious customs in late Mesopotamian history.

2. The Neo-Babylonian Empire and Its Odd Splendor

The Neo-Babylonian Empire took shape in the 7th century BCE, after the fall of the Assyrians. Nebuchadnezzar II became its most famous ruler.

Under his reign, Babylon became a city of massive walls, grand gates, and towering temples. Some people say Babylon's walls were so wide that a chariot with four horses could ride on top with room to spare. Even if that seems like an exaggeration, there is no doubt Babylon was a grand place.

During ceremonies, priests performed rituals to honor the god Marduk, the chief deity of the city. On certain feast days, the king would enter Marduk's temple, take the hand of the statue, and "walk" with the god. This tradition might sound strange, but it was meant to show that the king ruled with the blessing of Marduk. Failing to perform these rituals properly could be seen as a sign that the king lost divine favor.

Nebuchadnezzar II also ordered many large projects, such as rebuilding the famous Ishtar Gate. This gate was decorated with glazed bricks showing dragons and bulls—symbols of Babylon's gods. The bright blues and golds of the gate must have shocked visitors. For the Babylonians, color and art were ways to show wealth and devotion to their gods.

---

3. The Hanging Gardens: Fact or Fable?

When people think of Babylon, they often think of the Hanging Gardens, one of the "Seven Wonders of the Ancient World." These gardens were said to feature lush plants growing on terraces, watered by a clever system of pumps. Some stories claim Nebuchadnezzar II built them for his wife, who missed the green hills of her homeland.

Yet, historians are not entirely sure if the Hanging Gardens truly existed or if they were in Babylon at all. Some researchers suggest they might have been located in Nineveh, or perhaps they were an exaggerated tale told by travelers. Whether real or myth, the idea of a massive, leafy garden in the middle of a dry region is quite strange. It would have taken great skill to create such a wonder, with water constantly flowing to keep plants alive on tall terraces.

Imagining these gardens helps us see how people in ancient times combined real achievements with fantastic stories. Even if they were partly legend, the tale of the Hanging Gardens shaped how later generations viewed Babylon as a place of beauty and mystery.

4. Nabonidus: The Odd King Who Worshipped the Moon

After Nebuchadnezzar II, one of the last Neo-Babylonian kings was Nabonidus. He was an unusual ruler because he favored the moon god Sin over Marduk, Babylon's main deity. This caused friction with Babylonian priests, who expected the king to honor Marduk as the top god. Nabonidus spent much of his time away from the capital, living in Arabia and building temples to Sin. Some sources say the people in Babylon grew unhappy with him.

This religious choice was quite odd for a Babylonian king, as it disturbed the long tradition of worshipping Marduk. It might be similar to an important leader today suddenly deciding to honor a less popular belief instead of the traditional one. Nabonidus's actions weakened his support in Babylon, and he became known as the "king who neglected Marduk." This likely made it easier for the Persian conqueror Cyrus the Great to take the city without much resistance in 539 BCE.

5. The Rise of the Persian Empire

The Persian Empire began to grow east of Mesopotamia, in what is now Iran. Under the Achaemenid Dynasty, the Persians became a major force.

Cyrus the Great united various tribes and conquered lands far and wide. He defeated the Medes, then the Lydians, and finally the Neo-Babylonian Empire. One of the strangest and most admired things about Cyrus was his policy of tolerance toward conquered peoples. Instead of destroying local religions or traditions, he often allowed them to continue. For example, after taking Babylon, he let the local gods remain honored, which helped him gain favor among the priests.

Yet, Persian rulers were also known for their strict control. They set up satrapies, or provinces, each governed by a satrap (a kind of governor). This was a new and efficient way to manage a huge empire. In each province, local customs were allowed, but they had to pay taxes and obey the king's orders. This balance of freedom and tight governance was a hallmark of Persia. It might seem normal to us now, but at the time, it was a unique approach that made the empire stable and strong.

---

6. Cyrus the Great and Surprising Tactics

Cyrus is remembered not just for his conquests, but also for how he treated the peoples he conquered. We can find an ancient cylinder, called the Cyrus Cylinder, which some call an early statement of human rights. It talks about how Cyrus freed captured peoples and helped them rebuild temples. While this may sound noble, we should remember it also served as good propaganda. By showing kindness, he reduced the chance of revolts.

There are strange stories about his battle tactics. One legend says that when Cyrus fought the Lydian King Croesus, he used camels to frighten the Lydian cavalry, because horses are said to be afraid of the smell of camels. Whether this is fully true or not, it is an example of how Cyrus used creative methods. He was also skilled at diplomacy, winning over local leaders rather than just crushing them by force. In a time when might often made right, this was an unusual style that earned Cyrus respect and even some affection among his subjects.

7. Darius I: The Organizer with Grand Projects

After Cyrus, another major figure in Persian history was Darius I. He took control after some turmoil, possibly by defeating rivals who claimed the throne. Darius was known as a master organizer. He divided the empire into provinces more formally, introduced standard coins (the daric), and built roads to connect distant lands.

One of his most impressive projects was the Royal Road, stretching over 1,500 miles. Along this road, there were stations where royal messengers could change horses, eat, and rest. This let messages travel surprisingly fast for ancient times. Greek historian Herodotus said, "Nothing stops these couriers from covering their allotted stage in the quickest possible time, neither snow, rain, heat, nor darkness." That might remind us of modern mail slogans, but it happened long ago. It was quite a feat to have such an organized system.

Darius also built grand buildings at Persepolis, one of the empire's capitals. The palace complex there had huge columns and detailed carvings of people from many nations bringing gifts. This art tells us the Persian kings wanted to display their power through architecture. Yet, the empire's grandeur could be viewed as strange by smaller nations, who must have wondered how such a massive kingdom held together.

---

8. Xerxes and the Odd Details of His Rule

Xerxes I, the son of Darius, is famous for battles against the Greeks. He continued many of his father's policies, but also dealt with revolts within the empire. Ancient sources tell some strange stories about Xerxes. One says that when crossing the Hellespont (the water between Asia and Europe) to invade Greece, a storm destroyed his bridge of boats. Xerxes became so angry that he ordered the sea to be "whipped" and cursed it for disobedience. Whether this truly happened or not, it paints a picture of a king with a fierce temper who believed even nature should obey him.

Xerxes was also known for massive building projects at Persepolis. Some tales say he forced workers to labor under harsh conditions. Others mention he had lavish feasts where food was plentiful, and wine flowed freely. For the Persians, the king was almost like a god-figure with absolute power. Some might find it strange that one man could demand so much from so many, but in ancient Persia, the king's word was law.

---

9. The Royal Road and Its Messengers

The Royal Road was not just a simple path; it was a lifeline for the empire. Officials placed guard posts and rest stations at intervals. Messengers, sometimes called "angarium," carried official letters and decrees. They rode on horseback, day and night. This allowed the king to communicate with distant governors, get news of rebellions, and send commands quickly. Such an efficient system was rare in the ancient world.

It might sound simple to us today, but for the time, sending a message hundreds of miles away in a few days was a huge achievement. The empire's control over wide regions depended on this. If the Persians had not set up this road and its stations, local rulers might have acted without the king's knowledge. So the Royal Road was a key to keeping the empire united under one ruler, which in itself seems like a big job given the many cultures and languages within Persia's borders.

---

10. Peculiar Persian Customs: Food, Feasts, and Celebrations

Persian rulers loved grand feasts. Herodotus wrote that Persians often drank wine in large amounts and discussed important matters at banquets. Once they decided on something while drunk, they would talk about it again the next day while sober, to see if it still seemed like a good idea. If so, they acted on it. This might be a strange way to make decisions, but it was part of their culture.

They also had interesting dining habits. Persian nobles might sit on cushions or low chairs around a table filled with various dishes—meat stews, flatbreads, vegetables, fruits, and sweets. They enjoyed spices and sauces, which made their cuisine rich in flavor. Feasts were social events where people made deals, discussed politics, and built alliances. In a land so large, inviting local leaders to a royal feast was one way to keep them loyal.

Persians were also known to celebrate Nowruz (the new year). This spring festival involved cleaning the house, wearing new clothes, and sharing food with family. Though it continues in some form into modern times, its roots go back to ancient Persian beliefs about renewal and the coming of spring. Imagine the empire's roads filled with travelers heading to visit family or shrines at this time, creating a sense of unity across many provinces.

---

11. Zoroastrian Beliefs: Fire as a Sacred Element

The main religion in ancient Persia for a long time was Zoroastrianism, based on the teachings of the prophet Zoroaster (or Zarathustra). This faith taught about a supreme god named Ahura Mazda, who represented goodness, and an evil spirit named Angra Mainyu. The struggle between good and evil was a core theme. People were expected to choose the side of good through right thoughts, right words, and right actions.

One strange aspect for outsiders was the sacred fire used in Zoroastrian temples. Fire was a symbol of purity and truth. Priests, called magi, tended these fires day and night so they would never go out. Some travelers found it odd to see people bowing before fire, but for Zoroastrians, it was a way to honor the presence of Ahura Mazda. Temples had inner rooms where the main fire was kept, and only certain priests could enter. This secrecy added to the air of mystery around their worship.

---

12. The Magi: Priests with Hidden Knowledge

The magi were Zoroastrian priests who studied sacred texts and performed rituals. They also served as advisors to kings. Their role was powerful, and many people in the empire and beyond viewed them as wise men with secret knowledge. The word "magic" may even come from "magi," due to the priests' reputation for astrology and performing ceremonies that seemed mysterious.

Magi sometimes traveled with the army, offering blessings before battles. They interpreted omens, like the flights of birds or the way the flames flickered. For some, this was superstition, but the Persians took it seriously. Even the king might decide on war or peace based on a magus's reading of a sign. This might seem odd today, but in ancient times, many rulers believed the gods or higher powers guided events, and the magi were the experts at reading those signs.

---

13. Royal Court Life and Court Intrigues

Life at the Persian royal court could be glamorous. The king lived in palaces with thick rugs, carved decorations, and gold vessels. Yet, it was also a place of intrigue. High nobles, governors, and even family members schemed for power. Some wrote letters to the king praising themselves while blaming rivals. Others bribed court officials to gain influence. A single word from the king could mean a high position or a death sentence.

The Persians had a tradition that nobody could approach the king uninvited. If someone did, they could be executed on the spot—unless the king decided otherwise. This harsh rule might seem extreme, but it was meant to protect the king from threats and keep order. It also gave the king an almost divine status. People had to bow deeply or prostrate themselves before him, sometimes kissing the ground or the edge of his robe.

14. The Immortals: Elite Soldiers with a Strange Name

One of the most famous units in the Persian army was the Immortals. They were called "Immortals" because their number was always kept at exactly 10,000. If one died or was wounded, another soldier would immediately replace him, giving the impression that their ranks never shrank. They wore scale armor, carried spears, bows, and swords, and had a reputation for discipline and skill.

The Immortals also served as the king's personal guard. When the king traveled, they marched with him to ensure his safety. Some stories say they wore masks or carried special face coverings, but this might be more legend than fact. Still, the idea of a constantly renewed elite force is striking. It gave the Persian army a feeling of unstoppable power. Facing an enemy that seemed never to lose men, at least in appearance, must have been terrifying.

---

15. Towers of Silence: Bizarre Funeral Practice

In Zoroastrian belief, dead bodies were considered unclean. They could pollute sacred elements like fire and earth. So, Zoroastrians in ancient

Persia developed a method of placing the dead in special structures called "Towers of Silence." These were circular, open-air buildings on hilltops. The bodies were left there to be exposed to the sun and eaten by birds, usually vultures. Later, the remaining bones were placed in a pit in the tower's center.

To some outsiders, this custom looked gruesome or disrespectful. But for Zoroastrians, it was the best way to avoid contaminating earth or fire with a corpse. It also matched their view that the body was empty once the spirit left. Though different cultures have various ways of handling death, the Tower of Silence stands out as a unique method, tied deeply to the idea of purity and the fear of polluting nature's sacred elements.

---

16. Women in Persian Society

While we often picture ancient empires as strictly male-dominated, Persian women could hold some power, especially in noble families. Royal women might own land, manage estates, and even supervise workers. If a queen mother or a royal wife gained the favor of the king, she could influence decisions at court. Yet, ordinary women likely had fewer freedoms and were expected to focus on family life and household tasks.

Some ancient records mention Persian women who traveled the Royal Road with servants and guards. They might have visited temples or gone to see relatives in other provinces. This seems more freedom than some neighboring societies allowed. Of course, we should remember that most information comes from Greek or later sources, so our picture might be incomplete. Still, it is interesting to note that Persian noblewomen sometimes appeared in important public roles, which might seem surprising for that era.

---

17. The Persian Wars from Another View

Greek histories often describe the Persian Wars (like the battles of Marathon, Thermopylae, and Salamis) from the Greek side. They portray the Persians as vast armies in fancy clothing, led by harsh kings. From the Persian side, though, these wars were attempts to expand their borders or punish Greek city-states that had supported revolts.

Some Persian records hint at a sense of bewilderment about the Greeks, who fought among themselves but united against Persia. The Persians might have seen the Greeks as rebellious subjects or annoying raiders from the western edge of the empire. This clash of cultures led to many myths and half-truths. For instance, the story of Xerxes whipping the sea might be Greek propaganda to show the Persian king as foolish. In reality, these wars were complicated, with each side telling stories that made the other look strange or weak.

18. Persian Art, Architecture, and Strange Symbols

Persian art often showed rows of figures from different parts of the empire, each wearing local dress and carrying gifts. This was a way to say, "Look how many peoples we rule." In relief carvings, you might see scenes of the king in combat with lions or mythical beasts. Some think these pictures symbolized the king bringing order to chaos.

The architecture at Persepolis featured tall columns topped with double-headed bull capitals. Entering such a hall could feel overwhelming. Brightly colored walls, polished floors, and shining metal decorations gave a sense of regal power. The Persians also carved inscriptions in cuneiform, using languages like Old Persian, Elamite, and Babylonian. That way, people from many regions could read the king's proclamations.

This mix of styles, languages, and symbolism might look odd to a traveler who was used to simpler, smaller kingdoms. But to the Persians, it was a statement that they were a global power, uniting many lands under one throne.

19. Myths, Legends, and Propaganda

Like all empires, Persia had its share of legends. Some stories praised the great kings as chosen by the gods. Others warned about certain rulers who were cruel or lost the favor of Ahura Mazda. We should remember that many records came from the king's scribes or from Greek writers who saw Persia as an enemy. So, facts could be twisted into propaganda. For example, a Persian scribe might describe a victory in glowing terms, while a Greek historian might call the same event a brutal conquest.

These myths and tales shaped how people in the empire viewed themselves and their king. They also shaped how neighboring lands viewed Persia. When Greek armies finally defeated the Persians, the Greeks wrote stories that made their own heroes shine. In turn, Persians might have told tales of Greek trickery or cunning. The truth probably lies somewhere in between. Either way, the result is a collection of strange and dramatic stories that still fascinate us.

CHAPTER 4

Marvelous Myths: Odd Traditions from Ancient Greece

In this chapter, we explore the world of Ancient Greece. When we think of Greece, we might picture philosophers, democracy, and majestic temples. But behind these familiar ideas lies a wealth of strange beliefs, bizarre rituals, and curious stories. The Greeks were famous for their myths about gods, heroes, and monsters. They also had unusual customs in politics, warfare, and daily life. Let us dive into this land of city-states, each with its own laws and habits, and discover some marvelously odd details from ancient Greek history.

1. The Greek City-States: A Patchwork of Customs

Unlike large empires such as Persia, Ancient Greece was split into many city-states (poleis). Athens, Sparta, Corinth, Thebes, and others each had their own government, army, and traditions. This made Greece a place of variety. One city might value art and philosophy, while another might focus on military strength.

Because of this patchwork, Greek customs could vary widely. Some cities had kings or tyrants, while Athens became known for its form of democracy—although it was limited to free male citizens. Women, slaves, and foreigners could not vote. This might seem unfair to us, but at the time, Athens was still seen as a radical experiment in self-rule.

These differing systems often led to conflicts among the city-states. Yet, they also shared a common language and religion. The Greek gods were worshipped across the region, and certain myths were known everywhere, though with local twists. This blend of unity and diversity gave Greek culture a weird mix of cooperation (such as the Olympic Games) and competition (constant wars and rivalries).

2. The Olympic Games: Strange Beginnings

The Olympic Games began in Olympia, in honor of Zeus, the king of the Greek gods. These games were held every four years and attracted athletes from different city-states. The competition included running, wrestling, boxing, chariot racing, and more. One strange fact is that many events were performed in the nude. Greek men believed the human body was a thing of beauty and that competing naked showed courage and equality among athletes.

Women were not allowed to watch the Olympic Games. The penalty for a married woman caught at the games could be death. Yet there was a separate festival for women called the Heraean Games, in honor of the goddess Hera. These differences might look odd, but they reflect the roles of men and women in Greek society. Nudity, which might seem shocking to us in a public event, was normal for Greek athletics, tied to ideas of honor, freedom, and the admiration of the ideal physique.

---

3. Mythical Monsters and Their Meanings

Greek myths are full of strange creatures: the half-man, half-bull Minotaur; the many-headed Hydra; the winged horse Pegasus; and the snake-haired Medusa, whose gaze turned people to stone. While these monsters may look like fantasy stories to us, they held symbolic meanings for the Greeks. They often represented chaos, challenges, or sins that heroes had to overcome.

For example, the Minotaur lived in a labyrinth, a maze so complex that no one who entered could find the exit. This maze might symbolize the fear of getting lost in the unknown. The hero Theseus defeats the Minotaur, showing human bravery and intelligence conquering brute force. Another example is the story of the Hydra. Each time the hero Heracles cut off one head, two more grew back. This could represent problems in life that get worse if you do not find the right solution. These myths taught lessons, but also provided entertaining tales of gods, monsters, and the heroic spirit.

4. Gods Who Acted Like Humans

A strange thing about the Greek gods is how human they were in their behavior. Zeus, Hera, Poseidon, Athena, and others might have great powers, but they also had petty arguments, jealousies, and love affairs. Zeus was famous for disguising himself to pursue mortal women, angering his wife Hera, who took revenge on his lovers or their children. Poseidon got into fights with other gods over territory, and Artemis punished hunters who saw her bathing.

These stories might seem silly, but they were a big part of Greek religion. People built temples, offered sacrifices, and held festivals to honor these gods. They believed the gods could protect or punish them, depending on how they were treated. Each god had a domain—Zeus over the sky, Poseidon over the sea, Demeter over the harvest, and so on. The fact that the gods seemed flawed and emotional made them more relatable to the Greeks, although it is certainly peculiar to picture divine beings acting out so many dramas.

---

5. The Oracle of Delphi: Puzzling Prophecies

One of the strangest aspects of Greek religion was the Oracle of Delphi. People from across the Greek world visited this sanctuary to ask questions of the god Apollo. The oracle was given by a woman called the Pythia, who sat on a tripod over a crack in the earth. Fumes rose from the ground, and under their influence, she would speak in riddles or cryptic phrases.

Priests then interpreted her words for visitors. These messages were often ambiguous. For example, when King Croesus of Lydia asked if he should go to war with Persia, the oracle is said to have replied: "If you cross the river, you will destroy a great empire." Croesus thought it meant he would defeat Persia, but it turned out the empire he destroyed was his own. This story shows the confusing nature of oracle prophecies. People might twist the meaning to fit their hopes, only to discover too late that they had misunderstood.

Why the Pythia behaved this way is still debated. Some suggest natural gases caused hallucinations. Others think the priests staged part of it. Regardless, the oracle's fame spread far, and city-states competed for her favor, offering gifts to Apollo and hoping for a lucky prophecy.

---

6. Spartan Society: Tough and Unusual

Sparta is often remembered as a city of warriors. From a young age, Spartan boys entered the agoge, a rigorous training program that taught them discipline, endurance, and combat skills. They slept in barracks, ate sparse meals, and faced harsh punishments for mistakes. Stealing food was encouraged, but getting caught was punished. This taught them cunning.

Spartan girls also had more freedom compared to women in other Greek cities. They were expected to exercise and stay fit so they could bear strong children. Some Greek visitors were shocked to see Spartan women in short tunics, running and training in public. Yet Spartans believed that healthy women produced healthy warriors.

One of the strangest customs was the Spartan idea that dying in battle was the greatest honor. Cowards faced shame and might be forced to wear special clothing or be excluded from public events. This emphasis on warfare shaped every part of Spartan life. Their dedication to martial excellence was extreme, making Sparta different from other Greek cities where art, trade, and philosophy had a bigger role.

---

7. Athenian Democracy with Odd Rules

Athens claimed to be the birthplace of democracy, but it had some unusual features. Only free adult males with Athenian parents could vote. Women, slaves, and foreigners (metics) were excluded. Citizens met in an assembly on a hill called the Pnyx, where they debated and voted by show of hands. Important decisions about war, laws, and finances were decided this way.

There was also a strange practice called ostracism. Each year, Athenians could vote to banish one citizen for ten years. Everyone wrote a name on a broken piece of pottery called an ostrakon. If any single name got enough votes, that person was forced to leave. The idea was to protect the city from powerful individuals who might turn into tyrants. Yet, it could also be misused to get rid of rivals. It must have felt odd to be popular one day and then exiled the next if the assembly decided you were too dangerous.

---

8. The Mystery Cults: Eleusinian and Dionysian Rites

Aside from the main gods, some Greeks joined secret mystery cults. Two well-known examples were the Eleusinian Mysteries in honor of Demeter and Persephone, and the Dionysian rites in honor of Dionysus. These cults involved secret ceremonies, initiations, and promises of a better afterlife for members.

The Eleusinian Mysteries took place near Athens, where priests reenacted the story of Demeter searching for her daughter Persephone, who was taken by Hades to the underworld. Initiates underwent sacred rituals that we still do not fully understand, as they swore oaths of secrecy. The promise was spiritual renewal and hope after death.

The Dionysian rites were wilder. Followers of Dionysus might dance, drink wine, and enter a state of frenzy. Some celebrations involved wearing animal skins or masks, and in myths, the god's followers tore wild animals apart with their bare hands (a practice called sparagmos). These stories may sound gruesome, but they highlight how the Greeks used ecstatic worship to connect with the divine. It was very different from the calm image we might have of Greek temples.

---

9. Theater and Its Unusual Origins

Greek theater began as religious festivals honoring Dionysus. Actors wore large masks and performed on open-air stages. Tragedies told stories of gods and heroes, often ending in death or disaster to teach moral lessons or make people feel strong emotions. Comedies, on the other hand, mocked politicians, celebrities, and everyday life.

It might seem odd that the same god who inspired wild dancing and frenzy was also honored by serious plays. But theater started as a ritual, and the masks worn by actors may have been a nod to the idea of divine possession or transformation. The first actors, or "hypocrites," had to switch masks to show different roles. Some comedic plays had chorus members dressed as frogs, wasps, or clouds, dancing and singing silly songs. This mix of sacred and humorous is unique, showing how Greek culture blended deep respect for the gods with a playful spirit.

10. Philosophers with Strange Ideas and Lifestyles

Ancient Greece gave us famous philosophers like Socrates, Plato, and Aristotle. But there were also odd thinkers such as Diogenes the Cynic, who lived in a large jar or barrel in Athens. He rejected worldly goods, going about barefoot, owning almost nothing. One story says that when Alexander the Great visited him and offered to grant him any wish, Diogenes told the powerful conqueror to "stand out of my sunlight."

Other philosophers promoted unusual doctrines. Pythagoras, known for his theorem in math, also led a secret brotherhood with strict rules. They believed in the transmigration of souls (reincarnation) and avoided eating beans because they thought beans contained the souls of the dead. While we might remember Pythagoras for geometry, his cult-like group had many strange rules about diet, daily habits, and spiritual purity.

Philosophy in Greece was not just about abstract thinking but also about how to live. That often meant living in ways that others found eccentric or shocking, like sleeping in public, refusing to wear shoes, or having no possessions to show one's devotion to truth or virtue.

11. The Strange Banquets: Symposia

We might picture banquets as formal dinners, but in ancient Greece, men attended gatherings called symposia to discuss ideas, recite poetry, and drink wine. The Greeks usually drank wine mixed with water, thinking it barbaric to drink it pure. At these symposia, guests reclined on couches, ate snacks, and passed a wine bowl around.

One odd custom was the game of kottabos. Players would fling the last drops of their wine at a target, trying to hit it with a little splash. It was a bit like throwing darts with liquid. These gatherings could be both intellectual and rowdy. Philosophers might debate the meaning of life, while someone else sang a silly song or recited lines from Homer. Slaves served food and refilled cups. Women were generally not present unless they were entertainers or companions called hetairai. These women could be skilled in music or conversation, giving them a higher status than ordinary slaves, but still lower than free men.

---

12. Warfare Customs: The Hoplite and the Phalanx

Greek warfare might seem straightforward—lots of city-states fighting. But it had its own odd customs. The hoplite soldier was a heavily armed foot soldier with a bronze helmet, a round shield (called a hoplon), a spear, and a short sword. Hoplites fought in a tight formation called the phalanx. Shoulder to shoulder, each man's shield protected himself and part of his neighbor, creating a wall of shields and spears.

What might seem strange is that battles were often planned in open fields, and each side usually agreed to meet at a certain time. The Greeks also had rules about treating the dead. After a battle, both sides usually paused to allow each other to collect their fallen. This might appear civilized compared to later forms of total war. Still, fighting in a rigid phalanx was terrifying, as the front lines clashed in close quarters, with little room to maneuver.

13. The Shocking Thebes Sacred Band

In the city of Thebes, there was an elite military unit called the Sacred Band. It was made up of 150 pairs of male lovers (300 men in total). The idea was that lovers would fight more bravely to protect each other. It might seem shocking or strange for an army to be formed this way, but the Thebans believed the bond between these men made them loyal and fearless.

The Sacred Band was highly respected for its effectiveness. It famously defeated the Spartans at the Battle of Leuctra in 371 BCE, breaking Sparta's long-held dominance. The idea that love could create a powerful fighting force was both odd and impressive to other Greeks. Later, when the Sacred Band was finally defeated by Philip II of Macedon (father of Alexander the Great), Philip supposedly mourned their loss, praising their courage and devotion to one another.

---

14. Strange Punishments and Laws

Greek city-states had their own laws, and some punishments appear odd. In Athens, certain crimes could result in being sold into slavery if the person could not pay a fine. In Sparta, there was a law requiring men to marry by a certain age or face public shaming. In some places, heavy stones were placed in the marketplace for criminals to stand on while being ridiculed. The public nature of these punishments aimed to discourage wrongdoing by shaming offenders.

There were also odd rules like sumptuary laws that limited how much you could spend on funerals or festivals. Many Greeks believed in moderation. Too much display of wealth could bring envy or the anger of the gods. So lawmakers tried to control lavish spending. Today, it might seem unusual for the government to limit how fancy a funeral can be, but for some city-states, it was part of maintaining social harmony.

15. Bizarre Medical Practices: The "Wandering Womb"

The Greeks made strides in medicine, especially with figures like Hippocrates. But they also held strange beliefs. One was the idea of the "wandering womb." Some doctors thought a woman's womb could move around her body, causing hysteria or other problems. To cure this, they might recommend certain smells or even marriage, hoping to "settle" the womb. This sounds silly now, but in ancient times, the human body was a mystery.

Greek physicians also used herbs, diets, and surgery tools that were advanced for their day. Yet, mixing observation with superstition led to strange treatments. For headaches, they might suggest drilling a small hole in the skull (trepanning). Sometimes it helped by releasing pressure, but it also risked infection or death. Such practices remind us that ancient medicine was a blend of real insight and guesswork.

---

16. Alexander the Great's Surprising Habits

Though more connected to Macedonia, Alexander the Great spread Greek culture far beyond Greece. He admired Homer's epics and slept with a copy of the "Iliad" under his pillow. He also adopted Persian customs, wearing Persian robes and encouraging his men to marry Persian women. This shocked many Greeks, who saw Persian ways as foreign or "barbaric." Alexander believed blending cultures would help unite his empire.

He also founded new cities named after himself (Alexandria) or his horse (Bucephala). Some stories say that after a victorious battle, he would hold large feasts and games, mixing Greek and local traditions. His soldiers sometimes grew resentful, feeling that Alexander was becoming too much like the Asian kings he conquered. Still, his habit of combining cultures was unique for a conqueror of his time. This shows how flexible Greek customs could become, even if it seemed bizarre to old-fashioned Greeks.

17. Funeral Games and Elaborate Burials

In many Greek stories, we hear of funeral games held to honor a fallen hero. For example, in Homer's "Iliad," after the death of Patroclus, Achilles hosts chariot races, boxing matches, and other contests. People believed that such games pleased the spirit of the dead and demonstrated the respect owed to them. Real Greek city-states sometimes held athletic events or feasts in memory of important figures.

As for burials, some Greeks buried their dead with small coins placed on or near the mouth. This was fare for Charon, the ferryman who took souls across the river Styx in the underworld. If a person did not have the coin, they might be trapped on the wrong side of the river. This idea might seem like a fairy tale, but it shows how strongly myth affected real customs. Families took care to provide the dead with what they might need in the afterlife, blending practical funeral practices with mythic beliefs.

---

18. Daily Life: Strange Foods and Customs

Greek diets were based on bread, olives, wine, cheese, vegetables, and fish. Meat was rarer, often eaten during religious sacrifices, where part of the animal was offered to the gods and the rest shared by the community. One surprising custom was the practice of "pharmakos," where at certain festivals, a person might be chosen to be a scapegoat. They were sometimes paraded around, mocked, or even driven out of the city to rid it of bad luck or sin.

Dress was usually simple: men and women wore a chiton or peplos made of linen or wool, fastened with pins or belts. But some wealthy Greeks enjoyed bright dyes like purple, which was expensive. Another interesting detail is that most Greeks, even poor ones, had slaves. Slavery was common, and it often included people captured in war or born into slavery. This might feel odd or disturbing, but it was part of Greek daily life and the economy.

19. Weird Superstitions: Curses and Magical Spells

Many Greeks believed in the power of curses and spells. They wrote curse tablets (katadesmoi) on thin sheets of lead, asking gods or spirits to harm an enemy or affect a trial. These tablets might be rolled up and placed in a grave or a well, believed to be closer to the underworld. Some asked for vengeance or demanded that someone lose a court case or fail in business.

People also sought out love spells, hoping to make someone fall for them. Herbs, charms, and amulets were used to protect against the evil eye or bad luck. While we often associate ancient Greece with rational philosophy, everyday folks had plenty of superstitions. It is a reminder that not everyone was a logical thinker like Aristotle. Magic and religion mixed in curious ways, affecting how people behaved and dealt with misfortune.

---

20. Reflections on the Quirky World of the Greeks

Ancient Greece was a place of high culture and strange customs. City-states constantly vied with each other in war and art, producing epic poetry, grand temples, and new forms of government. Yet at the same time, they believed in oracles who spoke in riddles, worshipped gods who acted like jealous humans, and performed wild rituals to honor gods of wine and frenzy.

This clash of sophistication and superstition gave Greece its unique flavor. The Greeks achieved great advancements in philosophy, science, and math. But they also practiced odd medical treatments, had secret cults, and used curses to solve personal problems. From the naked athletes of Olympia to the silent hoplites marching in a phalanx, Greek life was full of contrasts.

Even today, many of these ancient Greek traditions remain fascinating or puzzling. We can see how their myths shaped Western storytelling, how their democracy idea influenced modern governments, and how their theaters laid the groundwork for drama. But we should never forget the stranger sides—like men flinging wine drops at targets, or entire city-states organized around harsh military training. These oddities remind us that history is never just about progress and great ideas; it is also about the weird ways people lived, believed, and celebrated their world.

CHAPTER 5

Roman Oddities: Strange Stories from the Eternal City

Rome started as a small village near the Tiber River, but it grew into one of the greatest powers of the ancient world. The Romans built impressive roads, aqueducts, and stadiums, and they had strong armies that conquered lands far and wide. But behind the famous achievements, there were many unusual customs, quirky beliefs, and odd tales that make the history of Rome both fascinating and strange. In this chapter, we will look at some of these weird facts—from the times of kings and the Republic to the days of mighty emperors.

1. A Curious Beginning: Romulus and Remus

Roman legend says that Rome was founded by the twin brothers Romulus and Remus. As babies, they were left by the river, but a she-wolf saved them and cared for them. Later, the two brothers fought over where to build their city. Romulus killed Remus and named the city "Rome" after himself.

This story might sound like a fairy tale, but the Romans believed it explained their city's bold spirit. The symbol of a wolf nursing two human babies became a popular image in Roman art. It is certainly strange to think that an entire city traced its origins to a story of a wolf acting like a mother. But it shows how myths shaped Roman identity, giving them a heroic yet wild beginning.

2. The Roman Kings and Weird Ceremonies

Before Rome became a republic, it was ruled by a series of kings. These kings performed unusual ceremonies. For example, the city of Rome was said to have a boundary around it called the pomerium. Nobody could bury the dead or carry weapons inside this sacred boundary. When a king wanted to expand the city's territory, he performed a ritual involving plowing a special furrow to mark the new line. It sounds simple, but it was treated with great seriousness—breaking the boundary was considered an offense against the gods.

One of the strangest kings was Tarquinius Superbus, also known as Tarquin the Proud. He was said to be cruel and arrogant. A famous story says he once used a clever trick to conquer a city: he sent his son to pretend to be a deserter and trick the enemy from the inside. The king himself also performed weird acts like cutting the heads off tall poppies in his garden. When asked why he did this, he said it was a message to kill the top leaders of a rival city. This kind of cryptic behavior might seem odd, but it shows how cunning and suspicious Roman kings could be.

---

3. The Early Republic and Its Strange Positions

After the last king was overthrown, Rome became a republic, run by elected magistrates and the Senate. But some positions in the Roman Republic were strange by modern standards. For example, there was the role of the dictator: a single leader given full power for six months in times of crisis. This might sound scary, but the Romans saw it as a necessary way to act quickly during emergencies. Once the crisis ended, the dictator was supposed to give up power and return to normal life.

There were also offices like the tribunes, who could veto decisions they thought unfair to the common people (plebeians). The tribune's body was considered "sacred," so harming a tribune was a serious crime. Another odd office was the censor, who counted the population and could remove senators if they behaved badly. The censor also decided how much tax each person should pay based on wealth. This combination of moral watchdog and tax official seems unusual, but it was part of Rome's unique system to keep order.

---

4. Sacred Chickens and Reading Omens

The Romans believed heavily in signs from the gods, known as omens. Augurs (religious officials) would watch the flight of birds or examine the insides of animals to predict the future. One of the strangest customs involved "sacred chickens." Before a naval battle or important event, the commander would feed these holy chickens. If they ate eagerly, it meant the gods favored the plan. If they refused to eat, it was a bad sign.

There is a famous story about a Roman commander, Publius Claudius Pulcher, who became angry when the sacred chickens would not eat. He threw them into the sea, saying, "If they will not eat, let them drink!" The battle that followed went badly for the Romans, and many believed it was because he disrespected the omens. This tale shows how strongly Romans trusted supernatural signs, and how ignoring them could lead to disaster—or at least rumors of it.

---

5. Lupercalia: The Odd Festival of Fertility

One of the most bizarre festivals in Rome was Lupercalia, celebrated in mid-February. It honored the god of fertility and the legendary she-wolf who nursed Romulus and Remus. Priests, called Luperci, would gather at the sacred cave (Lupercal) where the wolf was said to have cared for the twins. They would sacrifice goats and a dog, then cut strips from the goat hides.

Next, these priests ran around the city, gently whipping people—especially women—with the goat-skin strips. Women believed that if they were struck, it would help them become pregnant or have an easier childbirth. As strange as it sounds, many Romans happily took part in this wild festival, seeing it as a tradition that brought health and fertility. The atmosphere was chaotic, like a rowdy street party that also had serious religious meaning.

---

6. Gladiator Games: More Than Brutal Fights

Gladiators were usually slaves or prisoners of war trained to fight in arenas. The fights could be brutal, but there was more to them than just violence. These combats were often part of funeral ceremonies or major public festivals, with a religious side that might surprise us. Some Romans believed that spilling blood honored the spirits of the dead or satisfied the gods.

Over time, gladiator games grew larger, moving from small gatherings to huge shows in amphitheaters like the Colosseum. Emperors would sponsor these games to gain popularity. The events included exotic animals and staged naval battles (naumachiae) when the arena was flooded with water. While it might seem purely violent, these events combined entertainment, ritual, and the idea of showing Rome's power over beasts and enemies.

However, not everyone liked the gladiator spectacles. Some writers complained that the people became too fond of blood and gore. Still, the games remained a big part of Roman culture for centuries.

---

7. Peculiar Punishments and Laws

Roman law was advanced in many ways. It introduced ideas like "innocent until proven guilty." However, punishments could be very cruel. One shocking method was crucifixion, where criminals (especially slaves or rebels) were nailed or tied to a cross until they died. Another punishment for parricide (killing a parent) involved placing the criminal in a sack with a dog, a monkey, a snake, and a rooster, then throwing it into a river. This bizarre act was meant to show how terrible the crime was, but it is surely one of the strangest punishments in history.

Romans also had strict rules about social status. A wealthy citizen might only face a fine for a crime, while a slave could face torture or death for the same offense. This shows that while Roman law aimed for order, it was not always fair by modern standards.

8. The Roman Baths: Social Hubs with Odd Customs

Public baths (thermae) were a central part of Roman life. People of all social classes visited baths to relax, exercise, and socialize. A typical bath complex had a gym area, hot rooms, warm rooms, and cold pools. People would apply oil to their skin, then scrape it off with a strigil (a curved tool). While this might seem strange, it was their way of cleaning.

Bathhouses could be huge, decorated with mosaics, statues, and gardens. Some even had libraries and snack bars. But there were also odd customs: Romans talked business, politics, and gossip while almost naked or wrapped in towels. Mixed bathing—men and women together—did happen in some periods, though it was often frowned upon or regulated. For outsiders, these bathhouses might have seemed both luxurious and a bit scandalous.

9. The Peculiar Feasts: More Than Just Eating

Roman banquets could be lavish affairs lasting many hours. Wealthy hosts showed off by serving rare foods like flamingo tongues, dormice (small rodents) stuffed with nuts, and exotic fish. Guests reclined on couches around a low table and ate with their fingers or spoons (forks were not common yet). Slaves brought in course after course, along with wine mixed with water.

Some hosts liked to impress (or shock) guests with surprising dishes. One famous story involves the writer Petronius describing a feast where a roasted pig, seemingly whole, was cut open at the table. Live thrushes flew out, creating a bizarre spectacle. While this may be partly fictional, it shows the lengths Romans went to for a unique experience. Vomiting in a nearby bowl to continue eating was not unheard of among the very rich, though it is debated how common this really was. Either way, Roman feasts were definitely more than just simple dinners.

10. Strange Family Structures and Naming Customs

Roman society placed great importance on the family (familia). The paterfamilias (father of the family) had absolute authority over his household. He could even decide whether a newborn baby would be raised or exposed (left outdoors to die or be taken in by someone else). Though harsh, this practice was accepted in many ancient cultures.

Roman naming customs were also unusual. Men often had three names: praenomen (personal name), nomen (family or clan name), and cognomen (a nickname or branch of the family). For example, Gaius Julius Caesar: Gaius was his personal name, Julius his clan, and Caesar was originally a nickname that became a family name. Women, on the other hand, typically used the feminine form of their father's clan name, sometimes with "the Younger" or "the Elder" if there were two daughters. This could lead to confusion, as many daughters in the same household would share the same name.

11. Vestal Virgins: Sacred Keepers of the Flame

One of the most special religious roles in Rome was that of the Vestal Virgins. These were priestesses who served Vesta, the goddess of the hearth (fire). Their main job was to keep the sacred flame in the Temple of

Vesta burning. If the flame went out, Romans believed something terrible might happen to the city.

Vestal Virgins took a vow of chastity for 30 years. If they broke it, the punishment was being buried alive. This severe rule showed how important their purity was to the Romans. On the plus side, Vestal Virgins had many privileges. They could own property, move freely, and even pardon criminals. People saw them as living symbols of Rome's safety. To us, this role might seem both respected and restrictive, but in Rome, it was considered a great honor.

---

12. Emperor Worship and Strange Deifications

In the Roman Republic, leaders were just important citizens. But during the Empire, starting with Augustus, emperors often encouraged a cult of personality. Some emperors were declared "divine" after death by the Senate. Temples were built to honor them, and priests offered sacrifices to their spirits. For Romans, this was both political and religious: honoring the emperor's spirit helped unify the empire around a single figure.

Certain emperors took this idea to odd extremes. Emperor Caligula was said to dress as various gods and demand worship. Emperor Domitian had people address him as "Lord and God." Emperor Commodus named months after himself and claimed he was Hercules reborn. These acts might seem ridiculous now, but they reflected the absolute power some emperors held. People who refused to worship the emperor risked punishment. This mix of politics and religion created strange scenes of people bowing to living men who claimed divine status.

---

13. Mad Emperors: Excesses and Odd Behavior

Rome's emperors came in many types, but the so-called "mad" ones draw the most attention for their strange behavior. Caligula, who ruled in the first century CE, is famous for wild stories: he might have tried to make his horse, Incitatus, a consul or a priest. Some sources claim he built a marble stall for the horse and fed it gold-flecked oats. While historians argue about the truth, these tales show how people viewed Caligula as erratic and power-hungry.

Nero is another emperor known for bizarre acts. Stories say he sang and played the lyre during the Great Fire of Rome. He also built a massive palace called the Domus Aurea (Golden House), with an enormous statue of himself. Though the "fiddling while Rome burned" might be exaggerated, Nero's reputation for cruelty and love of lavish things is well-documented. Romans feared him, yet they also enjoyed the public works and games he sponsored.

---

14. Slavery and Gladiators: Strange Opportunities

Rome's economy depended on slaves, who performed many jobs. Some slaves worked in harsh conditions on farms or in mines, but others served as teachers, accountants, or household managers. Freed slaves could become citizens, though with limited rights. Oddly, some slaves even gained wealth if they had valuable skills.

Gladiators, though usually slaves, could become famous like sports stars. The best gladiators won money, gifts, and the admiration of the crowds. A few even earned their freedom and became trainers or wealthy citizens. This contrast—slaves who were both despised and celebrated—shows how complicated Roman society was. It might seem contradictory to us, but for Romans, it was normal that a small number of slaves could rise in status if they had luck or special talent.

---

15. Roman Military Discipline and Peculiar Practices

The Roman army was well-known for its discipline. Soldiers trained hard, marched long distances in formation, and built fortified camps each night. They also had harsh punishments for cowardice. One feared practice was "decimation," where every tenth soldier in a unit found guilty of desertion or mutiny was executed. This penalty was meant to scare the rest into obedience.

On the battlefield, Roman generals used surprising tactics. They built bridges quickly across rivers, even floating ones, to surprise the enemy. Julius Caesar famously built a bridge across the Rhine River in just ten days, then took it down after marching his troops across, simply to show Germanic tribes that Rome could reach them any time. These feats, while impressive, also seem a bit over-the-top, reflecting Rome's desire to show power in dramatic ways.

---

16. Roads and Milestones: The Empire Connected

"All roads lead to Rome" is a famous saying, and it has some truth. The Romans built a massive network of roads—straight when possible—across their empire. These roads were marvels of engineering, with layers of stones for drainage. Along them, milestones marked distances, telling travelers how far to the next town or to Rome itself.

They also set up inns or way stations. Some travelers complained about bedbugs, theft, or poor food at these spots, but overall, the road system allowed trade and communication to flourish. Roman legions could move quickly to trouble spots. Couriers carried messages from the emperor to governors at high speed. The idea of placing stone markers might seem basic, but it was groundbreaking for an empire that spanned three continents.

17. Everyday Oddities: Clothing, Names, and Toilets

Daily Roman life had its own quirks. Men wore tunics, and citizens wore togas—a heavy, draped garment that could be quite awkward. Women wore stolas. Togas were usually bright white, unless you were in mourning or had a certain rank. The bigger your toga, the more cloth you displayed, showing off wealth.

Public toilets were also a curious part of Roman life. They were often large rooms with rows of stone seats that had holes leading to a drainage system. People would sit side by side with no partitions. A shared sponge on a stick served as toilet paper, rinsed in a water channel. Modern readers might find this lack of privacy strange, but to Romans, it was normal. It was also a chance to chat or socialize while taking care of personal business!

---

18. The Strange Cult of Mithras and Other Foreign Gods

Rome welcomed many gods from conquered lands. One mysterious religion that became popular was the cult of Mithras, likely from Persia. It involved secret rituals in underground temples called Mithraea. Members performed initiations, shared sacred meals, and worshipped Mithras, often shown slaying a bull.

Only men could join, and soldiers favored Mithras, seeing him as a protector in battle. Little was written about these rites, adding to the mystery. Archaeologists have found Mithraic temples with altars and images of Mithras. Why it attracted so many Romans is not fully clear, but it might have offered a sense of brotherhood and personal salvation. This is just one example of how Roman spirituality could be quite open-minded, mixing different gods and beliefs into a sometimes bewildering religious landscape.

---

19. Peculiar Entertainment Beyond Gladiators

Romans enjoyed many entertainments besides gladiator games. Chariot races at the Circus Maximus were huge events, drawing crowds of over a hundred thousand people. Teams had colors—Blue, Green, Red, and White—and fans showed loyalty similar to modern sports teams. Riots sometimes broke out if people felt races were unfair.

Romans also loved theater, but their plays sometimes included slapstick humor and rude jokes. Pantomime performers told stories through dance and gestures, wearing masks. Audiences could be rowdy, throwing food or hissing at actors they did not like. Another strange entertainment was public executions staged as mythological scenes. A criminal might be dressed as a character who died tragically in a legend, and then actually be killed in front of the audience. This might seem horrible to us, but it was viewed as part of the spectacle in ancient Rome.

---

20. Enduring Oddities: The Roman Legacy

Rome eventually fell in the West around the 5th century CE, but its culture left a lasting impact on Europe and beyond. Roads, laws, languages, and ideas from Rome shaped many future societies. Yet, it is easy to forget how weird Rome could be. From sacred chickens to public baths, from making an emperor into a god to hosting banquets with very odd dishes, the Romans blended practicality with superstition, refinement with brutality.

Looking at these oddities helps us see that even the most influential civilizations had strange sides. They worshipped many gods, feared omens, performed harsh punishments, and enjoyed spectacles that many today would find shocking. In modern times, we still admire Roman architecture and law, but we might be puzzled by some of their behaviors. That is what makes history so interesting: discovering how people lived, even in ways we might never expect.

Rome's story is a mixture of greatness and eccentricity. It taught the world about governance and engineering, but it also gave us tales of mad emperors, bizarre festivals, and peculiar rituals. By exploring these odd facts, we keep alive the full picture of ancient Rome: not just a center of power and progress, but also a place of deep superstition, grand feasts, and unforgettable strangeness.

CHAPTER 6

Eerie Egypt: Hidden Secrets and Bizarre Rituals

Ancient Egypt captures our imagination with its towering pyramids, mysterious hieroglyphs, and powerful pharaohs. Yet, beneath the grand monuments lies a wealth of strange practices that might seem puzzling to us now. From the cult of animal gods to elaborate mummification methods, the Egyptians lived in a world filled with ceremony and symbolism. In this chapter, we dive deep into these eerie customs, discovering how they viewed life, death, and the gods who ruled over all creation.

---

1. The Nile and the Shaping of Odd Traditions

Egypt depended on the Nile River. Each year, it flooded the land, leaving fertile soil behind. Egyptians believed this cycle mirrored the gods' gifts. They developed complex irrigation systems and planned their calendar around the Nile's flooding. This closeness to the river also shaped their beliefs. They saw the annual flood as a sign that the gods were watching over them.

But life along the Nile came with peculiar traditions. Some festivals involved throwing statues or offerings into the water to please the river gods or ensure a good flood. People prayed to Hapi, the spirit of the Nile's floods, and offered thanks when the waters rose enough for good harvests. It might seem odd to us that an entire society relied on a river's yearly cycle for survival, but for Egypt, the Nile was everything, and they showed their respect in unique ways.

---

2. Strange Beginnings: The God-Kings Called Pharaohs

Egypt's rulers were not just kings; they were also seen as gods on Earth. The term "pharaoh" originally meant the royal palace but came to refer to the ruler. Egyptians believed the pharaoh upheld ma'at—order, truth, and balance. Without him, chaos could rise. This gave the pharaoh immense power, but also heavy responsibilities.

Pharaohs performed daily temple rituals to keep the gods happy. They sometimes took on the persona of certain gods, dressing in special outfits or performing symbolic actions. For example, a pharaoh might break open the soil with a ceremonial tool, showing that he brought fertility to the land. These acts might seem theatrical, but to Egyptians, they were essential for cosmic balance. The idea that one person could hold the key to harmony between heaven and earth is certainly a unique viewpoint.

3. Gods Everywhere: Animals and Unusual Deities

The Egyptian pantheon is famous for gods with animal heads: Anubis with a jackal head, Horus with a falcon head, Thoth with an ibis head, and so on. These gods mixed human and animal features, symbolizing their powers. The jackal, for instance, prowled near cemeteries, so Anubis was linked to death and embalming.

It was not just the big gods—many local towns had their own animal gods. Cats were sacred to Bastet, a protective goddess. Crocodiles were worshipped in some places as symbols of Sobek, the crocodile god. People sometimes kept these animals in temples, feeding them special meals and adorning them with jewels. To us, it might sound odd to pamper a crocodile or cat as a living symbol of a god, but for Egyptians, caring for these animals was a holy act. They believed the gods could live within these creatures or watch through their eyes.

4. The Pyramids: Tombs or Portals?

The giant pyramids, especially those at Giza, are among the most iconic structures on Earth. Built as tombs for pharaohs like Khufu, Khafre, and Menkaure, these massive monuments contained hidden passages and burial chambers. Some were originally covered in white limestone, making them shine in the sun. While many see them as simple tombs, the Egyptians believed they helped the pharaoh ascend to the afterlife and possibly join the sun god Ra.

Oddly, the largest pyramid, the Great Pyramid of Khufu, has such precise construction that historians still marvel at how it was done with ancient tools. Workers had to haul giant stones from distant quarries. Some weird theories claim aliens built them, but most experts say skilled Egyptian laborers completed the task over decades, using ramps and sleds. The real mystery might be the number of secret chambers or the exact design logic. Even now, the pyramids keep some secrets locked away behind thick walls.

---

5. Mummification: Protecting the Body for Eternity

Perhaps the most eerie aspect of ancient Egypt is mummification. Egyptians believed the body had to be preserved so the spirit (ka) and soul (ba) could reunite after death, allowing the person to live on in the afterlife. Embalmers removed the organs—liver, lungs, stomach, and intestines—and stored them in canopic jars with protective god heads. The brain was often taken out through the nose and discarded, as Egyptians thought it was not that important!

The body was then dried with natron (a type of salt) for many days before being wrapped in linen bandages. Spells and amulets were placed between the layers for protection. The entire process could take up to 70 days. Families paid different amounts depending on how fancy they wanted the mummification to be. While it might seem creepy, it was a deeply spiritual process for Egyptians. They believed this ritual guaranteed eternal life. Without it, a person's soul could be lost forever.

---

6. Animal Mummies: Millions of Sacred Creatures

Strangely, humans were not the only ones mummified. Egyptians also mummified animals—cats, birds, crocodiles, baboons, and even beetles.

Some were buried with their owners as pets, while others were offerings to gods. For instance, cat mummies were common offerings to Bastet, and ibis mummies were offered to Thoth. Archaeologists have found entire cat cemeteries with thousands of mummified felines.

In some cases, the demand for animal mummies led to mass breeding of these creatures just to be sacrificed. This might sound disturbing, but for Egyptians, it was an act of devotion. They believed giving these mummified animals to the gods would bring blessings. Today, we look at rows of cat mummies in museums and wonder at a culture that saw the divine in so many creatures.

7. The Book of the Dead: A Guide to a Strange Afterlife

Egyptians believed the afterlife was complex. They needed instructions to safely travel through the underworld and reach the Field of Reeds, a paradise where they could farm and relax as they did on Earth. These instructions were often written on papyrus scrolls or on the walls of tombs, known as the Book of the Dead (though Egyptians called it the "Book of Coming Forth by Day").

These texts included spells to avoid demons, pass through gates guarded by snake-headed creatures, and pass the final judgment by Osiris. In one famous scene, a person's heart is weighed on scales against a feather of truth. If the heart was heavier (due to sin), a monster called Ammit—part crocodile, part lion, part hippo—ate it, and the soul was destroyed. If it balanced, the soul entered paradise. It might sound like a scary test, but for Egyptians, it was vital to live a moral life so that they could pass. They took these beliefs so seriously that even in daily life, they tried to behave with ma'at (balance and goodness).

8. Tomb Curses: Fact or Fiction?

The idea of "mummy curses" is popular in movies, but were ancient Egyptians really writing spells to harm tomb raiders? Some tomb inscriptions do threaten harm to anyone who disturbs the burial. For instance, a curse might say, "The gods shall punish those who trespass." Most tombs, however, had prayers or blessings rather than explicit curses. The Egyptians wanted to protect the dead from robbers but also sought to preserve peace for the deceased.

Despite this, tomb robbery was common throughout Egyptian history because the tombs held precious items—gold, jewelry, and other valuables. Some tombs show signs of repeated looting. The modern idea of a "curse" might come from real warnings plus sensational stories. Perhaps the eeriest part is that many archaeologists who discovered tombs died years later from various causes, leading people to link their deaths to curses. In reality, it was likely disease, infection, or coincidence.

9. Opulent Obelisks and Their Travel

Obelisks are tall, pointed pillars often placed at temple entrances. They were carved from a single block of stone, usually granite, and covered with hieroglyphs praising gods or pharaohs. Moving these giant monuments from quarries to temple sites was a huge job. Workers floated them on barges along the Nile or dragged them on sleds.

Later, foreign rulers took some obelisks away. For example, Roman emperors transported several obelisks to Rome, setting them up in public places. The idea that an entire empire would move a giant stone pillar for decoration seems quite odd. But these obelisks were prized trophies, showing off a conqueror's power. Even now, we can find Egyptian obelisks in places like Paris, London, and New York, far from the desert land where they were first raised in honor of the sun god Ra.

---

10. Funerary Boats: Sailing to the Afterlife

Egyptians believed the afterlife might require a journey across cosmic waters. Pharaohs often placed full-sized boats in or near their tombs. These "solar boats" symbolized the sun god Ra's boat that sailed across the sky by day and through the underworld by night. One famous example is the Khufu ship found near the Great Pyramid, carefully dismantled and buried.

The idea of burying a boat might seem strange, but it was a statement of faith. If the pharaoh needed to sail with Ra or journey to distant realms of the underworld, he would have a royal vessel ready. The Khufu ship was so well-preserved that modern experts reassembled it, discovering it was a masterpiece of ancient shipbuilding, about 44 meters long. This level of detail for a boat never meant to sail in real water is a testament to how deeply Egyptians believed in the afterlife.

---

11. Animal Cults: Sacred Bulls and More

Among the many animal cults, the Apis bull in Memphis was one of the most prominent. The Apis bull was seen as a living manifestation of the god Ptah (and later associated with Osiris). When a special calf with specific markings was found, priests declared it the new Apis. It lived in luxury, fed the best food, and wore jewelry. People came from all over to ask for blessings.

When the Apis bull died, it received a grand funeral and a carefully prepared tomb. The cost might seem outrageous for a single animal, but

Egyptians felt it was a divine being. Some travelers from Greece and Rome found this practice both impressive and strange. They saw crowds weeping for a bull, dressing it in gold, and performing lengthy funerals. It highlights how Egyptian religion merged animals and gods in ways that outsiders often found bewildering.

---

12. Temples as Cosmic Models

Egyptian temples were not just places to pray. They were designed as models of the universe. The rooms grew darker and more cramped as one moved deeper inside, symbolizing the journey into the realm of the gods. Sacred lakes beside temples represented the primeval waters of creation. Columns might be carved to look like bundled reeds or lotus flowers, reflecting the marshy environment where life began in Egyptian mythology.

Priests in these temples carried out daily rituals, washing statues of the gods and offering food, incense, and prayers. Ordinary people could not enter the holiest areas, but they might gather in courtyards or present offerings. To us, the idea that the building itself represented the structure of the cosmos is quite grand. Yet, for Egyptians, each architectural detail mattered, linking the earthly realm to the divine.

---

13. Marriage and Family: Odd Rules and Roles

Egyptian society placed strong value on family. Many Egyptians married young, and unlike in some ancient cultures, women had considerable rights. They could own property, divorce, and even serve as rulers (like the famous Hatshepsut). However, some royal families practiced sibling marriage to keep the bloodline "pure." This was especially true among pharaohs, who saw themselves as gods and believed marrying within the family kept the divine line intact.

To outsiders, sibling marriage was shocking, but the Egyptians had done it for centuries among royals. They also had relaxed attitudes about inheritance. Women could inherit land and pass it on to their children. This mixture of advanced rights for women but also acceptance of incest in the royal line shows the complexity of Egyptian culture.

---

14. The Mystery of Akhenaten's Odd Religion

Akhenaten was a pharaoh of the New Kingdom who tried to shift Egypt's religion to worship Aten—the sun disk—almost as a single god. He closed temples to other gods and built a new capital city called Akhetaten (modern-day Amarna). Art from this period shows him with an elongated head and skinny limbs, hugging his family under the rays of the sun.

This might have been the earliest attempt at monotheism in history, or close to it. But it was very unpopular with many Egyptians who loved their traditional gods. After Akhenaten's death, his successors (including the famous Tutankhamun) reversed these changes, reopened old temples, and destroyed records of his rule. The sudden shift and the odd art style have puzzled scholars for centuries. Some wonder if Akhenaten had a genetic disorder or simply wanted a new style. Either way, his reign stands out as a strange moment in Egyptian history.

---

15. Hairstyles, Wigs, and Cone Perfumes

Both men and women in Egypt often shaved their heads for cleanliness and wore wigs. These wigs could be thick with tight curls. They were made from human hair or plant fibers. Wealthy Egyptians had fancy wigs braided with gold or beads, while poorer people used simpler versions. Shaving the head also helped with the heat and to avoid lice.

Another odd custom was the use of scented cones made of fat or wax mixed with perfume. People wore these cones on their heads during banquets or festivals. As the evening went on, the cones slowly melted, releasing a pleasant smell. This might seem strange—imagine walking around with a melting cone on your head—but it was how Egyptians kept cool and fragrant in the desert climate.

16. Music, Dance, and the Power of Hathor

Music and dance were central to Egyptian celebrations. Harps, flutes, and percussion instruments accompanied dancers who performed for gods, pharaohs, and guests at feasts. Hathor, the cow-headed goddess, was connected to music, joy, and love. Temple drawings show women shaking sistrums (rattle-like instruments) to honor her.

Sometimes, music and dance had a mystical purpose. In certain rituals, dancers wore masks of gods or animals to represent divine powers on Earth. The boundary between performer and deity could blur, which might feel spooky to modern viewers. But for Egyptians, these performances brought the gods closer and ensured their favor.

17. The Weighing of the Heart and Judgment

As mentioned, the Egyptians believed the dead had to pass through the Hall of Two Truths, where their heart was weighed against the feather of Ma'at. This final judgment decided if they reached the blissful Field of Reeds or faced destruction. The heart was thought to be the seat of intelligence and emotion (they did not value the brain as much).

During the mummification process, embalmers left the heart in the body because the soul would need it at judgment. To keep it safe, they might place a heart scarab amulet over the chest, inscribed with spells telling the heart not to speak against its owner. To us, it is peculiar to imagine an amulet that instructs the heart to remain silent about a person's sins. Yet, it shows how Egyptians prepared for every detail of the afterlife, hoping to avoid a nasty surprise when facing the gods.

---

18. Grave Goods and Shabti Servants

Egyptian tombs often contained all sorts of items for the afterlife: food, furniture, jewelry, and even toys. Pharaohs and rich nobles filled their burial chambers with gold, beds, chariots, and weapons. People believed they would need these things in the next world.

One especially odd feature is the presence of "shabtis"—small figurines shaped like mummified humans, each holding tools. These figures were meant to act as servants or workers for the deceased in the afterlife. If the gods called upon the dead to do labor, a magic spell could bring the shabti to life to do the work instead. This was so important that some tombs have hundreds of shabtis, ensuring the dead could relax in paradise. It is basically an ancient form of having "backup workers" on call!

---

19. The Rosetta Stone: Unlocking Weird Writings

For a long time, hieroglyphs were a mystery because nobody could read them after ancient Egyptian civilization declined. Then, in 1799, the Rosetta Stone was found. It had the same text in Greek, Demotic (a later Egyptian script), and hieroglyphs. Scholars used it to decipher hieroglyphs for the first time in modern history.

The texts revealed many strange beliefs, rituals, and stories. We learned about how Egyptians recorded daily life, prayers, and even jokes. Hieroglyphs themselves can seem odd: pictures of birds, eyes, and snakes standing for sounds or ideas. But once translated, they show a complex society that used writing for trade records, tax lists, love poems, and religious spells. Without the Rosetta Stone, much of Egypt's bizarre and wonderful culture would have remained hidden.

---

20. Lasting Mysteries and Fascination

Ancient Egypt lasted for thousands of years, through different kingdoms, invasions, and shifts in power. Yet it maintained a distinctive culture, with consistent religious beliefs about gods, the afterlife, and the importance of order. Pharaohs rose and fell, pyramids were built, and new temples appeared. Even today, we continue to make discoveries that shed light on how these people lived.

The strangest parts of Egyptian culture—mummifying animals, worshipping crocodiles, wearing perfume cones, burying boats, and more—remind us of how diverse human beliefs can be. While we might find these customs eerie or puzzling, to ancient Egyptians, they were part of a larger system that kept the world in balance and guided them after death. Their monuments still stand as silent witnesses to a civilization that saw magic, religion, and daily life as deeply connected.

That is what makes ancient Egypt so fascinating: behind every statue and inscription, there is a blend of beauty and mystery. The Egyptians believed life continued beyond the tomb, so they prepared carefully, leaving behind art, texts, and tombs that speak to us across millennia. Even though we live in a very different age, we can still feel the strange pull of Egyptian beliefs—haunted by the sense that there is more to life than what we see, and that, in some corner of eternity, the pharaohs still sail with the sun.

CHAPTER 7

Barbarian Nations: Surprising Facts About Europe's Early Tribes

When we hear the word "barbarian," we might picture wild warriors attacking the Roman Empire or living in uncivilized, harsh lands. The Romans often used the term "barbarian" for any group that did not speak Latin or Greek, so it included many different peoples. But these so-called "barbarian nations" were not just one large, unruly mass. They were made up of tribes with their own customs, religions, and leaders. They lived in different parts of Europe, from the dense forests of Germania to the misty islands of Britain.

In this chapter, we will explore the surprising facts and strange practices of some of these tribes: the Celts, the Germanic peoples, the Goths, and others who made their mark on ancient Europe before medieval times. We will learn how many of their beliefs and ways of life were very different from the Romans'—and sometimes quite shocking.

1. Understanding the Term "Barbarian"

The term "barbarian" comes from the Greek word "bárbaros," which meant someone who spoke a language the Greeks found unintelligible—sounding like "bar-bar." The Romans took this idea and used "barbarian" to label anyone outside their empire. However, the tribes beyond Rome's borders had complex cultures. They had their own laws, trade networks, and even art styles that might seem wild to outsiders, but were highly meaningful to them.

Far from living in constant chaos, many tribes formed alliances or confederations. They negotiated with the Roman Empire and, in some cases, even served in Roman armies. Some chieftains became wealthy from trade or from raiding. When we look at these groups more closely, we realize they were not just mindless warriors. They had social rules, religions full of odd gods and spirits, and traditions that might appear strange to outsiders then—and to us now.

2. The Celts: Head-Hunting and Strange Rituals

The Celtic peoples once spread across much of Europe, from what is now Spain and France (Gaul) to parts of the British Isles and Central Europe. They had a reputation for being fierce warriors. The Romans described them as tall, with long hair and big moustaches. But beyond the warlike image, Celtic culture was rich and full of surprises.

One of the strangest facts about some Celtic tribes was their practice of head-hunting. Warriors believed that the head was the seat of a person's spirit or power. So, taking an enemy's head as a trophy was a way to capture that power. Archaeologists have found evidence of skulls displayed on wooden poles or hung in houses. These trophies might seem grim, but in Celtic culture, they were respected symbols of victory and strength.

The Celts also held druids in high esteem. Druids were priests, judges, teachers, and keepers of lore. They memorized long poems and laws, passing them orally to the next generation. Because they relied on oral knowledge, we do not have many written records from the druids themselves. Much of what we know comes from Roman sources, who sometimes portrayed them as doing human sacrifices. For instance, Julius Caesar claimed that druids burned criminals inside large wicker structures. While historians debate the accuracy of these stories, they do show that the Celts had religious rituals the Romans found shocking.

---

3. Celtic Women and Surprising Freedoms

Compared to many ancient societies, Celtic women often enjoyed a higher status. They could own property, initiate divorce, and even lead tribes into battle. One famous example is Queen Boudicca (or Boadicea) of the Iceni in Britain. After the Romans mistreated her and her daughters, Boudicca led a revolt in the 1st century CE, burning Roman towns like Camulodunum (Colchester) and Londinium (London). She shocked the Romans with her fierce leadership.

Boudicca's story shows that the Celts did not always fit the Roman idea of how societies should be run. Having a warrior queen was unthinkable for many Romans, but for the Britons under Boudicca, it was a call to unity against foreign rule. While her uprising ultimately failed, her legacy lived on as a symbol of resistance and a reminder that Celtic societies could have powerful female rulers.

---

4. Celebrations and Festivals: Samhain and Beltane

Celtic tribes marked the changing seasons with festivals that connected everyday life to the spirit world. Two of the most famous Celtic festivals are Samhain and Beltane.

- **Samhain** (pronounced "SAH-win") happened around the end of harvest (late October to early November). People believed the boundary between the living and the dead grew thin at this time. Spirits could cross over more easily. Families lit bonfires to ward off evil and to honor their ancestors. People might wear costumes or disguises to protect themselves from wandering ghosts or fairies. It is easy to see how this tradition may have influenced modern Halloween customs.

- **Beltane** took place around May 1st, celebrating the coming of summer and the fertility of the land. Huge fires were lit, and cattle were driven between them to protect them from disease. People danced around bonfires and performed rituals to encourage a fruitful growing season. Beltane was also a time for matchmaking games, hinting at romance in the warmer months.

These festivals might seem magical or mysterious. They show how the Celts blended daily life—like farming and herding animals—with a deep respect for unseen spiritual forces.

5. The Germanic Tribes: Fierce Honor and Strange Oaths

North and east of the Celts lived the Germanic peoples: tribes like the Suebi, Cherusci, Goths, Vandals, and many more. The Romans often feared them, remembering disasters like the Battle of the Teutoburg Forest (9 CE), where Germanic warriors ambushed and destroyed three Roman legions. But Germanic culture was not just about war—it also included complex loyalty systems, feasts, and laws passed down through generations.

One odd feature was the Germanic tradition of the **comitatus**, a group of loyal warriors sworn to a chief or king. These warriors pledged to fight to the death for their leader, and in return, he shared treasure, food, and honor with them. It was almost like a family bond formed by oaths rather than blood. Failing to protect your chief was considered a great shame, worse than death.

Germanic law often included **trial by ordeal**, where a person accused of a crime might hold a hot iron or plunge a hand into boiling water. If the wound healed cleanly, they were judged innocent—if infected, guilty. Such customs might sound harsh, but they reflected a deep belief that the gods or fate would reveal the truth in these trials.

6. The Goths, Vandals, and Wild Migrations

Over time, several Germanic tribes began migrating for new lands or fleeing other nomadic groups (like the Huns). The **Goths** split into the Visigoths and Ostrogoths, moving southward and eventually sacking Rome in 410 CE under their leader Alaric. The **Vandals** marched through Gaul (now France) into Spain and even crossed into North Africa, capturing Carthage. From there, they launched raids across the Mediterranean.

The word "vandalism" today comes from the Vandals' reputation for destroying buildings and art, especially when they sacked Rome in 455 CE. However, some historians argue that the Vandals were not always as destructive as the term suggests. They may have been brutal conquerors, but they also tried to govern their new territories, adopting local customs and blending their culture with that of the people they ruled.

For the Romans, watching these tribes move across their empire was terrifying. It seemed like the end of the civilized world. But for the tribes, it was a chance to find better farmland, avoid pressure from other invaders, or simply grab the wealth of the crumbling Roman territories. Some of their customs—like naming kings, forming new kingdoms, and creating laws—show that "barbarian" did not always mean chaotic. They could organize societies that lasted for centuries, such as the Visigothic Kingdom in Spain.

---

7. Daily Life: Houses, Food, and Clans

How did these "barbarians" live when not at war? Many tribes lived in small villages, surrounded by fields where they grew grains or kept animals. Their houses were often wooden huts with thatched roofs. Large families lived together, sometimes with animals nearby to keep them safe and warm. In colder climates, sharing heat with animals might have been necessary, though it sounds odd to us today.

For food, they ate bread from barley or wheat, along with vegetables, dairy products, and meat when available. Hunting and fishing were also common.

They drank ale or mead (a drink made from honey), and feasts were important social events. A chief would hold a feast to reward warriors or celebrate a victory, offering roasted meats and abundant drink. These gatherings helped keep bonds of loyalty strong.

Clans or extended families formed the backbone of society. Being loyal to kin was essential. If someone harmed a member of your clan, it was your duty to seek compensation or revenge. This led to feuds or "blood feuds," which could last for years unless settled by paying a "weregild" (man-price). The weregild was a set amount of money or goods paid to end the feud. It might seem like a strange idea—to put a price on a person's life—but it was a way to avoid endless revenge killings.

---

8. Beliefs in Gods, Spirits, and Magic

Germanic and Celtic tribes had rich mythologies. Before Christianization, the Germanic peoples worshipped gods like Odin (Woden), Thor, Freya, and others. They believed the world was held together by Yggdrasil, a great cosmic tree, and that brave warriors went to Valhalla after death in battle. Meanwhile, Celtic mythology included gods like Lugus (Lugh), Dagda, and Morrigan, as well as nature spirits dwelling in rivers, springs, and forests.

Rituals often took place outdoors or in sacred groves, not always in temples. Sacrifices of animals (and sometimes humans) were offered to win favor from the gods or ensure good harvests. Charms and amulets were worn to protect against evil spirits. Some tribes believed in shape-shifting and carried tales of men turning into wolves or bears (these might have been related to warrior cults who wore animal skins for battle). To outsiders, these beliefs seemed wild, but for the tribes, the spirit world was woven into everyday life.

People also feared witches or sorcerers who could cast harmful spells. Some performed protective magic to keep enemies or disease away. Others used runes (like the Germanic runic alphabets) not just for writing but for divination, carving them on stones or pieces of wood to seek the guidance of the gods.

---

9. Battle Tactics: Ambushes and Fearsome Charges

Roman historians described Celtic and Germanic warriors as terrifying in battle. Some fought naked or wore minimal clothing to show bravery, while painting their bodies or spiking their hair with lime. The Celts, for instance, might blow loud trumpets to unnerve the enemy. The Germanic tribes often relied on ambushes in forests, using their knowledge of local terrain.

A favorite tactic was the **shield wall**, where warriors locked their shields together to form a protective barrier. The front lines clashed with spears and swords, while others threw javelins from behind. War chiefs might carry special standards (like the boar symbol among the Celts or the draco among some Germanic tribes), which were more than just flags—they were believed to carry the tribe's spirit. If a standard fell, it meant a great loss of honor.

Yet, not every tribe used the same methods. Some, like the Goths, became skilled horsemen. Others adapted Roman techniques after serving in Roman armies. Over time, these "barbarians" learned to build siege engines, adopt metalworking for better weapons, and even mint coins. So while we might picture them as primitive, they were quite capable of learning and adapting.

---

10. Strangeness in Dress and Appearance

Some Roman writers mocked the way barbarian tribes dressed. Celts liked bright colors and patterns, especially plaids or striped woolen cloth. They made jewelry of gold or bronze—torcs (neck rings) were common among high-ranking warriors. The dramatic moustaches of Gallic warriors were so famous that Roman coins sometimes showed them.

Germanic peoples favored simpler clothing, often a tunic and trousers made from wool or leather. But they too wore jewelry, sometimes from silver or iron. A strange detail is that some tribes bleached their hair to make it appear blonde, which the Romans found odd. They might also rub animal fat or lime into their hair to make it stiff and spiky. Such hairstyles may have had a religious or symbolic meaning, or simply served to look fierce in battle.

For the Romans—who prized togas and neatly cropped hair—these flamboyant styles seemed uncouth. But from the perspective of the tribes, their clothing and body art were marks of pride, identity, and rank.

11. Trading with the "Civilized" World

Despite conflicts, there was also trade between the barbarians and Rome. Celtic and Germanic tribes traded amber, furs, slaves, and agricultural products in exchange for Roman wine, oil, pottery, and luxury goods. The presence of Roman coins and goods in faraway tribal lands shows these connections were quite extensive.

Some tribes grew wealthy by acting as middlemen, passing goods from the north or east to Roman markets. Others used Roman coinage to pay their warriors or to show off wealth at feasts. Over time, the lines between "Roman" and "barbarian" blurred. Some tribal chiefs wore Roman-style clothing or built houses influenced by Roman villas. Meanwhile, Roman soldiers posted on the frontiers began to adopt local customs, even marrying women from tribal communities.

This blending might be surprising, given how often the two sides fought. But it shows that everyday life was not always about warfare. Merchants, travelers, and diplomats created links of culture and commerce. Sometimes, the same tribe that raided a Roman town one season might trade peacefully the next.

---

12. Influence on Language and Culture

Even after Rome fell, the legacy of the barbarians lived on in Europe. Germanic languages—like English, German, Dutch, and the Scandinavian languages—evolved from the tongues these tribes spoke. Celtic languages, though fewer in speakers now, survive in Irish, Scottish Gaelic, and Welsh.

In many parts of Europe, place names still carry traces of ancient tribal settlements. Archaeology reveals art styles, like the swirling La Tène style of the Celts, which influenced designs on weapons and jewelry for centuries. Tribal laws and customs also laid foundations for medieval legal systems. For example, the "Salic Law" of the Franks impacted inheritance rules in parts of Europe much later.

It is funny to think how a group once labeled barbarian could shape entire languages, laws, and cultural patterns for ages to come. But that is exactly what happened as these tribes carved out their own kingdoms on the ruins of the Western Roman Empire.

---

13. Strange Burial Customs and Grave Goods

Just like other ancient cultures, many barbarian tribes had unique burial practices. The Celts often placed the dead in underground chambers with rich grave goods—fancy weapons, pots, and sometimes chariots. In one famous find, the "Vix Grave" in France, a Celtic princess was buried with a massive bronze krater (a vase for mixing wine) likely from Greece, showing how far trade goods traveled.

Germanic tribes also buried warriors with their weapons, horses, or even entire boats. The boat burials of the later Vikings (a separate Germanic group in the north) are famous, but earlier tribes might also have placed the dead in ships or in special wagons. Some graves have large stone circles or standing stones marking them. The belief was that the deceased would need these possessions in the afterlife or that burying them properly showed respect and avoided hauntings.

In certain cases, archaeologists find evidence of human or animal sacrifice at these graves. A chief might be buried with his servants or slaves so they could continue to serve him beyond the grave. While this practice disturbs us today, it was part of some ancient cultures' views on loyalty and the afterlife.

14. Transition to Christianity: Odd Blends of Faith

Over time, many of these tribes converted to Christianity. The Goths were among the first, partly thanks to a missionary named Ulfilas (Wulfila), who created a Gothic alphabet to translate the Bible. Other tribes converted for political reasons—allying with Christian kingdoms—or because of the influence of captured Roman citizens who spread Christian beliefs.

Yet, the process of conversion was often slow and blended with old customs. A tribe might build a church, but still celebrate old pagan festivals. They might accept the Christian God, but also keep charms against forest spirits. This mixture of beliefs led to unique forms of folk Christianity. For instance, the Frankish King Clovis converted to Catholic Christianity around 496 CE, which helped him gain support from the Roman Church in Gaul. But many of his people likely held onto old gods in secret for a time.

The blending of pagan and Christian traditions could look strange: a feast day for a saint might fall on the same date as a tribal harvest festival. People might pray in a church, yet also bury items with the dead for the afterlife. This slow mixture shows that "barbarian" religions did not vanish overnight—they merged into new cultural practices that shaped medieval Europe.

15. Unusual Kings and Warriors

With the fall of the Western Roman Empire, many barbarian chiefs became kings of new realms. The Frankish King Charlemagne (8th–9th century) is often called the "Father of Europe" for uniting large parts of the continent. Though he lived in a later time, his ancestors were once considered barbarians by the Romans.

Other tribal kings, like Theodoric the Great (an Ostrogoth), tried to preserve Roman culture in Italy even as they ruled as "barbarian" monarchs. The Vandals in North Africa had kings who minted coins with their images, copied from Roman-style coinage. This odd situation—barbarian kings imitating Roman emperors—showed how the old empire's culture still had prestige, even among the very people who toppled it.

Warrior elites in these kingdoms often wore Roman military belts or brooches but combined them with tribal motifs. They might speak a mix of Latin, local languages, and possibly Greek. In big banquets, they praised their own ancestors' heroic deeds while enjoying Roman wines. This cultural mash-up created a fascinating blend of old Roman civilization and new tribal identities.

---

16. Quirky Superstitions and Folklore

Folk tales among the barbarian tribes were full of heroes, giants, dwarfs, and magical items. We see echoes of these stories in later Germanic and Norse epics, like "Beowulf" or the "Nibelungenlied." These poems mention monsters like Grendel (in "Beowulf") or dragons that guard hoards of gold. Though these are literary works from the early medieval period, they grew from older oral traditions.

One odd belief was that certain people could have the "evil eye," casting curses by just looking at someone. Amulets against the evil eye were common. Another fear was that the dead might rise as restless spirits. Some graves show heavy stones placed on top of the body, perhaps to keep them from climbing out.

Seasonal rites to appease nature's forces also continued. People might leave offerings at sacred trees or wells to ensure good harvests or to cure illnesses. These traditions lived on, even as official religion changed. In remote areas, travelers sometimes noted strange rituals combining Christian prayers with old pagan symbols, creating a cultural patchwork that can still be sensed in European folklore today.

---

17. Impact on Europe's Map

As these tribes migrated and set up kingdoms, they reshaped Europe's political map. The Angles, Saxons, and Jutes went to Britain, forming the early basis of England (Angle-land). The Franks consolidated power in Gaul, giving rise to France (Francia). The Burgundians settled in eastern Gaul, the Vandals in North Africa, the Visigoths in Spain, and the Ostrogoths in Italy. Over centuries, these realms would change again, but the roots of many modern European nations trace back to these "barbarian" kingdoms.

While some kingdoms collapsed quickly (the Vandals in North Africa fell to the Byzantine Empire in 534 CE), others endured. The Frankish realm expanded under Charlemagne, shaping much of Western Europe's future. Even the name "England" is a reminder of the Angles, a Germanic tribe once called barbarians by the Romans. It is strange how groups viewed as uncivilized ended up forming the foundation for modern states.

---

18. Artistic Expressions: Metalwork and Animal Styles

Barbarian tribes are also known for their distinctive metalwork, often called the "Animal Style" in archaeology. They decorated items—swords, helmets, brooches, belts—with intricate patterns of interlaced animals, swirling lines, and geometric shapes. This art style seems chaotic at first glance, but it required skill and careful planning.

For example, the famous Sutton Hoo ship burial in England (early 7th century) revealed stunning artifacts with gold and garnet inlays, featuring stylized birds and beasts. While Sutton Hoo is from a slightly later period, it shows how earlier Germanic or Anglo-Saxon art reached a high level of craftsmanship.

These designs might have had symbolic meanings—certain animals could represent clan totems, or the swirling shapes might reflect mythological concepts. To Romans used to columns and arches, this style was bizarre, but for the tribes, it was a proud statement of identity and belief.

19. The Curious Fate of the Huns

Though not Germanic or Celtic, the Huns had a big impact on barbarian movements. They arrived from Central Asia in the 4th century, driving Goths and other tribes westward. Led by Attila, the Huns terrorized parts of the Roman Empire, demanding gold and tribute. Attila earned the name "Scourge of God" among Christians, who saw him as a punishment for Rome's sins.

The Huns themselves had strange customs (from the Roman viewpoint). They were skilled horse archers, rarely staying in one place for long. Some accounts claim they practiced cranial deformation—binding infants' heads to create a distinctive skull shape. Others described them as scarred from childhood, with lines on their cheeks or foreheads. While these might be exaggerated, they painted a fearsome image of a mobile, relentless force.

Attila's death in 453 CE caused the Hunnic Empire to collapse quickly. Without his leadership, the Huns scattered. But the chaos they caused had already reshaped Europe's tribes. Many Germanic groups found new homes within Roman lands, or carved out kingdoms in the power vacuum left by Rome's decline.

20. Looking Back at the "Barbarians"

When we think of the barbarian nations, we see a tapestry of tribes each with its own culture, religion, and way of life. Rome's perspective painted them as wild and uncultured, but archaeology and historical research tell a more complex story. They had laws, crafts, trade, and beliefs that were different from Rome's, not necessarily lesser.

These tribes introduced new elements into Europe's cultural mix. Their art styles, languages, and heroic legends shaped the medieval period. Many of their practices—like the Celtic festivals that influenced modern holidays—still echo in today's world. The image of the savage barbarian with unkempt hair, wearing animal skins, is only part of the story. In reality, these tribes had their own codes of honor, rich mythologies, and advanced techniques in metalwork and trade.

It is amazing to realize how much they impacted Europe, from the fall of Rome to the rise of the early medieval kingdoms. Names like Alaric, Boudicca, Attila, and Clovis still spark images of conquests and rebellions. But behind every fierce battle was a community of farmers, artisans, and families with beliefs and traditions that might seem strange yet reveal a fascinating chapter in human history.

Thus, the "barbarian nations" were more than simple destroyers. They were complex societies with odd customs, warrior pride, strong ties to family and the spirit world, and a willingness to adapt. Understanding them helps us see that history is often written by those in power. Being labeled a "barbarian" sometimes just means being on the outside of someone else's empire. And what we call "crazy" or "wild" in their culture might be a valued tradition that shaped Europe in ways we still see today.

CHAPTER 8

Medievaι Curiosities: Knights, Castles, and Strange Events

When we think of the Middle Ages, we might imagine knights in shining armor, towering castles, and damsels in distress. We picture kings, queens, and crusaders battling for glory or God. Yet, behind these dramatic images, medieval life was filled with odd customs and events that might surprise us today. From bizarre medical practices to unusual trials and superstitions, the people of the Middle Ages had their own unique ways of handling everyday challenges.

In this chapter, we will explore some of the strangest aspects of medieval Europe: the oddities of feudalism, the daily life in castles and villages, the curious roles of knights, and the weird beliefs that shaped medicine and justice. We will also peek at the spread of new ideas that started to change the medieval world toward the end of this era.

1. The Feudal Pyramid and Strange Loyalties

Feudalism shaped how medieval society was organized, especially in Western Europe. At the top was the king, who technically owned all the land. He gave large estates (fiefs) to nobles or lords, who in turn promised loyalty and military service. Those nobles might then grant smaller fiefs to knights, who again swore to serve their lord. At the bottom were peasants or serfs who worked the land.

What is strange is how much this system relied on personal oaths and ceremonies. A knight would kneel before his lord, place his hands between the lord's hands, and swear fealty. This bond was deeply serious—breaking it was considered treason, a crime punishable by death. Yet, these layers of loyalty could be confusing, especially if a noble owed loyalty to two different lords who began to fight each other. In times of conflict, it created bizarre situations where knights had to decide which oath was more important.

Feudalism also led to local "laws" set by lords who might be harsh or fair, depending on their temperament. A peasant under a cruel lord had little hope of justice, but a kind lord might protect them. This personal tie was both the strength and weakness of feudal society, often leading to conflicts that seem odd to our eyes, such as entire villages switching allegiance because of a marriage alliance or a disputed inheritance.

2. Castles: More Than Just Fortresses

We often picture castles as big stone fortresses with tall towers and moats. Indeed, many were built for defense, with thick walls, arrow slits, and drawbridges. But castles were also homes for lords and their families. Inside, there were great halls for feasts and gatherings, private chambers, and sometimes even a small chapel.

Life inside a castle could be surprisingly crowded. Servants, guards, family members, visiting nobles, and their retinues all lived in close quarters. Castles were not always the cleanest places. Before modern plumbing, waste was dumped into moats or cesspits. Some castles had "garderobes," which were little rooms with holes that emptied outside the walls. Imagine the smell and the flies in the summer! It might seem strange that a place so grand lacked basic hygiene by our standards, but that was normal for the time.

Another odd feature was that early medieval castles might be wooden motte-and-bailey structures rather than stone. The "motte" was a raised earth mound with a keep (a small fortress) on top, and the "bailey" was a courtyard enclosed by a fence. Over time, stone replaced wood, creating the massive stone castles we think of today. But even these stone castles were cold, dark, and damp, which might not match our romantic ideas of castle life.

3. Knights and Their Peculiar Code of Chivalry

Knights were heavily armored warriors, often riding warhorses. Gaining knighthood involved training as a page and a squire, learning not just combat skills but also manners and social customs. When finally dubbed a knight, a person pledged to follow the code of chivalry.

Chivalry included ideas like bravery, loyalty, defending the church, and protecting the weak. But in practice, knights could be rough, especially during wars or raids. The code of chivalry was often more of an ideal than a reality. Nonetheless, it shaped how knights were expected to behave, leading to strange rituals.

For instance, before being knighted, a young squire might have to keep an all-night vigil in a chapel, praying in full armor. Some knights wore colors or tokens from ladies they admired as a sign of devotion. They might fight in tournaments wearing scarves or ribbons from their beloved. If we imagine sweaty knights charging each other with lances while wearing a lady's silk favor on the arm, it seems quite odd, but it was part of medieval romance culture.

---

4. Tournaments: Dangerous Sport or Public Party?

Medieval tournaments were big events that combined competition, celebration, and sometimes political alliances. Knights competed in the joust—where they rode towards each other with lances, trying to unhorse their opponent—and in melees, where groups of knights fought in teams. At first, tournaments were quite violent. Knights could die, or be held for ransom. Armor and weapons were real, and the lines between sport and actual battle could blur.

Over time, rules were added to make tournaments safer (or at least less deadly). Blunted lances were introduced, and special armor called "tournament armor" offered more protection. Yet, accidents still happened. King Henry II of France died in 1559 from a jousting wound, showing how dangerous these events could remain even in later centuries.

Despite the risks, tournaments were huge social gatherings. Ladies watched from stands, minstrels played music, and merchants sold food and trinkets. Winning knights gained fame, prizes, and sometimes the favor of important nobles. It might seem strange to us to treat armed combat as a festive event, but in the Middle Ages, tournaments were a major form of entertainment for the nobility.

---

5. The Church's Powerful Role: Saints, Relics, and Pilgrimages

During the Middle Ages, the Christian Church held great influence. Bishops and popes could crown kings, excommunicate powerful nobles, and shape daily life through church rules. People believed strongly in heaven, hell, and purgatory. They also believed that saints could protect them or perform miracles if honored properly.

Relics—objects associated with saints—became extremely important. Churches claimed to have pieces of saints' bones, scraps of their clothing, or even drops of their blood. These relics were often displayed in ornate containers and could attract pilgrims from far away. The faithful believed that praying near a relic could heal illness or bring good fortune. Some relic claims were very odd: multiple churches claimed to have the same saint's skull, for example. Despite doubts, pilgrims would travel great distances, sometimes risking robbery or disease along the way.

Pilgrimages themselves were another curious part of medieval life. A peasant or a noble might set off to Jerusalem, Rome, or Santiago de Compostela, hoping to gain spiritual merit or be cured of sickness. The journey could take months or years. Pilgrims wore badges or carried symbols (like the scallop shell for Compostela) to prove their purpose. At times, entire roads were lined with inns, hospitals, and shrines catering to these travelers, making pilgrimage routes almost like medieval highways.

---

6. Strange Medical Practices: Leeches and the Four Humors

Medieval medicine was a mix of ancient theories, superstition, and religion. Doctors believed in the "four humors": blood, phlegm, yellow bile, and black bile. Illness was caused by an imbalance of these humors, so treatments aimed to restore balance. One common remedy was bloodletting, sometimes using leeches. People believed that removing "bad blood" could cure fevers or infections.

Herbal remedies were also common. Monasteries kept herb gardens and copied medical texts, preserving some knowledge of healing. But there were also bizarre cures. For example, doctors might prescribe ground-up mummies (real or fake) as a medicine called "mumia." Some believed powdered stones or gems had healing power. Others recommended prayers or wearing amulets inscribed with holy words.

Surgeries were risky due to lack of sanitation. Amputations or trepanning (drilling holes in the skull) were done without modern anesthesia—often just wine or strong liquor to numb the pain. It might sound horrifying, but it was the best they had. The idea of washing hands or using sterile tools did not fully catch on until much later.

---

7. Bubonic Plague: A Terrifying Mystery

No discussion of medieval oddities would be complete without the **Black Death**, which struck Europe in the mid-14th century. This bubonic plague killed an estimated one-third of the population. People had no real understanding of germs. Some blamed bad air, planetary alignment, or God's wrath. Flagellants roamed the streets, whipping themselves to atone for sins they thought caused the plague.

Others tried bizarre cures—burning herbs, using aromatics, or even carrying sweet-smelling flowers (a practice that might have inspired the nursery rhyme "Ring a Ring o' Roses"). In some places, people blamed minority groups like the Jews, accusing them of poisoning wells, leading to terrible persecutions. The fear and chaos were immense, and social order broke down in many regions.

This tragic event shows how medieval people, lacking scientific knowledge, turned to superstition or violence. Yet, the Black Death also changed society. Labor shortages gave peasants more bargaining power, and old feudal ties began to weaken. Even from a catastrophe, new social changes rose, illustrating how medieval life was in constant flux—even if the reasons behind it often seemed strange or irrational.

---

8. Medieval Justice: Trial by Combat and Trial by Ordeal

Justice in medieval times could be brutal and odd. We already mentioned trial by ordeal among barbarian tribes, but it continued in parts of medieval Europe. A suspect might have to pick a stone out of boiling water or walk over hot ploughshares. If the burns healed cleanly, it was a sign from God of innocence. If they got infected, guilt was assumed.

Trial by combat was another method. Two people in a dispute fought, sometimes to the death. The idea was that God would favor the righteous side. These combats could be private affairs or public spectacles. Nobles or knights fought in full armor. For commoners, it might be a brutal fistfight or a clash with simple weapons. The outcome, of course, often depended on skill and strength rather than innocence.

Certain places even had special laws. For example, in the Holy Roman Empire, some city-states had their own unique ordeals or punishments. Thieves might have their hands cut off, adulterers might be paraded in public, and accused witches could face drowning tests. All these reflect a time when the line between religion, superstition, and law was thin, and people truly believed the supernatural could reveal truth.

---

9. Courtly Love: A Weird Blend of Romance and Rules

In the medieval courts of nobles, a concept called **courtly love** developed—an idealized form of love where a knight pledged service to a lady, often of higher rank or even a married woman. The knight wrote poems, performed deeds of bravery in her honor, and treated her as a distant, almost holy figure. Physical consummation was not the main goal in the literature (though reality might differ).

This tradition gave rise to chivalric romances, stories of knights like Lancelot pining for King Arthur's queen, Guinevere. Troubadours in southern France composed songs praising the beauty and virtue of noblewomen. It might sound sweet, but it also created awkward situations. A real lady might have multiple knights seeking her favor, leading to jealousy or scandal.

Courtly love introduced new ideas about romance in European culture. However, it was mostly an aristocratic game, far removed from the lives of ordinary peasants, who had little time for poetic rules about love. Still, it shaped medieval literature and helped define "romantic love" as we often see it today, though it came with plenty of odd rules and contradictions.

10. Oddities of Monastic Life

Monks and nuns withdrew from worldly life to focus on prayer and service. But monastic communities had their own strange quirks. They followed strict rules (like the Rule of St. Benedict) which dictated when to pray, eat, sleep, and work. Some orders practiced silence, only speaking when necessary. Others believed in self-denial to a radical degree, wearing hair shirts or whipping themselves to avoid temptation.

Monasteries also became centers of learning, copying ancient texts and storing manuscripts in scriptoria. This was crucial for preserving knowledge from earlier civilizations. But the monastery routines might look odd to an outsider—waking before dawn for vigils, chanting psalms many times a day, and keeping limited contact with the outside world.

Despite vows of poverty, many monasteries became wealthy from land donations. They produced their own beer, wine, cheese, and bread. Pilgrims gave money to see relics, and local lords might sponsor lavish chapels. So, a "humble" monastery could accumulate great riches, leading to corruption in some cases. This contradiction between the ideal of a simple spiritual life and the reality of wealth is one of the more curious aspects of medieval monasticism.

11. Crusades: Holy Wars with Strange Encounters

The Crusades were a series of religious wars to retake the Holy Land from Muslim rulers, beginning in the late 11th century. Many knights and nobles saw it as a sacred duty. But once they reached the Middle East, they encountered cultures very different from their own—Byzantine Greeks, Turks, Arabs, Jews, and others.

Some crusaders were shocked to find advanced cities with libraries, hospitals, and public baths. They also discovered new foods like spices, sugar, and coffee (though coffee became more common later). These encounters led to odd mixtures of war, trade, and cultural exchange. While the Crusades were often brutal, they also brought back ideas about science, medicine, and philosophy from the Islamic world to Europe.

Crusaders sometimes formed strange alliances. At times, they allied with certain Muslim groups against other Muslim or Christian factions if it served their political interests. The story of the Crusades is more tangled than just "Christian vs. Muslim." The result was a messy but significant meeting of cultures, leading to changes in European thinking—although many crusaders returned home with tales that sounded both wondrous and terrifying.

---

12. Witch Hunts and Superstition

Belief in magic and witches continued into the late Middle Ages. Though the worst witch hunts would come later (in the early modern period), medieval people already feared witchcraft. Church laws often condemned "maleficium" (evil magic). Some regions held trials for suspected witches.

One strange custom was using a "witch's bridle" or a "scold's bridle" to punish women accused of nagging, gossiping, or witchcraft. It was a metal mask with a gag that could pierce the tongue. This was a cruel way to silence someone. While not always about witchcraft, it shows how fear and superstition could lead to bizarre punishments.

In times of crisis—famine, plague, or war—people looked for scapegoats. They might blame witches for casting spells that ruined crops or caused diseases. Sadly, innocent women (and sometimes men) suffered. Though not as widespread as later witch trials, these medieval accusations hint at how fear led to harsh consequences for those labeled "different" or suspected of secret powers.

13. Gilds and Curious Work Practices

Medieval towns had **gilds** (or guilds) for different trades: bakers, blacksmiths, weavers, and more. These guilds set rules for how their craft should be done, who could become an apprentice or a master, and the quality of goods. An apprentice spent years learning under a master, living in the master's house and doing chores alongside craft training. After proving skill with a "masterpiece," the apprentice could become a master and join the guild.

This system had odd rituals, like formal ceremonies to mark the step from apprentice to journeyman, then to master. Some guilds celebrated feast days of patron saints related to their trade. Bakers might honor Saint Honoré, for example. The guilds also controlled prices, wages, and competition. In some towns, no one could sell bread unless they belonged to the baker's guild.

Though guilds maintained quality, they also stifled innovation at times by restricting who could work or how. To us, it might seem unusual that a single group decided every detail of a trade—like how many apprentices a master could take, or what design was allowed for shoes or pots. Yet, in the medieval mindset, this protected the community from bad workmanship and ensured fairness (at least among guild members).

14. Odd Laws and City Life

Medieval towns were cramped, with narrow streets and houses that might lean over the road. With no proper sewage systems, people often threw waste into the street, causing foul smells and disease outbreaks. City laws sometimes tried to curb these problems with fines for dumping trash in public. But enforcement was weak.

In some cities, laws regulated clothing. Sumptuary laws prohibited lower classes from wearing expensive fabrics or certain colors. Nobles and wealthy merchants wanted to preserve social distinctions, so they banned "commoners" from dressing too finely. For instance, wearing ermine or satin could be restricted to certain ranks. This might seem odd to us—telling people what they can wear—but it was part of keeping social order.

Nighttime city life could be dangerous. Thieves, gangs, and no streetlights made walking around risky. Some towns enforced curfews, and gates might close after a certain hour. Watchmen patrolled, but crime was still high. People carried lanterns or torches if they had to go out, but most stayed indoors. The concept of policing was rudimentary; often, citizens were expected to catch criminals themselves, or the local lord's bailiff might do so with a small group.

---

15. Heraldry: Strange Symbols on Shields

Heraldry developed in the medieval period as a way to identify knights in battle or tournaments. Knights put unique coats of arms on their shields, banners, and surcoats (the cloth worn over armor). These often featured animals, mythical creatures, or geometric shapes in bright colors. Each design was unique, belonging to a family or an individual.

The rules of heraldry were quite detailed. Certain color combinations were allowed, like metal (gold or silver) on color (red, blue, black, green) or color on metal, but not color on color or metal on metal (with exceptions). This might sound overly strict, but it helped viewers see the designs clearly from a distance.

Some crests were strange—like a boar's head with wings, or a two-headed eagle. Others included punning references to the family's name. For instance, a knight named "John Rose" might feature roses on his coat of arms. Over time, these symbols became important legal markers. A person's right to bear certain arms might be disputed in heraldic courts. It is odd to think people went to court over who could put a lion or a fleur-de-lis on their shield, but it was serious business to medieval nobility.

---

16. Universities and Scholastic Puzzles

During the High Middle Ages, the first universities appeared in places like Bologna, Paris, and Oxford. Students studied grammar, rhetoric, logic, arithmetic, geometry, music, and astronomy—known as the "liberal arts." After mastering those, they might move on to theology, law, or medicine.

University life was peculiar. Students were often young men, living in crowded lodgings, with strict rules about curfews and drinking. Lectures were given in Latin. One strange practice was public disputation, where a student had to defend a thesis against opponents, sometimes for hours. The style was very formal and logical, reflecting the "scholastic" method, which involved detailed arguments to reconcile faith and reason.

Famous scholars like Thomas Aquinas tried to merge Christian doctrine with Aristotle's philosophy. This sounds odd to us—imagine spending days debating how many angels can dance on the head of a pin. But such questions were serious attempts to explore the nature of God, matter, and existence. While some see medieval scholastics as overly fixated on trivial points, they laid groundwork for intellectual debate that paved the way for future scientific thinking.

---

17. Traveling Minstrels, Troubadours, and Jokers

Entertainment in medieval times included wandering performers: **minstrels** (musicians and singers), **troubadours** (poet-musicians in southern France who sang about courtly love), **jongleurs** (jesters and acrobats), and more. They traveled from castle to castle, town to town, sharing news, stories, and songs.

Feudal lords often hired a **fool** or **jester** who could entertain them with jokes, riddles, and satirical commentary. Oddly, jesters sometimes had the freedom to mock nobles or even the king without punishment—because it was their "fool's privilege." This turned the jester into both an entertainer and a sort of social critic.

Imagine a feast in a great hall, the lord and lady seated at the high table, knights and guests on benches, while a jester in colorful motley leaps about, juggling or making puns, and minstrels play lutes or harps. It might feel festive, but also chaotic, with the smell of roasted meats, the clang of drinking cups, and the flickering torchlight. This lively scene was typical of a medieval banquet, offering a break from the hardships of daily life.

---

18. Animal Trials: Yes, They Put Animals on Trial

One of the strangest medieval practices was putting animals on trial. In parts of Europe, if an animal caused harm—a pig that killed a child, for example—it could be arrested, assigned a lawyer, and tried in a church or secular court. Judges, priests, and lawyers took these trials seriously, excommunicating or even executing the animal if found guilty.

In some cases, infestations of pests like locusts or rats were summoned to court. A bishop or a priest might command them to leave an area, under threat of excommunication or curses. These rituals reflect a mindset where animals and insects could be held morally accountable or might be driven away by the church's power. It is bizarre to us, but for medieval people, who believed deeply in a moral and spiritual order covering all creatures, it made a certain sense—however odd.

---

19. Mumming and Festival Foolery

Festivals and celebrations in medieval Europe could be rowdy. **Mumming** was a tradition where people dressed in costumes or masks, sometimes performing plays or pantomimes at Christmas or other feasts. They went house to house, expecting food or drink in return for their show. Over time, this merged with local customs, leading to carnival-like events with feasting, drinking, and general merriment.

During certain holidays like the Feast of Fools or Carnival, social order could be reversed. A peasant might be crowned "king" for a day, or people might wear costumes mocking priests and nobles. Such behavior was tolerated briefly, giving the lower classes a chance to blow off steam and poke fun at authority. Afterwards, the normal rules resumed. This custom might seem chaotic or disrespectful, but it served as a safety valve for social tensions.

20. Dawn of a New Age: Strange Shifts Toward the Renaissance

As the Middle Ages neared their end (around the 14th and 15th centuries), Europe began seeing changes that would lead to the Renaissance. Trade with the East grew after the Crusades, bringing new ideas and goods. The Black Death, though devastating, restructured societies and labor systems, weakening feudal bonds. Universities spread knowledge, and scholars rediscovered classical texts from Greece and Rome, spurring new thinking.

Gothic architecture soared in cathedrals like Chartres and Notre-Dame, showcasing advanced engineering for higher vaults and larger stained-glass windows. Chivalry shifted as gunpowder made knights less dominant on the battlefield. Princes and kings hired new professional armies, changing feudal loyalties forever.

All these transformations set the stage for the Renaissance, a period of "rebirth" in art, science, and culture. Looking back at the medieval world, we see a mix of superstition and faith, violent warfare and romantic ideals, lavish feasts and dire poverty, strict social hierarchies and moments of festive chaos. It was an age of contrasts, shaped by beliefs that might seem bizarre to us now but were very real to the people living through it.

Medieval life was neither entirely "dark" nor entirely "chivalrous." It was a tapestry woven of many threads: devotion, fear, wonder, cruelty, and creativity. Whether we look at knights defending a castle, peasants praying for a good harvest, monks copying sacred texts, or townsfolk dancing in a wild festival, we find a world that fascinates us with its strangeness. Through that strangeness, we see echoes of our own humanity—seeking purpose, security, and joy in a world full of danger and mystery.

CHAPTER 9

Dark Times: Weird Legends and Unusual Beliefs

In this chapter, we will look at the period often labeled as the "Dark Ages" or the late medieval era—roughly spanning from around the 5th century to the early 15th century—focusing on some of the strangest legends and beliefs that people held. We will explore superstitions, folklore, and the ways people tried to explain the scary or mysterious things happening around them. Some of these beliefs overlap with the medieval customs we saw in the last chapter, but here we will dive deeper into the bizarre stories people told to make sense of their hardships, from monstrous creatures to doomsday fears.

These so-called "dark times" were not literally without progress or light, as there were many positive cultural developments. But for many living through wars, plagues, and social upheaval, the world could feel frightening. This sense of fear encouraged odd explanations for disease, strange social panics, and a mix of Christian teachings with older pagan superstitions. Let us explore these weird legends and unusual beliefs that flourished in Europe and beyond during this era, bearing in mind that what we might see as wild or spooky was, for them, a way to understand a confusing world.

1. A Time of Uncertainty and Fear

During the late Middle Ages, Europe faced repeated waves of the Black Death, constant local wars, and religious conflicts. Life was fragile. People saw entire villages vanish due to plague or raiding armies. Crops sometimes failed, leading to famine. Local lords fought each other or launched bigger wars, such as the Hundred Years' War between England and France. With so much chaos, it was no surprise that people turned to all sorts of beliefs—holy relics, magical objects, and rumor-fueled legends—to find answers or hope.

One of the strangest outcomes of this environment was the spread of rumors about supernatural causes for everyday problems. A sudden illness might be blamed on a witch's curse. A crop failure could be the work of demons or fairies. If a child went missing, some folks whispered about werewolves or monstrous creatures lurking in the woods. These beliefs, though irrational to us, made sense in a world where scientific knowledge was limited, and divine or evil forces seemed very real.

---

2. Monsters and Creatures of the Night

Stories of monsters were common in medieval Europe, especially in rural regions where dense forests and dark nights made it easy to imagine hidden beasts. Wolves roamed many parts of Europe, so the legend of the **werewolf** grew strong. People believed that a person could be cursed or use black magic to turn into a wolf at night, hunting children or livestock. Though some werewolf trials did happen in later centuries, the seeds of these stories were planted in the so-called "dark times," fed by fear of the unknown in shadowy forests.

Another fearsome legend was the **vampire**, though the medieval version was sometimes different from the modern pop-culture vampire. People believed that a dead person with an unclean soul might return from the grave to suck the life or blood from the living. To prevent this, villagers could place a stone in the corpse's mouth, stake it to the coffin, or bury the body facedown. These customs might seem wild, but they were ways to ensure the dead could not rise again to harm the living.

Still, not all creatures were evil. Some were just odd. Many bestiaries—medieval books describing animals—listed mythical beasts like the **unicorn** or the **griffin** next to real animals. Illustrations showed them in bright colors, often with moral lessons attached. A unicorn's horn, for example, was thought to detect poison in water. Merchants sometimes sold "unicorn horns" that were actually narwhal tusks, and people believed they had special protective powers.

3. Fairy Folk and Hidden Realms

In many parts of Europe, older pagan traditions continued. People believed in fairy folk, elves, or hidden spirits dwelling in hills, forests, or lakes. These were not always cute or kind. In Celtic lands, for example, the **síde** (fairies) could be dangerous. Travelers warned each other not to wander into certain rings of mushrooms (fairy rings) or to disturb ancient mounds believed to be fairy homes.

Parents told children stories of changelings: a sickly fairy child left in place of a healthy human baby. If a baby suddenly fell ill or behaved oddly, some believed fairies had swapped it. In some areas, folks performed odd rituals to drive out the fairy child, hoping to get their real baby back. These beliefs could lead to cruel treatment of sickly children or those with disabilities, as desperation took hold in times of uncertainty.

Legends of hidden realms also inspired travelers' tales. Some knights or adventurers claimed to have stumbled upon the Fairy Queen's court or a mysterious otherworld. They might return with strange gifts or curses. These stories reflect the medieval blend of Christianity (with its angels and demons) and older pagan ideas of magical worlds just beyond human sight.

---

4. Doomsday Prophecies and Millennial Fears

Another feature of these "dark times" was the frequent prediction that the world would end soon. Medieval Europe was deeply religious, and biblical prophecies about the Apocalypse (from the Book of Revelation) were taken very seriously. Each new disaster—a plague outbreak, a devastating war, or a comet in the sky—could be interpreted as a sign of the End Times.

Around the year 1000, there were widespread stories (some say exaggerated by later historians) of panic over the world's end. People believed that a thousand years after the birth of Christ or his crucifixion might mark the final judgment. While modern scholars debate how widespread this panic really was, we do know that medieval chroniclers wrote about doomsday quite often.

Even later, in the 14th century, when the Black Death struck and the Hundred Years' War raged, many believed they were living in the last days. Some turned to extreme penance, such as the **Flagellants** who marched from town to town whipping themselves. Others built fortunes, thinking only of the present moment. Doomsday fears fed a sense that anything could happen, making all sorts of odd beliefs or cults more appealing.

---

5. Saints and Their Extraordinary Legends

We have already mentioned how important saints were. In these dark times, tales of saintly miracles spread everywhere, offering hope and wonder. Saints were thought to heal the sick, cure blindness, stop storms, and protect towns from invading armies. Some stories became very strange, mixing real events with fanciful exaggerations.

For instance, legends grew about saints who defeated dragons or performed bizarre feats. **Saint George** was famed for slaying a dragon in many stories, though historically, it is more symbolic than literal. Other saints might be linked to natural wonders, like a fountain springing from the ground where they knelt to pray. People also collected stories of "incorruptible" saintly bodies that did not decay, seeing this as a sign of holiness. These remains were placed in elaborate reliquaries, attracting huge crowds of pilgrims.

Some saints were believed to protect specific groups—like **Saint Elmo** for sailors, or **Saint Blaise** for throat ailments. Communities had processions and festivals honoring their patron saints, sometimes carrying the saint's relics through the streets to ward off plagues or hailstorms. While this might sound superstitious, for medieval folk, it was a crucial part of survival and community identity.

---

6. Heresies and Strange Sects

The Catholic Church dominated religious life in medieval Europe, but not everyone followed its official teachings exactly. Some groups formed what the Church called "heresies," developing unusual beliefs or rejecting certain doctrines. One example is the **Cathars** in southern France during the 12th and 13th centuries. They believed in two opposing forces: a good spiritual God and an evil material god. They saw the physical world as corrupt. This clashed with Catholic teachings.

The Church responded with the **Albigensian Crusade** (named after Albi, a town in southern France), a brutal campaign to wipe out Catharism. The Inquisition also started rooting out heresy, using interrogation and punishment. People who confessed might do penance, but stubborn heretics could face execution. The logic was that saving one's soul was more important than preserving physical life.

Outside the Church's structure, other odd sects popped up—some praising new self-declared prophets or claiming direct revelations from God. In times of disaster, it was easy for a charismatic leader to gather followers with promises of divine protection or secret knowledge. The Church often saw such movements as dangerous, leading to hunts for heretics that spread fear and suspicion in local communities.

---

7. Relic Manias and Odd Pilgrim Souvenirs

We already know relics were highly prized. But the demand for relics grew so intense that some people faked them. Dishonest merchants sold feathers claiming to be from an archangel's wing or lumps of wood claimed to be from the True Cross. Nobles and bishops competed to own the most impressive relic to draw pilgrims to their churches, boosting local income.

One bizarre relic was the **Holy Prepuce** (the supposed foreskin of Jesus). Multiple churches in Europe claimed to possess it, which created confusion. Equally strange were the "milk of the Virgin Mary," "tears of Christ," or "hair of the apostles." While these might make us raise our eyebrows, medieval Christians saw them as precious treasures connecting them to holy figures.

Pilgrims themselves gathered odd souvenirs. Some carried lead badges shaped like the shrine they visited, pinned to their hats or cloaks. If you went to Canterbury, you might get a badge of St. Thomas Becket's mitre (bishop's hat). Pilgrims returning from Jerusalem sometimes wore a palm frond or had palm leaves embroidered on clothes, signifying they were "palmers." These items were not just keepsakes but proof of pious journeys that could earn respect.

8. The Dance of Death and Obsession with Mortality

With the high mortality rates from plague, famine, and war, medieval art developed an obsession with death. The **Danse Macabre** (Dance of Death) motif showed skeletons dancing with people of all ranks—kings, knights, peasants, and nuns—reminding viewers that death comes for everyone. Such images decorated church walls, manuscripts, and sometimes even homes, a constant reminder of life's fragility.

Another example is the use of **memento mori** (Latin for "remember that you must die"). This phrase accompanied images of skulls, hourglasses, or decaying corpses to urge people not to be proud, since life could end at any moment. While this might seem grim, it was a way of coping. By focusing on death, medieval people hoped to live more piously and be ready for the afterlife.

Writers and poets also dwelt on this theme. They composed moral plays where personifications like Death, Justice, or Mercy argued over a sinful human soul. Common folk told ghost stories or recounted near-death visions of heaven and hell. In these dark times, fear of death was not just an abstract worry but a daily reality, shaping art, literature, and everyday conversation in strange ways.

9. The Cult of the Black Madonna

One odd phenomenon was the popularity of **Black Madonna** statues or paintings—representations of the Virgin Mary with dark or black skin. These images appear in churches across Europe (for example, in

Montserrat, Spain; Częstochowa, Poland; and other places). Some are said to be naturally dark because of age or smoke from candles, while others were intentionally created with dark features.

Believers often attached special miracles to these Black Madonnas, claiming that they had cured diseases, protected the region from invaders, or granted fertility. Scholars debate whether these images link to older pagan earth goddesses or if the color was purely symbolic for humility or sorrow. Whatever the reason, these icons drew pilgrims from far and wide, and legends surrounded them with tales of healing and wonder.

To modern eyes, it might look unusual that medieval Europeans, who mostly depicted biblical figures as fair-skinned, would revere black-skinned statues of Mary. But these local devotions show how broad the range of beliefs and artistic traditions could be. People were eager to find any sign of divine favor in a harsh world, including unusual images that claimed supernatural powers.

---

10. Astrology, Alchemy, and the Heavens

Science, as we know it, did not exist in the same way during the Middle Ages. Instead, people relied on a blend of learning from ancient texts, church teachings, and a large dose of superstition. **Astrology** was hugely popular. Many believed the stars and planets influenced human events. A king might consult astrologers before a battle or a marriage arrangement. Ordinary folk might plan weddings or journeys based on favorable planetary alignments.

Alchemy also flourished. Alchemists tried to find the philosopher's stone, which supposedly could turn base metals into gold or grant immortality. While most of these pursuits did not succeed, alchemists did develop early lab techniques and discovered chemicals. Their texts were full of cryptic symbols—dragons, suns, moons—that symbolized different substances or phases of the work.

Even the great scholars we now admire, like **Roger Bacon** or **Albertus Magnus**, might mix logical studies with alchemy or astrology. They did not see a conflict between faith and these pursuits. Instead, they viewed the cosmos as a grand, God-created puzzle where hidden forces like celestial movements or secret potions could reveal divine truths.

11. Magical Charms and Folk Healers

For everyday problems—aches, fevers, missing livestock—many people did not rely on university-trained doctors (who were few and often expensive). Instead, they turned to local wise women or cunning folk who knew spells, herbal cures, and protective charms. These folk healers combined Christian prayers with older pagan practices, saying a charm to Saint So-and-So while also sprinkling herbs.

Amulets were worn for protection: small bags with saint medals, bits of cloth, or even scraps of writing from holy texts. Some believed that wearing a piece of parchment inscribed with special words or symbols would ward off evil spirits or the evil eye. Others pinned small crosses or images inside their clothes. If a child was sick, the mother might whisper a protective formula passed down from her grandmother.

At times, the Church tried to crack down on these magical practices, labeling them as superstitious or heretical. But in many rural areas, the lines between official religion and folk magic blurred. Priests might themselves use holy water in ways that resembled old pagan blessings. If the crops were failing, a priest could lead a procession through the fields, sprinkling water and chanting prayers, in a ritual not so different from older fertility rites.

12. Sin-Eaters and Odd Funeral Customs

Death customs varied widely. One strange practice, reported in some parts of Britain and possibly in other places, was the idea of a **sin-eater**. A person (often poor) was paid to eat a piece of bread or some food placed on the chest of the deceased, symbolically absorbing their sins so the dead person could pass on purified. This might have been rare or local, but it shows how creative people could be in trying to handle sin and the afterlife.

Other funeral customs included waking the dead—sitting with the body overnight, praying or telling stories to comfort the family. Some believed that if the body was left alone, evil spirits could enter it, or the spirit could wander. So, a constant vigil was kept. People might place coins on the eyes of the deceased to keep them closed, reflecting an old belief that the eyes could open and watch the living otherwise.

In places heavily touched by plague, funeral customs became rushed or abandoned. Mass graves were used, leading to rumors of undead corpses or ghosts haunting the living. Some said that if a corpse was not properly buried, it might turn into a revenant—a wandering dead spirit seeking revenge.

---

13. The Strange Tale of the Children's Crusade

Around 1212, something truly bizarre happened—often called the **Children's Crusade**. A boy named Stephen from France and another named Nicholas from Germany each claimed they had divine visions telling them to lead a crusade to the Holy Land. Large numbers of children and young people joined them, believing the sea would part so they could walk to Jerusalem.

Of course, that did not happen. Instead, many children died of hunger or disease on the journey. Some were sold to slave traders. Historians debate the details—whether all participants were truly children or also included poor adults. But the legend of thousands of innocent youths marching to free the Holy Land remains one of the strangest episodes in medieval history.

This event highlights the intense religious fervor of the time, where even children believed they could do miracles if God willed it. It also shows how rumors and visions could quickly gather a following in a world desperate for hope. To modern eyes, the idea that entire groups of children would trek hundreds of miles on faith alone is both tragic and bewildering.

---

14. Flagellant Movements and Self-Punishment

We mentioned the Flagellants briefly in connection to plague. These were groups of people who publicly whipped themselves to atone for the sins they believed caused God's wrath. During plague outbreaks, Flagellant bands wandered from city to city. They wore simple robes, sang hymns or prayers, and beat themselves with whips, chanting that God might spare humanity from more suffering.

At first, the Church tolerated them. But some Flagellants grew extreme—accusing priests or bishops of corruption, claiming they had special divine revelations. They disrupted public order. The Pope eventually condemned their processions, seeing them as dangerous and heretical. Still, the Flagellant idea did not vanish. Even in later centuries, certain devout groups practiced self-flagellation, thinking it a holy act that imitated Christ's sufferings.

This intense form of devotion reflects the mindset of the time: when faced with massive death and fear, punishing one's own body was seen as a way to beg for God's mercy. It might sound horrifying, but many people believed it was a direct path to spiritual purification and a miraculous end to catastrophes.

---

15. Rituals to Repel the Undead

Vampire and revenant beliefs led to a variety of burial rituals meant to keep the dead from walking. Archaeologists sometimes find skeletons with rocks or bricks forced into their mouths, or stakes driven through their chests. In Poland and other parts of Eastern Europe, so-called "vampire burials" show that local communities took these fears seriously.

A suspected vampire might be dug up if villagers believed unexplained deaths were happening at night. They would check the corpse for signs of fresh blood or an un-decayed appearance. If they "confirmed" vampiric traits, they mutilated the corpse—cutting off its head or burning it. This was done to protect the living.

We might see this as gruesome and irrational. But in an age without scientific medicine, if a villager died unexpectedly, the community needed an explanation. Blaming a restless corpse was one way. It gave them a course of action: find and neutralize the threat. This phenomenon endured, in some places, well beyond the Middle Ages.

---

16. The Legend of Prester John

Amidst all the chaos, Europeans longed for a powerful Christian ally somewhere in the East. This desire sparked the legend of **Prester John**, a mythical king-priest who ruled a rich Christian kingdom beyond the Islamic lands. Rumors claimed his realm overflowed with gold and wonders. Some said he had a fountain of youth or magical creatures. Others believed his army could help conquer the Holy Land.

Letters supposedly written by Prester John circulated in Europe, describing fantastic lands filled with giants and dragons but also devout Christians. Explorers and envoys tried to find him, traveling to Africa or Asia in the hope of forging alliances. Of course, no one ever found this mythical king. Over time, the legend shifted—some explorers placed him in Ethiopia, others in India.

The fact that so many took this story seriously shows how eager medieval people were for hope of a grand Christian empire that could stand up to threats. They did not have accurate maps or knowledge of distant lands, so it was easy for stories of an unknown Christian paradise to take root.

---

17. Dance Manias and Strange Collective Behavior

In certain regions during the late medieval period, odd cases of **dance mania** or "dancing plagues" were reported. Groups of people began dancing uncontrollably, sometimes for days, until they collapsed from exhaustion or died. One famous outbreak happened in 1374 in the Rhine region (modern Germany). Others occurred later, like the 1518 dancing plague in Strasbourg.

Explanations vary: perhaps ergot poisoning (a fungus on rye) caused hallucinations, or maybe mass hysteria from stress or fear drove people to these frenzies. In a time of limited medical understanding, onlookers often blamed demonic possession or divine punishment. The frantic dancers might beg for mercy or claim they heard heavenly music. Some towns tried playing more music to help them dance it out, while others prayed over them or locked them in churches.

Such events highlight the psychological strain of the age. People living with constant threats sometimes experienced collective breakdowns. Without modern science, it turned into a bizarre spectacle, fueling rumors of curses, witches, or dancing devils.

---

18. Courtly Bestiaries and Mythical Landmarks

We mentioned bestiaries, but medieval geography books were also filled with wonders. Some described places like the **Magnetic Mountain**, where ships' iron nails were ripped out by its magnetism, causing the vessel to fall apart. Others told of the **Fountain of Youth**, the **River of Gold**, or a land of one-eyed men called **Cyclopes**.

Travelers like **Sir John Mandeville** (who may or may not have been a real person) wrote accounts of journeys through Asia and Africa, describing monstrous races with dog heads or no heads at all, but faces on their chests. These tall tales mixed with real details of exotic animals like elephants or giraffes, forming a confusing mix of truth and fantasy.

Nobles read these travelogues for entertainment. They also served a moral purpose—writers often added Christian lessons or warnings about sinful cities being destroyed. For instance, the city of Babel might be portrayed as filled with monstrous sinners. Though we see these as clearly fictional, medieval readers, lacking reliable maps, might accept them as partly real or at least possible.

---

19. Legends of King Arthur's Return

In the British Isles, stories of **King Arthur** were more than just fairy tales; they fed national identity. Arthur, according to legends, had fought Saxon invaders and created a glorious realm with the Knights of the Round Table. Then he was mortally wounded and taken to the isle of Avalon. Many believed he would return one day to save Britain in its darkest hour.

This prophecy of a "once and future king" mirrored other European myths about heroes who did not truly die but slept in a hidden place—like **Frederick Barbarossa** in Germany or **Ogier the Dane** in Denmark. People in tough times pinned hopes on these legendary saviors, believing that if their country was threatened, the great hero would awaken.

Knights in the Middle Ages read romances about Arthur's quests, the Holy Grail, and the wizard Merlin. These stories mixed Christian ideas with old Celtic myths. They shaped chivalry and even political propaganda. Some kings tried to link themselves to Arthur, staging tournaments with Round Table themes. The idea of Arthur's eventual return was a comforting legend in times of strife and invasion.

---

20. The End of an Era and the Seeds of Change

By the 15th century, the medieval world was shifting toward what we now call the Renaissance. The old superstitions did not just vanish—witch hunts, odd cures, and weird beliefs continued. But new trade routes, the rise of strong national monarchies, and the gradual spread of printed books (after Gutenberg's press in the mid-15th century) began to challenge the "darkness."

Still, the era of weird legends and unusual beliefs left a permanent mark. It influenced literature, folklore, holiday traditions, and even modern entertainment. Stories of werewolves, vampires, and hidden fairies remain popular in books and movies. The fear of doomsday reappears in modern times under different forms. The medieval mania for relics echoes in how people still collect celebrity memorabilia, hoping to own a piece of someone great.

So, these "dark times" were not entirely dark. They were filled with creativity, imagination, and a strong urge to explain a frightening world. People told stories of monsters and saints, used relics and amulets for protection, and blended Christian faith with old pagan beliefs. While we might call it superstitious, for them it was a means of survival—both physical and spiritual.

Understanding these legends and beliefs helps us see how our ancestors coped with hardship. They had limited science or technology, so they built a worldview where anything was possible—miracles, curses, dragons, or dancing plagues. It is a testament to human resilience: even in the face of war and disease, people told stories and practiced rituals that gave them comfort or hope.

CHAPTER 10

Renaissance Wonders: Odd Details of a Changing World

The Renaissance is often described as a rebirth of art, science, and learning in Europe, roughly spanning the 14th to the 17th centuries. We might picture famous artists like Leonardo da Vinci and Michelangelo, new scientific ideas championed by Copernicus or Galileo, and a flowering of literature in the works of Shakespeare. Yet, beneath the shining achievements, the Renaissance also had its share of peculiar practices and surprising beliefs.

In this chapter, we will see how the Renaissance was not all polished humanism and rational thought. Old medieval superstitions did not vanish overnight. People still hunted witches, wore protective charms, and relied on astrology. At the same time, new inventions and discoveries brought fresh oddities: strange scientific theories, weird medical experiments, and daring voyages across the oceans. Let us explore this fascinating clash between old and new, as Europe transformed from the late medieval period into a time of exploration and creativity—while still holding onto some very odd habits.

1. The Renaissance: A Shifting World

By the 14th and 15th centuries, Italy's city-states like Florence, Venice, and Milan had grown wealthy through trade. This wealth funded art, architecture, and scholarship. Nobles and merchants competed to sponsor painters or sculptors, leading to breathtaking works. The spirit of **humanism** encouraged the study of classical texts from ancient Greece and Rome, bringing new respect for human potential.

But even as scholars rediscovered old philosophies, many Renaissance thinkers held onto medieval beliefs. The lines between science, magic, and religion were blurred. A great mathematician might also cast horoscopes. A brilliant physician might still believe in humors. So, while we see the Renaissance as modern, it was a transitional time full of contradictions and odd blends of knowledge.

2. Strange "New" Sciences: Alchemy, Astrology, and Beyond

Renaissance scientists carried forward medieval traditions like alchemy, but they refined them. Alchemists still sought the **philosopher's stone**, hoping to transmute base metals into gold or discover the elixir of life. Famous figures such as **Paracelsus** and **John Dee** blended chemistry, magic, and astrology, claiming to unlock nature's secrets.

Astrology remained highly influential. Princes and bishops consulted astrologers to pick auspicious dates for battles, marriages, or coronations. Even great minds like **Johannes Kepler**, who discovered the laws of planetary motion, worked as an imperial astrologer to pay the bills. It might seem contradictory for a pioneering astronomer to draw horoscopes, but it was normal for the era. Kepler was searching for cosmic harmony, seeing no big conflict between astronomy (the science) and astrology (the belief system).

Meanwhile, new inventions like the **printing press** spread knowledge quickly. Astrological and alchemical texts found wide audiences, fueling interest in hidden knowledge. This lively mix of old magic and new empirical observation shaped the Renaissance "scientific revolution," though it progressed in fits and starts, often leading to strange experiments.

3. Leonardo da Vinci's Odd Ideas and Machines

Leonardo da Vinci was a quintessential Renaissance man—painter, inventor, anatomist, and engineer. He famously designed flying machines, tanks, and even a diving suit in his notebooks. Yet, many of these ideas remained on paper, never built in his lifetime. Some were quite bizarre, like a giant crossbow or a mechanical lion that could walk and open its chest to reveal lilies.

He also studied anatomy, dissecting human corpses to understand muscle and bone structure. This was scandalous to some, as the Church frowned on such practices. Leonardo's notebooks feature detailed drawings of organs, fetuses in the womb, and skeletal frameworks. Yet, he never fully published these findings, keeping them mostly secret.

Despite his forward-thinking curiosity, Leonardo still lived in a world that believed in cosmic influences, and he sometimes wrote in code or mirrored script to hide his ideas. This secrecy might reflect fear of criticism or simply a habit of privacy. Whatever the reason, it added an air of mystery to his works, making him a figure of odd brilliance who mingled science with hints of the occult.

---

4. Court Life: Strange Etiquette and Fashion

Renaissance courts could be glamorous. Kings, queens, dukes, and nobles surrounded themselves with courtiers who wore colorful, extravagant clothing. In places like the French court under Francis I or the English court under Henry VIII, fancy banquets and dances showcased the latest fashions. Women wore wide, decorated gowns with tight bodices. Men sported padded shoulders, puffed sleeves, and codpieces—those odd pouches at the front of men's hose that exaggerated a certain area.

Etiquette was strict. One had to bow or curtsey at the right angle, never turning one's back on the monarch. Even how you held a goblet could matter. Mistakes in etiquette could ruin a courtier's reputation. Some courtiers spent hours perfecting their posture, gestures, and witty conversation. If that seems strange, remember these courts were like the social media of their day: everyone watched each other to see who was "on trend."

Court entertainment could be odd as well—elaborate masques, where courtiers wore costumes representing mythological figures, dancing in carefully choreographed steps. The lines between theater, pageantry, and real life blurred in these displays of wealth and power.

5. Extravagant Banquets and Food Oddities

Renaissance banquets could outshine even medieval feasts. Italian courts were famous for multi-course meals with decorative displays: peacocks re-dressed in their feathers after roasting, pies from which live birds flew out, and sugar sculptures shaped like castles or mythical creatures. Table manners became more refined—forks started appearing in Italy, though many Europeans mocked them as silly at first.

In France, the high table might feature sweet and savory dishes in strange combinations, like meats cooked with fruits and spices. Food coloring was common. Sauces were thickened with bread or almonds. The wealthy loved sugar, a luxury brought by trade from distant lands. Overconsumption of sugar led to rotting teeth becoming a status symbol, oddly enough, because it showed you could afford lots of sweets!

Meanwhile, poorer people stuck to simpler fare: bread, cheese, onions, perhaps a bit of salted fish or meat. The gap between rich and poor diets was huge. Yet, even peasants might have local festivals with special breads or pastries shaped in curious ways, honoring saints or marking harvest times.

6. Odd Medical Advances and Human Dissection

Though medieval practices lingered, the Renaissance pushed medicine forward in surprising ways. Doctors like **Andreas Vesalius** challenged ancient authorities by dissecting human corpses, publishing detailed anatomy books such as "De humani corporis fabrica" in 1543. Vesalius corrected errors from Galen (a 2nd-century Greek physician whose works dominated for over a millennium).

Still, old ideas about the four humors hung on. Doctors bled patients to balance humors, or used purges and emetics. Yet the new knowledge from dissections gradually improved surgery. **Ambroise Paré**, a French barber-surgeon, introduced better wound treatments, replacing boiling oil cauterization with gentler ointments. Such changes were revolutionary.

However, public dissections often drew crowds like a spectacle. Professors might lecture from a high chair while an assistant cut open the corpse below. The odor was terrible, and the risk of infection high. People even came to watch out of curiosity, treating it almost like a macabre show. It is hard for us to imagine, but for Renaissance onlookers, the chance to witness the secrets of the body was as thrilling as it was disturbing.

7. Witch Hunts Continue

The medieval fear of witches persisted and even intensified in some areas during the Renaissance. **Heinrich Kramer** wrote the infamous "Malleus Maleficarum" (Hammer of Witches) in 1486, a treatise on how to identify and prosecute witches. Although the Church did not universally endorse it, the book influenced many witch trials across Europe.

These trials often targeted women—especially widows, midwives, or herbal healers—though men were accused too. Torture was used to extract confessions. Accused witches might be blamed for bad weather, crop failure, or sudden illnesses. The rise of Protestant and Catholic conflicts, as well as social upheaval, sometimes fueled these panics.

Some areas, like parts of Germany and Switzerland, saw large-scale witch hunts with hundreds of executions. Others, like Spain under the Inquisition, were ironically more cautious about witchcraft accusations, focusing on heresy instead. It was an uneven phenomenon. But overall, the Renaissance was not a friendly time for those suspected of casting harmful spells, which seems contradictory to the era's emphasis on learning and progress.

8. Discovery of the New World and Weird Encounters

One of the biggest changes in the Renaissance was the "Age of Exploration." Europeans sailed across the Atlantic, encountering the Americas. Explorers like **Christopher Columbus** (1492) and later **Hernán Cortés**, **Francisco Pizarro**, and others reported back tales of strange lands, exotic fruits, and peoples with unfamiliar customs.

At first, many Europeans tried to fit these new discoveries into old frameworks. Some believed they might find monstrous races from medieval bestiaries—people with no heads, or dog-headed men. Though they did not find such creatures, they still spread sensational stories of "cannibal" tribes or gold-rich kingdoms like El Dorado.

The arrival of new foods—tomatoes, potatoes, maize (corn), cacao—eventually revolutionized European diets, but at first, many mistrusted these foreign plants. Some thought tomatoes were poisonous. Chocolate was introduced as a bitter, spiced drink from Mesoamerica, later sweetened with sugar to become a European luxury. All these novelties sparked curiosity and confusion. Christian missionaries, meanwhile, attempted to evangelize Indigenous peoples, labeling their rituals as devilish, which added another layer of bizarre misunderstanding.

---

9. Cabinets of Curiosity and Odd Collectors

With new trade routes, curious objects flooded into Europe: exotic shells, stuffed animals, strange plants, and artifacts from distant cultures. Wealthy nobles or scholars began creating **cabinets of curiosity** (also called Wunderkammer in German). These were rooms or display cases packed with oddities: dried lizards, mineral specimens, odd clocks, coral branches, mythical "mermaid" skeletons (really a sewn-together monkey and fish), and anything else considered rare or amazing.

Owners showed off their cabinets to impress guests, claiming it was a microcosm of the entire world. The line between real science and fantasy was blurred. A single collection might include genuine animal fossils alongside fabricated creatures. Some collectors spent fortunes acquiring rumored "dragon eggs" or the horn of a unicorn (a narwhal tusk).

These collections laid groundwork for modern museums but were extremely hodgepodge. Renaissance curiosity thrived on the bizarre, linking it with a thirst for knowledge. People genuinely believed studying these items might reveal secrets of nature or confirm biblical wonders. So, these cabinets of curiosity became hotspots of weird science and speculation.

10. Machiavelli's Surprising Realism

Politics during the Renaissance also shifted. The city-states of Italy, especially, engaged in complex diplomacy, spying, and alliances. **Niccolò Machiavelli**, a Florentine diplomat, wrote "The Prince" (published in 1532), offering blunt advice on ruling. He famously suggested it is better for a prince to be feared than loved if he cannot be both. He also said moral goodness might have to yield to cunning and ruthlessness in politics.

This shocked many who upheld the medieval ideal of a virtuous Christian ruler. Machiavelli's realism seemed cynical, even diabolical. Yet, his ideas reflected the cutthroat environment of Italian politics, where assassinations and betrayals were common. The "Machiavellian" approach—using deceit or cruelty if needed—clashed with older chivalric codes.

People found "The Prince" both fascinating and horrifying. Some called Machiavelli an agent of the devil; others saw him as a brilliant observer of human nature. In any case, his work was a radical break from medieval political theology, which tried to unite Christian virtue with governance. His blunt style remains odd and unsettling to this day.

11. Sumptuary Laws and Fashion Fines

Like in the Middle Ages, Renaissance governments passed **sumptuary laws** to regulate clothing, jewelry, and feasts. In places like Venice or Florence, sumptuary laws aimed to curb excessive luxury so that newly rich merchants did not outshine old noble families. Certain fabrics or colors were reserved for nobles. Fines were imposed if you wore clothes beyond your station.

These laws might say, for instance, that only nobles above a certain rank could wear velvet or pearls, or only the doge's relatives could wear gold-trimmed gowns. Some restricted how many courses you could serve at a wedding banquet. The logic was both moral (preventing vanity) and social (keeping classes distinct).

Despite such rules, many flaunted them anyway. We have records of repeated sums paid for wearing forbidden styles. People enjoyed showing off wealth in an era of rising commerce. Silk from the East, elaborate lace from Flanders, and fine leather from Spain fueled a fashion frenzy. The laws were often ignored or only lightly enforced, adding to the Renaissance's curious mix of flamboyance and official disapproval.

---

12. Religious Turmoil: Reformation Oddities

The 16th century brought the **Protestant Reformation**, led by Martin Luther, John Calvin, and others who challenged the Catholic Church. This caused massive religious strife in Europe, leading to wars and persecutions. But it also produced weird side effects. Some radical Protestants, like **Anabaptists** in Münster, briefly formed a communal society that forbade private property and practiced polygamy. Their city turned into a bizarre theocracy before being crushed by surrounding forces.

Catholics struck back, leading to the **Counter-Reformation**. The Council of Trent reaffirmed traditional beliefs, and new religious orders like the Jesuits emerged to promote education and missionary work. The Inquisition grew more active in Catholic regions, hunting heresy. In some places, superstitions or folk practices were banned if seen as too "pagan."

This era saw devout Catholics performing lavish baroque religious ceremonies, while strict Calvinists or Puritans stripped churches of decorations, seeing them as idolatrous. People debated theological points that might sound minor—like whether worshippers should kneel for communion—but these issues could cause fierce disputes. The combination of spiritual zeal and political power struggles led to bizarre alliances and violent conflicts all over Europe.

13. Galileo's Trials and the Clash of Ideas

Galileo Galilei famously improved the telescope and supported **Copernicus's** theory that the Earth orbited the sun. This challenged the centuries-old view that Earth was the center of the universe—a view tied to both classical philosophy and Church teaching. When Galileo published his findings, he got in trouble with the Roman Inquisition.

In 1633, Galileo was put on trial for heresy. He was forced to recant his stance that the Earth moves around the sun, and he spent the rest of his life under house arrest. The Church feared that if scripture was reinterpreted to allow a heliocentric universe, it could lead people to question more teachings.

This conflict was odd because many cardinals admired Galileo's work. The tension lay in how to reconcile new scientific evidence with older religious interpretations. Galileo tried to argue that the Bible was not a science textbook. But in an era of religious upheaval, the Church hesitated to accept radical changes. Thus, the Renaissance witnessed breakthroughs in science overshadowed by fears of heresy.

14. The Art of Poison: Political Murders and Secret Potions

Italian Renaissance courts gained a notorious reputation for poisoning rivals. The powerful **Borgia** family, especially Pope Alexander VI and his children Cesare and Lucrezia, were rumored to use poison to eliminate enemies. Though some stories may be exaggerated, the era's fascination with poisons was real.

Apothecaries sold substances like arsenic or antimony. Secret recipes circulated, disguised as cosmetics or medicines. A slow-acting poison might mimic natural illness, thus avoiding suspicion. Tales of "cantarella," a

Borgia poison, or "acqua tofana," said to be invented by an Italian woman named Giulia Tofana for wives who wanted to kill abusive husbands, spread far and wide.

While these stories sometimes blend rumor with fact, they highlight the dark side of Renaissance intrigue. Courtiers lived in fear, suspecting each other of plots. Poison offered a discreet weapon in a time when open violence might spark a feud or war. This gave rise to odd protective measures—like tasting cups, employing food tasters, or wearing amulets to counteract venom.

---

15. Festivals, Pageants, and Ridiculous Displays

Renaissance rulers loved public pageants to impress subjects and visitors. In places like Florence, elaborate **carnevale** celebrations featured masked balls, street performances, and horse parades. In Rome, the pope might sponsor grand processions during religious festivals, with floats depicting biblical scenes.

One bizarre tradition was the "**Battle of the Bridge**" in Pisa, where teams fought to push a cart across a bridge. In Florence, **calcio storico** was a violent ball game played in city squares. The Renaissance turned these events into spectacles with costumes, banners, and music.

At royal weddings, the feast might include mechanical scenery, like a stage that transformed from a garden into a seascape. Actors dressed as gods would descend from hidden platforms. Fireworks, newly adapted from Chinese technology, lit the night sky. All this cost a fortune, but it showcased a ruler's glory. People must have been both awestruck and perhaps a bit puzzled by the extravagance.

---

16. Opera's Strange Beginnings

Opera was born in the late Renaissance, combining music, drama, and spectacle. Early operas in Florence, like those by Jacopo Peri or Claudio Monteverdi's later works, retold Greek myths or pastoral stories with singing throughout. This was weird to some, as singing every line instead of speaking was a new concept.

Audiences at first included noble patrons, hearing these performances in private courts. Costumes were lavish, sets and stage machinery complicated. People installed trapdoors, flying harnesses, and wave machines to depict storms or underworld journeys. The illusions could be wondrous. However, some viewers found it odd that characters sang about mundane details, like receiving a letter or walking in a garden.

Over time, opera became hugely popular. By the 17th century, public opera houses opened in Venice. But in its infancy, it was an eccentric art form: part play, part concert, and part magical show. The fact that audiences embraced this blending of styles shows how the Renaissance love for creativity trumped old conventions.

17. The Printing Press and Weird Books

Johannes Gutenberg's printing press (mid-15th century) revolutionized information. Bibles and scholarly works spread fast, but so did bizarre pamphlets full of prophecies, rumors, or false news. The public ate up sensational stories of sea monsters or monstrous births. One popular theme was "**monstrous births**," describing babies born with extra limbs or heads—seen as omens of divine wrath. Some pamphlets used crude woodcut illustrations to shock or amaze readers.

People printed almanacs with astrology-based predictions for weather and harvests. Others published "cures" or "recipes" for success in love. The printing press, while an incredible step forward, also unleashed a flood of questionable texts. Satires, political propaganda, and scandalous tracts spread across Europe quickly.

Martin Luther famously nailed his 95 Theses to a church door (in 1517, as tradition says), but it was the printing of these theses that made them go viral. Soon everyone was reading or debating them. This dynamic environment, combining new technology with old credulity, led to an explosion of ideas—both wise and weird.

18. Mercenary Armies and Condottieri

In Italy and parts of Europe, city-states or nobles often hired **condottieri**—mercenary captains—to lead their armies. These soldiers of fortune fought for whoever paid best. Some became very powerful, like **Francesco Sforza**, who took control of Milan. This practice created an odd war culture where loyalty was negotiable, and battles could be less about honor and more about profit.

Condottieri sometimes switched sides mid-conflict if a better offer came along. Historians note that some battles ended with minimal casualties because mercenaries did not want to risk their valuable skill or the next paycheck. City-states liked them because they could wage wars without risking their own citizens. But it was a risky game—if a mercenary general grew too strong, he might overthrow his employer.

Despite the cynicism, condottieri had a flair for grand gestures. They held lavish courts, wore fancy armor, and lived in fortified castles. Their romantic image of knightly prowess clashed with the reality of them being "guns for hire." This mismatch is yet another Renaissance oddity: a chivalric facade hiding ruthless opportunism.

---

19. Explorers' Tales: Myths Meet Reality

From **Vasco da Gama** to **Ferdinand Magellan**, Renaissance explorers circled the globe, encountering new peoples and lands. They returned with astonishing tales of giant Patagonians, "cannibal" tribes, or cities built on water (like Tenochtitlan in Mexico). Some stories were accurate; others were embellished. Cartographers tried to map these finds, adding sea monsters or mermaids in uncharted waters.

Sir Walter Raleigh searched for El Dorado in South America, believing there was a city of gold. Explorers wrote about the Amazon warrior women, referencing Greek myths. Sailors claimed they saw monstrous fish or storms conjured by sea witches. These partly came from real experiences—like manatees might inspire mermaid tales—but also from the old medieval mindset that the world was full of marvels.

As a result, maps from the 16th century are a mix of improved coastlines and bizarre creatures in the open ocean. Slowly, repeated voyages corrected some myths, but new ones popped up. The line between science and legend stayed blurry. The Renaissance thirst for discovery was both rational (charting coasts precisely) and fantastical (searching for mythic gold).

20. Turning Point: Into the Modern Age

By the 17th century, Europe was on the cusp of great changes. The Renaissance, with its revival of classical learning and thirst for exploration, had reshaped art, politics, and science. Yet it had also clung to medieval superstitions—witch hunts still raged, many believed in astrological destinies, and monstrous birth pamphlets sold well. This contradiction was part of the Renaissance's charm: an age of Michelangelo's divine artwork and Machiavelli's ruthless politics, of Copernicus's cosmic revolutions and men who still believed in alchemy.

Nevertheless, seeds of the modern world were planted. **Francis Bacon** advocated inductive reasoning, championing the scientific method. **René Descartes** sought a philosophical foundation in reason alone, writing "I think, therefore I am." Gunpowder, navigational tools, and more advanced printing led to an interconnected world. Nations began to form stronger central governments, moving away from feudal fragmentation.

Looking back, it is remarkable that an era producing geniuses like da Vinci and Galileo also burned witches and revered unicorn horns. That tension is what makes the Renaissance so fascinating. In the next chapters, we will see how the Age of Exploration and the rise of global empires continued to birth new oddities and expansions of belief. But for now, let us appreciate the Renaissance as a time of wonder and contradiction—where people soared to new intellectual heights while keeping one foot planted in the spooky shadows of the medieval past.

CHAPTER 11

Age of Exploration: Strange Journeys and Shocking Discoveries

The Age of Exploration took place mostly between the 15th and 17th centuries. Explorers from Europe sailed across unknown oceans, hoping to find new lands, gold, spices, and glory. Although we often hear about the bravery of explorers like Christopher Columbus, Vasco da Gama, Ferdinand Magellan, or Sir Francis Drake, we do not always hear about the odd and shocking details of their travels. This was a time filled with misunderstandings, weird encounters, and surprising lessons.

Sailors risked their lives on small ships, facing storms, disease, and superstition. They brought back amazing tales of monstrous sea creatures, lands rich with gold, and people who looked or acted very different from Europeans. Many stories were exaggerated or based on fear and confusion. In this chapter, we dive into these surprising facts and bizarre moments from the Age of Exploration. We will see how explorers managed to sail far from home, what they believed about the oceans and lands beyond, and the wild encounters they had with new cultures.

1. Myths That Drove Explorers

Before the Age of Exploration truly began, many Europeans believed in mythical places like the Kingdom of Prester John (a Christian ruler supposedly in Africa or Asia), or islands populated by dog-headed men. Maps showed sea monsters and giant serpents. Explorers hoped to find lost Christian kingdoms or rivers of gold.

Christopher Columbus, for instance, read old texts describing lands to the west and believed he could reach Asia by sailing across the Atlantic. He thought he might encounter the Great Khan of China or find the biblical Earthly Paradise. Though it sounds strange now, these myths fired the imagination of sailors. Stories of precious spices like cinnamon, cloves, and pepper, along with pearls and other riches, gave them a strong reason to venture into the unknown.

This mixture of legend and greed pushed explorers to undertake dangerous journeys. They often carried letters from kings addressed to mythical rulers or unknown peoples. Today, it is easy to laugh at some of these ideas, but for them, tales of monstrous races or hidden empires were a serious motivation to set sail.

2. Odd Navigational Tools and Superstitions

Sailing uncharted seas required more than courage. Explorers used navigational tools like the **astrolabe** (to measure the altitude of stars) and the **cross-staff**. They also used **portolan charts**, which were maps with detailed coastlines, though these charts often showed only known regions. Beyond familiar waters, maps were blank or filled with drawings of sea creatures and warnings like "Here be dragons."

Sailors were full of superstitions. Whistling on a ship was thought to bring storms. A small carved statue of the Virgin Mary might be placed on the mast, or a saint's relic might be kept in a safe place, believed to protect from shipwrecks. Many sailors refused to learn how to swim, thinking it was pointless if you fell overboard in the vast ocean.

Also, there was fear of the **"magnetic lodestone"** principle. While compasses helped them steer, some sailors believed compasses were magical and that if you got too close to the North Pole, the compass needle or even iron nails in the ship might be torn out. Such strange ideas mixed real science with lingering medieval myths, creating an odd approach to navigation.

3. The Surprising Voyage of Columbus

When **Columbus** reached the Caribbean in 1492, he called the people there "Indians," thinking he was near India. This confusion stuck, and Europeans used the term "Indian" for many Indigenous peoples in the Americas for centuries. Columbus's misunderstanding might seem funny now, but it shaped history in big ways.

He also wrote reports describing how he believed he could be near the Earthly Paradise mentioned in medieval texts. He thought the mild climate, lush forests, and unusual fruits hinted that the Garden of Eden was not far. Some of his letters home included wild guesses about local people's customs. He assumed they might know about grand Asian empires or monstrous races further inland.

Oddly, Columbus refused to accept he had found a landmass unknown to Europeans. Until his death, he insisted he had reached Asia. This stubborn belief caused confusion among other explorers, who had to figure out that the lands Columbus visited were not Asia but continents later called North and South America.

---

4. Strange Foods and Bewildered Taste Buds

When European explorers arrived in the Americas, Africa, or Asia, they encountered foods that shocked them. In the **Caribbean**, they discovered chili peppers, which were spicier than anything Europeans had tasted before. In **Mesoamerica**, they found cacao beans, used to make a bitter chocolate drink. At first, many Europeans found this beverage strange and unappealing. Over time, they added sugar and created the sweet chocolate we know today.

In the **Andes** (South America), explorers found potatoes. The potato eventually became a staple in Europe, but at first, people were suspicious of it and thought it might be poisonous. Similarly, tomatoes were brought from the Americas to Europe, but many refused to eat them, thinking they were toxic ornamental plants.

These new foods, along with corn, peanuts, and vanilla, transformed diets around the world. It is hard to imagine Italian cooking without tomato sauce, or Irish cuisine without potatoes, but both ingredients came from the Americas. This exchange of plants and animals changed entire societies. Yet in the beginning, explorers were cautious or even frightened of these unfamiliar tastes.

---

5. Rumors of Monsters and Cannibals

Returning sailors told tales of giant cannibals, men with no heads, or tribes that had faces in their chests. Such stories often mixed real customs with fear and exaggeration. For instance, some Caribbean tribes did practice ritual warfare and captured enemies, which sparked rumors of cannibalism. The word "cannibal" itself came from a mispronunciation of the Carib people.

Amerigo Vespucci, who explored parts of South America, wrote letters describing what he saw (or claimed to see). Some of his accounts mentioned cannibal feasts or bizarre rituals. While there might have been a kernel of truth—some groups did practice forms of ritual violence—Vespucci's stories were often shaped to fascinate European readers eager for sensational tales.

This created a strange cycle: explorers expected to find savagery or monsters, so they interpreted local cultures in the worst possible light. Then the stories they spread fueled more explorers to seek "human oddities" across the seas. The result was a patchwork of half-truths and wild fantasies that shaped European views of distant peoples for centuries.

---

6. Portuguese Voyages Around Africa

While Spain focused on sailing west across the Atlantic, **Portugal** aimed to find a sea route to Asia around Africa. Explorers like **Bartolomeu Dias** and **Vasco da Gama** braved the unknown waters of the African coast. Dias reached the southern tip of Africa (the Cape of Good Hope) in 1488, proving it was possible to sail around the continent.

During these voyages, Portuguese ships sometimes anchored at small coastal villages, where they traded beads, metals, or cloth for gold, ivory, or slaves. European diseases began to spread, and local conflicts arose. Explorers were often baffled by the diversity of African cultures. Some, like **Prince Henry the Navigator**, funded missions partly due to myths of a rich Christian kingdom (maybe linked to Prester John) in sub-Saharan Africa.

Navigating the treacherous waters around the Cape was extremely dangerous. Storms tossed ships, and swirling currents confused navigators. Sailors told stories of ghost ships or demons. Over time, knowledge improved, but the early attempts were marked by fear and speculation, adding to the Age of Exploration's reputation for weird and perilous journeys.

---

7. The Circus-Like Arrival of Cortés in Mexico

Hernán Cortés arrived in Mexico (1519) with the aim of conquering the Aztec Empire. The Aztecs had never seen horses or cannons before, and the Spanish used these to create a frightening spectacle. Legends say that when Aztec emperor **Moctezuma II** first heard of the Spaniards, he wondered if they might be gods returning as prophesied in Aztec lore, though modern scholars debate how true that is.

Cortés marched inland, forming alliances with tribes who hated Aztec rule. The Spanish presence was bizarre to local people: men in shiny metal armor, riding animals that seemed half-man, half-beast. Firearms made thunderous noises and deadly smoke. Aztec warriors, however, also had powerful armies and impressive city-states.

The cultural misunderstandings went both ways. The Spanish found Aztec human sacrifice horrifying. The Aztecs, in turn, found the Spanish obsession with gold strange—why would foreigners kill and destroy for simple yellow metal? The clash led to the fall of the Aztec capital, Tenochtitlan, in 1521, forever altering the region.

---

8. Smallpox and the Tragic Columbian Exchange

One of the most significant and heartbreaking parts of the Age of Exploration was the **Columbian Exchange**—the movement of plants, animals, and diseases between the Old World (Europe, Africa, Asia) and the New World (the Americas). While some aspects were beneficial, like new food crops (potatoes, tomatoes, maize) and livestock (horses, pigs, cattle) introduced to the Americas, the disease exchange was devastating.

Smallpox, measles, influenza, and other illnesses arrived with European explorers and colonists. Native populations had no immunity to these diseases. Epidemics swept through entire communities, killing an enormous percentage of the Indigenous peoples in North and South America. This tragic loss of life was perhaps the single biggest factor in the swift European conquest.

Strangely, there were also lesser-known diseases that traveled from the Americas to Europe—like syphilis (though its exact origin is debated). The sudden changes in both hemispheres were so drastic that historians still study how societies adapted or collapsed in the face of these biological and cultural shocks.

9. Magellan's Voyage: A Fatal Circumnavigation

Ferdinand Magellan is credited with the first circumnavigation of the globe (1519–1522), though he did not survive the full journey. He set out with five ships, aiming to find a westward route to the Spice Islands (the Moluccas in present-day Indonesia). Along the way, his voyage was marked by storms, mutiny, starvation, and strange encounters with local peoples.

In the southern tip of South America, Magellan found a narrow passage (now called the Strait of Magellan). The crew saw large footprints on the shore, leading them to call the local people "Patagonians," believing them to be giants. There may have been some difference in height, but the Spanish likely exaggerated the stories for effect.

Magellan died in the Philippines, caught in local conflicts. Only one ship, the Victoria, made it back to Spain under the command of **Juan Sebastián Elcano**. The circumnavigation proved the world was larger than many had thought and that Asia could indeed be reached by sailing west around the Americas, although it was an incredibly dangerous route.

10. Encounters in the Pacific: Surprising Civilizations

Explorers crossing the Pacific encountered far-flung island societies. Spaniards and Portuguese were astonished to find local navigators in the

Polynesian region who traveled vast ocean distances using star navigation, wind patterns, and wave observations—often without written charts. This was a shock, as Europeans assumed they alone had advanced seafaring knowledge.

When the Spanish landed in the **Philippines**, they found a network of trade linking the region to China, Japan, and other parts of Southeast Asia. Marketplaces had porcelain, silk, spices, and intricate metalwork. Europeans realized that these were not "uncivilized" lands but places with complex societies.

Yet confusion remained: some Spanish explorers thought they might stumble on the legendary islands of gold or hidden cities filled with precious stones. They were eager to claim these lands for the Spanish crown. This blend of curiosity and greed often led to violent confrontations. The local peoples were baffled by European armor and guns, while Europeans marveled at islanders who navigated thousands of miles using only natural cues.

---

11. The Ill-Fated Search for El Dorado

No tale from the Age of Exploration is more famously odd than the hunt for **El Dorado**, the legendary city or kingdom of gold in South America. Explorers heard stories from Indigenous peoples about a king who covered himself in gold dust and dived into a sacred lake as part of a ritual. This rumor grew into a myth of an entire golden city.

Sir Walter Raleigh made two expeditions to find El Dorado along the Orinoco River in present-day Venezuela. Though he discovered waterfalls, rivers, and various tribes, he never found the fabled city. Others, like the Spanish conquistador **Gonzalo Pizarro**, also led disastrous expeditions into the Amazon jungle, losing countless men to disease, hunger, and hostile encounters.

These journeys, driven by greed and rumor, often ended in misery. Explorers trudged through swamps, faced venomous creatures, and starved. Yet the legend persisted, fueling more quests. It was a testament to the power of myth—how a single story could cause men to risk everything for a golden paradise that never truly existed.

12. Francis Drake's Pirate-Like Exploits

Sir Francis Drake was an English sea captain who sailed around the world (1577–1580). Though celebrated as a hero in England, to the Spanish he was more like a pirate. He raided Spanish settlements in the Americas and seized valuable cargoes of gold and silver.

One strange episode occurred in California (which Drake claimed for England and named "Nova Albion" in 1579). Drake had peaceful encounters with the Coast Miwok people, who were curious about these newcomers. Drake left only vague descriptions of where he landed, leading to centuries of debate over the exact bay in which he anchored.

Drake also claimed to see glimpses of unusual creatures along the Pacific coast, though these might have been distorted accounts of seals, sea lions, or local wildlife. The English public back home loved reading about his exploits, many of which sounded like grand adventures with heroic battles and exotic discoveries—though the Spanish saw him as a plunderer who caused chaos along their colonial routes.

13. Jesuit Missionaries and Their Surprising Reports

Jesuits (members of the Society of Jesus, founded in 1540) traveled widely during the Age of Exploration as missionaries. They wrote detailed letters about the peoples they encountered in Asia, Africa, and the Americas. Some Jesuits were genuinely curious, learning local languages, studying customs, and describing them in letters to Europe.

In **China**, Jesuit missionaries like **Matteo Ricci** adopted Chinese dress and studied Confucian teachings to gain acceptance at the imperial court. They shared Western math and astronomy, impressing Chinese scholars. Yet they also sent home tales of strange Chinese practices, elaborate ceremonies, and unique foods (like tofu and tea).

In **Japan**, Jesuits were stunned by the strict social codes and samurai culture. Some wrote about tea ceremonies and the widespread practice of ritual suicide (seppuku) among samurai. These reports fascinated Europeans, who had never imagined such customs. On the other hand, local governments sometimes grew suspicious of the missionaries, leading to persecutions or expulsions.

Jesuit letters were among the first in-depth written accounts of non-European civilizations that tried to understand them rather than just label them as savage or monstrous. Though not always free of bias, these writings opened European eyes to the complexity of other cultures.

---

14. Strange Animals Brought Back Home

During the Age of Exploration, sailors returned with living curiosities or exotic animal parts—parrots, monkeys, large tortoises, even llamas. Europeans were amazed by creatures like the **toucan** with its huge beak, or the **sloth** that moved so slowly. These odd animals were often displayed in royal courts or menageries.

In 1515, King Manuel I of Portugal sent a **rhinoceros** to Pope Leo X. This caused an uproar in Europe, as no living rhinoceros had been seen there since Roman times. The animal died in a shipwreck off the coast of Italy, but the Pope had wanted to see it. The famous German artist **Albrecht Dürer** made a woodcut of the rhino based on descriptions, leading to an iconic but somewhat inaccurate image.

Similarly, explorers brought back "tigers" (often jaguars), "strange goats" (llamas), and "monstrous birds" (cassowaries or ostriches). People flocked to see these animals, feeding rumors that the far corners of the globe teemed with wonders beyond imagination.

15. Disease on the High Seas

Sailing for months or years exposed crews to poor nutrition, bad water, and cramped conditions. **Scurvy**, caused by lack of vitamin C, was particularly deadly. Sailors' gums would bleed, teeth would fall out, and they grew weak. They had no idea that citrus fruits could prevent it until much later. Explorers often saw half or more of their men die during long voyages.

Other diseases like **typhus** or dysentery spread quickly on ships. Rats infested the holds, carrying fleas and lice. A single outbreak could decimate the crew. Some sailors who survived might arrive in distant lands only to face local illnesses like malaria or yellow fever.

In desperation, captains tried odd cures: forcing men to drink vinegar, or whipping them to "keep the blood flowing." Some ships carried live animals (chickens, goats) to provide fresh food, but these conditions rarely solved the deeper problem of vitamin deficiency and contaminated water. Despite these dangers, men still signed up for voyages, lured by promises of riches or the chance to escape poverty at home.

---

16. The Global Slave Trade's Dark Side

Tragically, the Age of Exploration also saw the rise of the **Atlantic slave trade**. As European powers established colonies, they demanded labor to grow sugar, tobacco, and other cash crops. When Native populations dwindled (largely due to disease and brutal treatment), Europeans began forcibly transporting millions of Africans to the Americas.

These African captives endured the horrific **Middle Passage** across the Atlantic, crammed into slave ships in inhumane conditions. Diseases were rampant, and death rates were extremely high. Survivors faced enslavement on plantations or in mines. This forced migration reshaped the populations of the Americas, with enslaved Africans and their descendants contributing massively to the cultural and economic landscape under cruel oppression.

It was an odd and terrible contradiction: the same explorers who "discovered" new lands under claims of glory and progress also enabled one of the largest systems of human exploitation in history. While many Europeans were fascinated by the wealth these colonies generated, they often turned a blind eye to the suffering of enslaved people.

---

17. Piracy and Privateers: Lawlessness on the Seas

The Age of Exploration also sparked an age of **piracy**. With treasure-laden galleons crossing the oceans, rogues and adventurers took to the seas in search of loot. Some pirates were officially sanctioned as **privateers**, holding letters of marque from a king or queen allowing them to attack ships of rival nations. Others were outright outlaws with no allegiance.

The Caribbean became a hotspot for piracy. Figures like **Blackbeard** or **Henry Morgan** (though Morgan was more 17th century) are legendary. They used small, fast ships to ambush slower treasure ships. Pirate hideouts on remote islands or hidden coves offered a place to repair vessels and share plunder.

To avoid pirate attacks, some galleons traveled in fleets escorted by armed warships. But pirates could still slip through. Stories circulated about buried treasure, pirate codes, and shocking cruelty on both sides. This lawlessness further spiced up the legends of the New World, turning the oceans into a dangerous stage where explorers, merchants, and pirates played out thrilling, and often brutal, dramas.

---

18. Cultural Blending and Strange Exchanges

Despite the violence and tragedy, the Age of Exploration also fostered surprising cultural blending. In the **Philippines**, for instance, Spanish rule led to a mix of local traditions with Catholic festivals. In places like Brazil, enslaved Africans blended their religions with Catholic saints, forming new faith expressions like **Candomblé**.

In Asia, Portuguese outposts in **Goa** (India) or **Macau** (China) combined European and local architecture, cuisines, and customs. Jesuit schools taught Western math and science to Asian students, while European merchants adopted local clothing or married local women.

These exchanges sometimes produced odd results: Europeans wearing cotton robes and eating spicy curries, or aristocrats in Japan adopting European guns and styles. Meanwhile, terms from Indigenous languages entered European vocabularies—words like "hammock," "barbecue," or "canoe" (from the Caribbean) became common. This cultural mixing was an unintended outcome of explorers searching for gold and spices but ended up sharing languages, foods, and lifestyles.

19. Misinterpreted Customs and Awkward Diplomacy

Diplomatic exchanges in new lands were often comical or tragic. European explorers might try to present a fancy gift, misunderstanding local customs. In some African kingdoms, the local king expected elaborate rituals. European envoys, unaware of the etiquette, could offend the court by refusing to bow deeply or by stepping on sacred ground.

In the **Americas**, a handshake might be meaningless to local leaders who expected a symbolic exchange of gifts or a shared feast. Explorers sometimes waved flags and read official documents in languages the locals did not understand, proclaiming the land claimed for their king. Meanwhile, the Indigenous people might have had no concept of "land ownership" in the European sense.

These cross-cultural failures led to confusion. Some local rulers used the Europeans for their own power struggles, while Europeans claimed they had been given control. It was a swirl of comedic errors with serious consequences, often ending in broken alliances or open conflict.

20. Legacy of the Age of Exploration

By the end of the Age of Exploration, Europeans had mapped much of the world's coastlines. New routes connected continents, and global trade networks emerged. Silver from the Americas fueled the Spanish Empire, spices from Southeast Asia enriched the Portuguese and Dutch, and sugar plantations in the Caribbean transformed European tastes.

Yet, the negative impacts were massive. Indigenous cultures were suppressed or destroyed, enslaved people were transported across oceans, and local economies were forced into colonial systems. The world was forever changed—crops like potatoes and corn fed growing populations in Europe, while European empires grabbed land in the Americas, Africa, and Asia.

The Age of Exploration was both an era of wonder and horror. Explorers returned with incredible stories that stretched the imagination, from giant "Patagonians" to monstrous fish, from golden cities to bizarre foods. At the same time, diseases, conquests, and slavery revealed the dark side of this global expansion. This odd mixture shaped our modern world in ways we still grapple with today.

Now that we have looked at these strange journeys and shocking discoveries, we can move on to Chapter 12 to explore the next phase: how these emerging empires turned their discoveries into colonies, and how their curious and often cruel expansions continued to shape history before modern times.

CHAPTER 12

Conquests and Colonies: Curious Events from Growing Empires

After the initial rush of discovery in the Age of Exploration, European powers moved to conquer and colonize the new lands they had found. Spain and Portugal led the way, quickly followed by the Dutch, English, and French. They set up colonies across the Americas, Africa, and Asia. This period saw the building of grand colonial empires—and also the rise of odd, sometimes shocking, events and systems.

In this chapter, we will dig into the curious facts around colonial administration, strange battles for territory, unusual alliances with local rulers, and the bizarre ways colonial societies tried to blend or sometimes violently suppress different cultures. We will see how trade thrived with new goods and how colonists, missionaries, adventurers, and enslaved laborers created a patchwork of cultures that often clashed. Though we are still a few centuries away from "modern" times, these colonial expansions laid much of the groundwork—both good and bad—for the world we know today.

1. The Treaty of Tordesillas: Splitting the World

Shortly after Columbus's voyages, Spain and Portugal faced a conflict over claiming lands in the New World. In 1494, they turned to the Pope for a solution, resulting in the **Treaty of Tordesillas**. This treaty essentially drew an imaginary line in the Atlantic: Spain got rights to most of the Americas (west of the line), while Portugal got what lay east of it (including Brazil and much of Africa and Asia).

This was a strange idea—two European kingdoms dividing the entire globe between them, ignoring the rights of the peoples living there. But it shows how the mindset of conquest worked. The line was poorly understood, and other European powers did not accept it. Still, it gave Spain and Portugal a sense of legality as they built their empires.

The treaty also led to odd boundary disputes. Portuguese explorers found that part of the South American coast lay east of the line, giving them Brazil. Over time, they expanded further west, often disregarding the original boundary. Meanwhile, Spain claimed vast swaths of land in the Americas, fueling both fortune and conflict.

2. Encomiendas: A Bizarre Labor System

In Spanish colonies, the **encomienda** system granted conquistadors the right to demand labor or tribute from Indigenous communities in exchange for "protection" and instruction in Christianity. In theory, it was meant to be a paternalistic system where Spanish lords looked after the well-being of their Indigenous subjects. In practice, it often resulted in forced labor and harsh conditions.

Some conquistadors became incredibly wealthy through encomiendas, exploiting Native labor in mines or plantations. Missionaries like **Bartolomé de las Casas** protested against the cruel treatment of Indigenous peoples. He wrote about their sufferings, shocking many in Europe who had never witnessed such brutality.

This system was strange because it tried to combine feudal ideas of lord and vassal with the reality of conquest in a foreign land. The Indigenous peoples had no tradition of feudal loyalty to these foreign "lords," leading to confusion and abuse. Over time, Spain replaced encomiendas with other forms of colonial rule, but the damage to Indigenous communities was already done.

3. Portuguese in Brazil: Sugar and Strange Settlements

Portugal's main colony in the Americas was **Brazil**, where they established sugar plantations along the coast. Portuguese settlers used enslaved Africans to grow and process sugar cane, creating a huge export business. Towns like **Salvador** and **Recife** became centers of trade and administration.

An odd aspect was the existence of "Quilombos"—communities formed by escaped enslaved people, such as the famous **Quilombo dos Palmares**. These communities defended themselves against Portuguese raids for years, showing resilience and forming unique social structures.

Another curious twist came from the Jesuits, who set up missions to convert local peoples like the Tupi or Guarani. In some areas, they formed **reductions**—protected settlements where Indigenous families lived under Jesuit supervision. Although these missions aimed to shield natives from slavers, they also imposed strict discipline and cultural change, creating a strange blend of Christian rules with local traditions.

4. The Race for Spices and Odd Alliances

Beyond the Americas, European powers also vied for control of **spice-producing regions** in Asia. The Portuguese built forts along the Indian Ocean coast, capturing key ports like **Goa** in India and **Malacca** (in modern Malaysia). They forced local rulers to allow Portuguese monopolies in pepper, cinnamon, cloves, and nutmeg.

Soon, the **Dutch** challenged them, forming the **Dutch East India Company (VOC)** in 1602. This company was granted powers by the Dutch government to wage war, make treaties, and govern territories. It aggressively took over islands in Indonesia, sometimes making brutal deals with local princes or carrying out bloody raids to secure spice monopolies.

The English also formed the **British East India Company**, seeking trade in India and beyond. All of these companies made odd alliances with local sultans or rajahs, sometimes providing them with European firearms in exchange for exclusive trade rights. These business-driven conquests turned seas and distant islands into battlegrounds of both diplomacy and violence, creating a web of unusual treaties that heavily favored European interests.

5. Strange Settlements of the French and English in North America

While Spain focused on Central and South America, the **French** and **English** competed for land in North America. The French established **New France** along the St. Lawrence River, focusing on the fur trade. They developed friendly ties with some Indigenous nations (like the Huron), exchanging metal tools and guns for beaver pelts. This alliance was odd to the English, who often saw Indigenous peoples more as obstacles than partners.

Meanwhile, the **English** set up colonies along the Atlantic coast, like **Jamestown** (1607) and **Plymouth** (1620). Jamestown settlers expected to find gold or a passage to Asia but ended up struggling with disease, hunger, and conflicts with the Powhatan Confederacy. The story of **Pocahontas** and **John Smith** is a famous (though partly mythic) example of how cultural misunderstandings shaped these early colonies.

The French also built forts along the Great Lakes and Mississippi River, forging alliances with various tribes. They shared Catholic missions, brandy, and trade goods, which changed local politics. These patchwork alliances led to strange bedfellows—some tribes siding with the French, others with the English, creating tangled alliances in future colonial wars.

---

6. Pilgrims, Puritans, and Peculiar Laws

In English colonies like New England, **Puritans** and **Pilgrims** arrived seeking religious freedom. However, once established, they enforced their own strict religious rules. Dancing, card playing, or celebrating Christmas could be banned. The colonists formed small, tight communities with mandatory church attendance and harsh penalties for dissent.

The **Salem witch trials** (1692) in Massachusetts were a bizarre outcome of these religious anxieties. Several young girls began having fits and accused neighbors of bewitching them. Hysteria spread, leading to over 200 accusations and 20 executions. The region's tense religious atmosphere, combined with local grudges and fear of the devil, fueled these trials.

Puritan communities held odd "town meetings" where church members governed local affairs. They also had unusual punishments like the **stocks** or the **ducking stool**, meant to humiliate offenders. Despite these strict rules, some colonists broke away to form more tolerant settlements, showing how diversity slowly emerged in these rigid societies.

---

7. The Dutch in the New World: New Amsterdam's Quirks

The **Dutch** also claimed parts of North America, calling it **New Netherland** (along the Hudson River). Their capital, **New Amsterdam**, on Manhattan Island, was a lively, multi-ethnic trading center by the mid-1600s. Dutch authorities welcomed merchants from various backgrounds, including Jews and free Black people, making it more tolerant than many English colonies.

Yet, the Dutch West India Company had strict goals: profit from the fur trade and shipping. Conflicts arose with local Algonquian peoples, leading to brutal wars. One Dutch governor, **Willem Kieft**, tried to impose heavy taxes on tribes, which sparked fighting that devastated the colony.

New Amsterdam had odd laws. For instance, residents could be fined for throwing garbage into the street or failing to maintain the wooden fence around their plot. Eventually, the English seized New Amsterdam in 1664, renaming it **New York**. The legacy of Dutch influence remains in place names (Brooklyn from "Breukelen," Harlem from "Haarlem") and a certain spirit of commercial openness that continued even under English rule.

---

8. The Lost Colony of Roanoke

One of the strangest colonial mysteries is the **Lost Colony** of Roanoke. Sir Walter Raleigh sponsored an English settlement on Roanoke Island (off modern North Carolina) in 1587. The governor, John White, returned to England for supplies. When he came back in 1590, the colony was deserted. Buildings stood empty, and the word "CROATOAN" was carved on a post.

No one knows for sure what happened. Some believe the colonists joined nearby Native tribes, perhaps the Croatoan. Others think they were killed or died of disease. The colony's disappearance sparked wild speculation: were they kidnapped by the Spanish, attacked by hostile tribes, or did they flee inland in search of better resources?

This bizarre vanishing act remained unsolved. Archaeologists still search for clues. The story of Roanoke stands as a symbol of the fragility of early colonies and how harsh conditions, poor planning, or misunderstandings could doom a settlement.

---

9. The Galleon Trade and Silver's Strange Path

Once Spain controlled much of the Americas, they extracted huge amounts of **silver**, especially from mines in Mexico and Potosí (in present-day Bolivia). They shipped silver across the Pacific in the **Manila Galleons**, trading it in the Philippines for Chinese silk, porcelain, and spices. This created a global trade loop.

Spanish silver from the New World ended up in **China**, where it became a main currency. Chinese goods (silks, ceramics) went to Europe and the Americas. The Spanish used the port of Manila (founded in 1571) as a crucial hub. On these galleons, life was risky: storms, pirates, and months at sea threatened the cargo and crew.

The silver trade had odd economic effects. In Europe, the influx of silver caused inflation (the "price revolution"). In China, silver became so vital that it changed tax systems. Meanwhile, local economies in the Americas were distorted as mining overshadowed other activities. This single metal connected distant peoples, but it also fueled exploitation and power struggles.

---

10. Catholic Missions and Forced Conversions

Catholic missionaries, particularly the **Franciscans**, **Dominicans**, and **Jesuits**, followed conquistadors into the Americas. They built churches, schools, and mission stations, aiming to convert Indigenous peoples to Christianity. While some missionaries genuinely cared for the well-being of local tribes, many forced conversions, destroying native temples and banning traditional rituals.

In places like **California**, Franciscan missions under **Father Junípero Serra** sought to gather Indigenous peoples into mission communities. But these missions also imposed strict rules. Many died from European diseases within the cramped living quarters. Over time, these missions became centers of colonial authority, with Indigenous labor used to build churches, farm fields, and raise livestock for the Spanish.

This forced religious assimilation was strange for tribes used to their own spiritual beliefs. Some resisted, others blended Catholic saints with local gods, creating new forms of worship. Today, many old mission buildings stand as tourist sites, but they hold a legacy of cultural loss and complex history that is not always obvious to the casual visitor.

---

11. Colonial Women and Mixed Cultures

Women in colonial societies faced unique challenges. European women were few in many colonies, so marriages with local women or enslaved women were common, creating mixed-heritage populations. In Spanish colonies, the **casta system** labeled individuals by their racial background (like "mestizo" for Spanish-Indigenous, "mulatto" for Spanish-African, and so on). This produced a complicated social hierarchy.

Some women, like the Spanish noblewomen traveling to the New World, maintained high status. Others became cloistered in convents if they lacked a dowry. Indigenous or African women might marry or have relationships with Europeans, gaining certain legal protections but often facing prejudice.

In places like **New Orleans** (French) or **St. Augustine** (Spanish Florida), free women of color sometimes ran businesses or owned property, exploiting legal loopholes. Meanwhile, the majority of enslaved women had little power. The cultural blending led to new music, dance, and language forms—like **Creole** languages that mixed African, European, and Indigenous words—revealing how women's roles shaped colonial life in strange and unexpected ways.

---

12. The Dutch Golden Age and Asian Colonies

During the 17th century, the **Dutch Republic** prospered. In Asia, the Dutch East India Company took control of lucrative spice islands, including the **Banda Islands** for nutmeg. They expelled or killed local inhabitants who resisted, then imported slaves or laborers to work the plantations. These brutal actions contradicted the Netherlands' reputation for tolerance in Europe.

In **Japan**, the Dutch were the only Europeans allowed to trade at a small island in Nagasaki's harbor called **Dejima**. The Japanese limited foreign contacts, suspicious of European intentions after conflicts with Catholic missionaries. The Dutch, adapting to these rules, developed unique cultural exchanges with Japanese scholars, who learned Western science (known as **rangaku**, "Dutch learning").

This odd arrangement meant the Dutch had a tiny base in Japan, cut off from the main city. They were required to follow strict protocols—no Christian worship, no leaving Dejima without permission, and they had to perform forced humiliations for the shogun occasionally. Still, it gave them exclusive trade, showing how a mix of cunning and compromise built their Asian empire.

---

13. Sugar Colonies and Savage Slave Codes

As Europeans established sugar plantations in the Caribbean and Brazil, the need for labor soared. Millions of Africans were enslaved and brought to work in harsh conditions. Colonies like **Barbados** or **Jamaica** under British rule, or **Saint-Domingue** under French control (later Haiti), ran massive sugar estates.

Planters enforced brutal slave codes, dictating every aspect of enslaved people's lives. Punishments for disobedience could be extremely cruel—whipping, branding, or worse. Yet enslaved people found ways to resist, through sabotage, running away to form **Maroon** communities, or preserving cultural identities in music and religion.

These sugar colonies also held surprising social complexities. Some free people of color owned property or even enslaved people themselves, creating odd layers of status. The sugar wealth built grand plantation houses, but it relied on unimaginable suffering. For the colonizers, it was normal business, while for the enslaved, it was a living nightmare that shaped the demographics and culture of the Caribbean for centuries.

14. Buccaneers and the Tortuga Oddity

Buccaneers were outlaws and privateers in the Caribbean, often French or English, who attacked Spanish ships and settlements. They used hidden bases like **Tortuga** Island off the coast of Hispaniola. Tortuga became a notorious haven for criminals, runaway sailors, and adventurers looking to strike at Spanish targets.

This strange community included hunters (who smoked meat using native Taino methods, which gave them the name "boucanier," later "buccaneer") and pirates. Over time, the French crown turned a blind eye, seeing them as a tool to weaken Spain. Tortuga developed its own rough society, with taverns, gambling dens, and a chaotic blend of cultures.

Buccaneers lived by a code sharing plunder and punishing disloyalty. Some ships allowed voting on important decisions, in a proto-democratic style. Women were scarce, and captive or local women faced harsh treatment. The success of these buccaneers in raiding Spanish colonies shaped the Caribbean's lawless image, fueling legends of hidden pirate treasures.

15. British East India Company: Rulers of an Empire?

Over in Asia, the **British East India Company (EIC)** began by trading in spices and textiles. Slowly, it gained political power in **India**. By forging deals with local princes, it secured trading posts like **Madras**, **Bombay**, and **Calcutta**. Company merchants armed themselves with private armies, interfering in local wars to protect or expand their interests.

A turning point came with the **Battle of Plassey** (1757), where the EIC forces, led by **Robert Clive**, defeated the Nawab of Bengal. This odd victory, aided by bribery and cunning, gave the Company control over one of India's richest regions. Soon, the EIC collected taxes, ran courts, and minted coins. It was a business acting like a government, with little oversight from Britain at first.

This corporate rule was full of bizarre contradictions: British "gentlemen" in wigs and waistcoats commanding Indian sepoys (troops), negotiating with local rulers, and sometimes disrespecting local customs. The tension built over the decades, leading to uprisings. The sheer strangeness of a corporation ruling millions of people was a hallmark of the colonial era's twisted power structures.

---

16. French Indochina and the Mandarin Mysteries

France also gained a foothold in Asia, particularly in Vietnam, Cambodia, and Laos—regions later called **French Indochina**. Early French missionaries and traders arrived in the 17th century, clashing with local rulers who distrusted Christian influence.

An odd story involves a French missionary, **Pigneau de Béhaine**, who backed a Vietnamese prince, **Nguyễn Ánh**, in a civil war in the late 1700s. The missionary raised funds and troops for his ally. Once Nguyễn Ánh became Emperor Gia Long, he rewarded the French with trade rights and advisory roles at his court.

This strange partnership led to deeper French involvement, culminating in full-blown colonization in the 19th century. Mandarins in the Vietnamese court wore traditional robes and hats, studied Confucian classics, and took pride in resisting foreign dominance. Yet French officials insisted on treaties that favored them. Over time, France forced open more ports and demanded concessions, showing again how a few determined foreign players could reshape an entire kingdom's policies.

17. The Weird Saga of New Sweden

Less known is that **Sweden** briefly held a colony in North America: **New Sweden** (1638–1655) along the Delaware River. Swedish settlers built Fort Christina (in present-day Wilmington, Delaware). They traded furs with local Lenape and Susquehannock tribes.

However, the colony was small and overshadowed by Dutch and English neighbors. The Dutch at New Netherland considered New Sweden an intrusion on their territory. Governor **Peter Stuyvesant** of New Netherland eventually sent a force to conquer it in 1655.

Swedish colonists who stayed became subjects of the Dutch, and then English, as colonies changed hands. They left small cultural traces—log cabin designs, Lutheran churches, some Swedish place names. It is an odd footnote that a European power like Sweden tried to carve out a slice of the New World, only for it to vanish in less than 20 years.

---

18. Culture Clash in the Colonies

Throughout the colonial empires, attempts to blend European customs with local practices produced strange outcomes. In **Latin America**, the "Virgin of Guadalupe" story emerged in Mexico, where an apparition of the Virgin Mary supposedly appeared to an Indigenous man, **Juan Diego**, in 1531. This symbol combined Catholic devotion with Aztec symbolism, becoming a unifying icon for Mexican identity.

In **French Canada**, Catholic missionaries found that the Huron or Algonquin might accept baptism but still keep traditional feasts. The resulting "mixed" Christianity alarmed some priests. Meanwhile, African enslaved communities in the Caribbean blended Christian saints with West African deities, forming religions like **Vodou** (in Haiti) or **Santería** (in Cuba).

Colonial authorities often tried to stamp out these "pagan" elements, but they persisted, creating hybrid cultures. Dances, languages, and festivals grew from these fusions—like Carnival in Brazil, with African drum rhythms and Catholic feast-day timing. Such cultural mixing was one of the few ways oppressed groups could maintain their heritage within a harsh colonial system.

---

19. Strange Attempts at Utopian Colonies

Not all colonies aimed just for profit or conquest. Some were founded on utopian ideals. The **Jesuits** in Paraguay established missions where Indigenous Guarani lived in communal settlements, supposedly free from outside exploitation. The Guarani learned European music, crafts, and reading, while Jesuits praised their discipline. Critics said the Jesuits ruled like overlords, controlling every aspect of daily life.

Another odd example is the **Plymouth Colony** (Pilgrims), who intended to form a godly community separate from the Church of England. Or the **Georgia** colony in the 1730s, envisioned by **James Oglethorpe** as a place where debtors from England could start anew, with strict bans on alcohol and slavery at first. However, these bans did not last, and Georgia became much like other Southern colonies.

These experiments highlight a recurring theme: colonists dreaming of building perfect societies in new lands, only to face the reality of climate, conflicts, and economic pressures. Over time, most "utopias" bent to the same patterns of exploitation and social hierarchy as elsewhere.

---

20. The Shifting Tides of Empire

By the 18th century, the global map had changed drastically. Spain dominated much of Latin America but faced rebellions and competition. Portugal's hold on Brazil remained strong, though it faced Dutch and French raids. The British and French battled for supremacy in North America and India. The Netherlands clung to profitable outposts in Indonesia and the West Indies.

Colonial wars—like the **Seven Years' War** (1756–1763)—spanned continents, with battles in Europe, America, Africa, and Asia. This was a truly global conflict. Meanwhile, local peoples tried to navigate or resist these colonial powers, sometimes playing one European rival against another.

As we near the later 18th century, new ideas of liberty and enlightened thinking began to spark revolutions. The system of conquest and forced labor faced growing criticism. Yet, it would take many more decades (and even centuries) for many colonies to gain independence. The legacy of these strange events—forced conversions, bizarre labor systems, surprising cultural blends—still affects us today.

Thus, the era of conquests and colonies was filled with contradictions: grand cities built on forced labor, religious missions that combined genuine charity with cultural destruction, and daring explorers who nonetheless carried disease and prejudice. In the next chapters, we will keep moving through time, looking at other parts of the world and the odd kingdoms, surprising facts, and ever-shifting beliefs that continued before the truly modern age arrived.

CHAPTER 13

Odd Kingdoms: Strange Tales from African Empires

Africa's history stretches back thousands of years, filled with powerful kingdoms, bustling trade routes, and surprising customs. Yet, many people do not know the fascinating stories behind early African empires and states. In this chapter, we will explore some of these "odd kingdoms" and highlight their unusual facts, peculiar beliefs, and hidden wonders. From the deserts of West Africa to the forests of Central Africa, from the highlands of Ethiopia to the savannas of the south, we will see how these empires grew, clashed, and thrived—long before modern times.

Though often called "mysterious," these civilizations left behind clear signs of advanced organization: grand cities, well-structured governments, strong armies, and impressive art. Their stories show us that Africa was never just a land of isolated tribes. Instead, it was home to countless complex societies that traded, warred, and exchanged ideas across long distances. As we dive into their peculiar customs and achievements, remember that what might look strange to us today was a normal part of life for them.

1. Ancient Ghana: Gold, Camels, and a Mysterious Capital

One of the earliest known empires in West Africa is often called **Ancient Ghana** (not to be confused with the modern country of Ghana, which took its name from this old kingdom). Flourishing around the 6th to 13th centuries, Ancient Ghana sat in the Sahel region, near important trade routes that connected North Africa to sub-Saharan Africa. Traders brought salt, cloth, and other goods by camel caravans, exchanging them for gold, which was abundant in Ghana's lands.

Some odd facts about Ancient Ghana:

- **Invisible Capital**: The capital, known as Kumbi Saleh, was said to be divided into two towns. One was for the king, the other for Muslim traders. Early Arab writers claimed they were six miles apart, though modern archaeology suggests they were closer. The idea of two separate towns gave rise to legends about a hidden royal city that outsiders rarely saw.

- **Camels as "Ships of the Desert"**: Ghana's wealth depended on camels carrying tons of salt bars across the Sahara. These journeys were dangerous, yet the empire thrived because of this trade. Camels were prized as they could go days without water, an almost magical trait to people outside desert regions.
- **Strict Court Ceremonies**: Ghana's king was treated like a semi-divine figure. People had to kneel and sprinkle dust on their heads in his presence. If that seems strange, remember that many medieval rulers used rituals to show power, and Ghana's king was no exception.

2. Mali Empire and the Legendary Riches of Mansa Musa

When Ancient Ghana declined, other powers rose, including the **Mali Empire** (13th–15th centuries). Mali stretched across a vast area of West Africa, controlling trade routes that carried gold, salt, and other products. The most famous ruler of Mali was **Mansa Musa** (early 14th century), often dubbed the richest man who ever lived.

Why did people think Mansa Musa was so wealthy?

- **Gold, Gold, and More Gold**: Mali's goldfields were among the richest in the known world. Mansa Musa controlled them, so the empire's treasury overflowed. When he made a pilgrimage to Mecca, he traveled with a massive caravan of camels loaded with gold, distributing it to the poor along the way. Stories say he gave out so much gold in Cairo that the local gold market crashed for years.
- **Timbuktu, Center of Learning**: Under Mansa Musa, the city of Timbuktu became a major hub of Islamic scholarship. Libraries, universities, and mosques flourished. However, outsiders often imagined Timbuktu as a hidden city of gold. That legend attracted explorers who thought they would see streets paved with gold. In reality, it was more a cultural and trading center—but still quite grand for its time.
- **Royal Etiquette**: Like Ghana, Mali's court had strict rules. Servants might carry a parasol to shade Mansa Musa from the sun, symbolizing his high status. Courtiers wore fine robes and performed bows to show respect. Though it seems formal and "fancy," it was normal for big African empires to mirror the pomp of other medieval courts around the globe.

---

3. The Rise of Songhai: Canoes, Magic, and a University City

After Mali's power waned, the **Songhai Empire** (15th–16th centuries) emerged along the Niger River. At its height under leaders like **Sunni Ali** and **Askia Muhammad**, Songhai was one of the largest empires in African history. Its capital, Gao, and the famous city of Timbuktu became centers of trade, religion, and learning.

- **River Power**: Songhai developed a strong river navy. Warriors used canoes to patrol the Niger River, giving them an advantage over enemies who stuck to land. Sunni Ali's reign was marked by bold conquests using both cavalry and these river forces.
- **Magic and Diviners**: Sunni Ali was rumored to have magical powers or the help of sorcerers. Some stories say he commanded spirits to fight for him. While this might sound odd, mixing warfare with superstition was not unusual. Many cultures believed leaders had spiritual backing.

- **The University of Sankore**: In Timbuktu, Songhai supported the University of Sankore, attracting scholars from many lands. They wrote books on math, medicine, law, and astronomy. For a while, Timbuktu rivaled famous centers of learning in the Islamic world. The idea of an African city with thousands of students and countless manuscripts surprised outsiders who expected only "tribes."

4. Eerie Legends of the Kanem-Bornu Empire

Located around Lake Chad, the **Kanem-Bornu Empire** (9th–19th centuries) lasted a remarkable length of time. Kanem was the earlier phase, eventually shifting to Bornu. Traders passed through from North Africa, the Nile valley, and beyond, making the empire wealthy. But there are some truly odd tales about its rulers:

- **The Saifawa Dynasty**: This ruling family claimed descent from a legendary hero or spirit. Some stories say they had ties to the Middle East, linking them to mythical ancestors. They used these tales to solidify their right to rule.

- **Strange Initiation Rites**: Oral traditions mention certain initiation rituals for warriors or courtiers. Although details are hazy, outsiders whispered of frightening ceremonies that tested loyalty. While much of this remains unverified, the legends show how Kanem-Bornu used mystery to maintain power.
- **Horses and Armed Cavalry**: Like other Sahelian empires, Bornu prized horses. Though Lake Chad's wetlands could be difficult for cavalry, riders adapted by guiding horses around marshy areas. Their strong cavalry units guarded trade routes, enforcing tolls. Some passing travelers spoke of Bornu cavalry who wore chain mail, which looked strange in a region known for heat and dryness.

5. Ethiopia (Aksum and Later Dynasties) and the Ark Legends

Moving to East Africa, we find the kingdom of **Aksum** (1st–8th centuries) and its successor states. Aksum, centered in what is now northern Ethiopia, was a powerful trading empire linking Africa with Arabia and beyond. Many unusual stories swirl around this region:

- **The Ark of the Covenant**: Ethiopian tradition claims that the Ark of the Covenant (from the Bible's Old Testament) was taken to Aksum. Even today, the Ethiopian Orthodox Church says the Ark rests in a chapel in the holy city of Aksum. Only one guardian priest can see it. Skeptics doubt this, but the belief is strong, adding an air of deep mystery to Ethiopian culture.
- **Queen of Sheba**: Another legend says that the biblical Queen of Sheba (Makeda) visited King Solomon in Jerusalem, bore his son, and that their lineage founded Ethiopia's royal house. True or not, medieval Ethiopian kings used this story to claim a grand heritage.
- **Rock-Hewn Churches**: In the 12th–13th centuries, King Lalibela built churches carved straight into the rock in a place now called Lalibela. Visitors marvel at how entire churches sit below ground level, chiseled from solid stone. People say angels helped with construction. This kind of amazing craftsmanship is rarely seen elsewhere.

6. The Empire of Great Zimbabwe: Hill Complexes and Cattle Wealth

In southern Africa, **Great Zimbabwe** (11th–15th centuries) astonished travelers with its massive stone walls and towers. These structures, built without mortar, formed the largest stone complex in sub-Saharan Africa at the time. But Great Zimbabwe's culture was not well understood by outsiders, leading to odd speculations.

- **Stunning Architecture**: The remains feature a royal enclosure, large curved walls, and a tall conical tower. Early European explorers could not believe Africans had built such structures. They claimed it was the work of Phoenicians, the Queen of Sheba, or other foreign powers—refusing to accept local genius. Archaeology has since proven that it was the center of a local Shona kingdom.
- **Rich Gold Trade**: Great Zimbabwe's wealth came from controlling goldfields and trade routes to the coast. Ivory and gold were exchanged for cloth and glass beads from Asia. The city's rulers also measured wealth in cattle. Owning large herds meant influence in society.
- **Mystic Spiritual Beliefs**: Oral traditions mention that ancestors' spirits guided the rulers, and ceremonies were held around sacred places. Ritual specialists performed dances and used spirit mediums to speak with the dead. This connection between leadership and ancestral spirits gave the king a mystical aura.

---

7. The Swahili City-States: Coral Palaces and Spicy Tales

Along the East African coast, **Swahili city-states** rose from around the 8th century onward. Places like **Kilwa, Mombasa, and Sofala** became thriving ports. With influences from Arab traders, local Bantu culture, and even Persian settlers, the Swahili towns were rich in trade and had a distinct fusion identity.

- **Coral Stone Architecture**: Wealthy Swahili merchants built houses and mosques from coral stone, giving a unique look to these coastal cities. Fine carvings adorned doors and walls. Some visitors described them as "pearls of the Indian Ocean," shining under the tropical sun.
- **Zanzibar and Spice**: The island of Zanzibar became known for trading spices like cloves, cinnamon, and pepper. The scents drifting from spice plantations earned it the nickname "Spice Island." Though large-scale spice farming developed more in later centuries, trade in exotic flavors was already happening in smaller forms, surprising travelers who expected only simple villages.
- **Cultural Fusion**: Swahili people spoke a Bantu-based language that incorporated many loanwords from Arabic and Persian. They also followed Islam but blended it with local customs. Outsiders found it odd that some Swahili women wore African-style clothing but also covered their hair with veils. The mix of local tradition and Islamic practice produced a cosmopolitan culture many did not expect in East Africa.

---

8. Kingdom of Kongo: A Royal Conversion and Weird Diplomatic Ties

In Central Africa, the **Kingdom of Kongo** (14th–19th centuries) was known for its organized bureaucracy and trade. Portuguese explorers met the Kongo king (the Manikongo) in the late 15th century, leading to unusual cultural exchanges.

- **Sudden Embrace of Christianity**: King Nzinga a Nkuwu converted to Christianity around 1491, taking the name João I. Later kings, like Afonso I, also embraced the faith. Some historians find it odd how quickly the Kongo court adopted European practices—though they often combined them with African traditions, leading to a unique fusion.
- **Diplomatic Missions to Europe**: Kongo sent ambassadors to Portugal and even to the Vatican. These envoys, dressed in a mix of Kongo and European garb, caused a stir. People in Lisbon were amazed to see African royals with knowledge of Portuguese language and etiquette.

- **Conflict Over Slavery**: Kongo's rulers had complicated relationships with the Portuguese over the enslavement of their people. They asked for priests and teachers, but Portuguese traders were more interested in capturing or buying slaves. This tension led to odd letters from Kongo kings to European monarchs, pleading for fair treatment. The clash of diplomacy and commerce made for a perplexing arrangement.

9. Benin Kingdom: Bronze Plaques and Fearsome Oba

The **Kingdom of Benin** (not to be confused with the modern Republic of Benin) was a powerful state in what is now southern Nigeria. Its art, especially the famous **Benin Bronzes**, is admired for intricate designs. The kingdom thrived on trade with Portuguese and Dutch merchants from the late 15th century onwards.

- **The Oba's Court**: The ruler of Benin was called the Oba, viewed almost like a god-king. The Oba's palace was a grand complex decorated with brass plaques that recorded historical events. Foreign visitors described strict protocols, with courtiers prostrating themselves fully on the ground.
- **Sacred Python**: Some accounts mention a giant python kept near the Oba's palace. Locals believed it had protective powers. Though possibly exaggerated, the story reveals how important symbolic animals were to the kingdom's identity.
- **Bronze Casting**: Benin artisans used the lost-wax casting method to create lifelike statues and plaques. Scenes showed warriors, nobles, or even Portuguese merchants wearing hats. Europeans who saw these bronzes were astounded at the level of skill, challenging stereotypes that African societies lacked complex artistry.

10. The Yoruba City-States: Ife's Sculptures and Eccentric Traditions

In southwestern Nigeria, the **Yoruba** peoples formed city-states like **Ife**, **Oyo**, and others. Ife is considered the spiritual heart of the Yoruba, while Oyo became a military powerhouse. Some customs and stories from these city-states stand out as especially unusual to outsiders.

- **Realistic Sculptures**: Ife is famous for terracotta and metal heads dated to the 12th–15th centuries. These heads are so realistic that when Europeans first discovered them, they thought they were from ancient Greece or Rome. The skill in capturing facial features with metal alloys and terracotta remains a mystery to many.
- **The Oduduwa Myth**: Yoruba tradition says that the world started at Ife when the god Oduduwa descended on a chain from the sky. He scattered earth on water and placed a cockerel to spread it, forming land. This creation story might sound fantastical, but it is a core belief for many Yoruba, connecting their city directly to divine origins.
- **Kingly Rituals**: Oyo's king, called the Alaafin, had complex ceremonies. Some Yoruba tales mention that certain kings were never to be seen eating in public. Others had to avoid certain colors. Such rules might look odd, but they reinforced the king's sacred aura.

---

11. Luba and Lunda: Sacred Kingship in Central Africa

Moving back to Central Africa, the **Luba** (16th–19th centuries) and **Lunda** (17th–19th centuries) empires emerged around the upper Congo region. These were famous for their art, especially carvings and ceremonial objects that symbolized sacred kingship.

- **The Lukasa "Memory Board"**: Luba royal advisers used lukasa boards—carved wooden tablets with beads and patterns—to recall complex historical events. They memorized genealogies, clan migrations, and important agreements. Outsiders found it bizarre that a simple board with beads could hold so much data, but for the Luba, it was a sophisticated memory tool.
- **Spirit Capitals**: Some Luba kings claimed their real capital was in the spirit world, and that the earthly capital was just a reflection. People believed that the king's body housed powerful spirits, which could bring rain or curses. This made the king both a political and a mystical figure.

- **Umbilical Cord Rituals**: According to some oral histories, when a royal child was born, the umbilical cord was kept as a sacred object. It symbolized a connection to ancestors. If that child grew up to be king, the umbilical cord was used in ceremonies to confirm his legitimacy—an odd practice, but deeply meaningful in Luba culture.

---

12. Monomotapa and the Search for Ophir

South of Great Zimbabwe, the **Mutapa** (or Monomotapa) state grew in the 15th century. It controlled goldfields and traded with Swahili towns. When Portuguese explorers heard of the region, they linked it to biblical tales of Ophir (the land of gold visited by King Solomon's ships).

- **Portuguese Myths**: Hoping to find King Solomon's mines, the Portuguese ventured inland, believing the Mutapa state held endless gold. Though gold was indeed mined, it was not the fantasy trove they pictured. Their disappointment led to conflicts and attempts to control local rulers.
- **Fortified Hills**: Like Great Zimbabwe, Mutapa's settlements had stone walls atop hills, giving them a defensive edge. People used these enclosures for rituals and protection. Legends told of hidden tunnels leading to secret chambers filled with treasure—likely exaggerated, yet they added mystique.
- **Mwari Cult**: In parts of the region, the Mwari (or Mwali) religion was practiced, worshipping a supreme creator. Oracles and priests carried out ceremonies in sacred caves. Outsiders found it unsettling to hear chanting echo from hidden caverns, but for local believers, it was a key link to the spirit world.

---

13. The Hausa City-States: Walls and Trading Might

In what is now northern Nigeria, the **Hausa city-states** included Kano, Katsina, Zaria, and others. These states thrived on trans-Saharan trade, famous for dyed cloth, leather goods, and grains. Some unusual features set them apart:

- **Massive City Walls**: Each city-state built tall walls of sun-dried mud bricks to protect from raids. Kano's wall was said to be so thick that two horsemen could ride side by side on top. People believed these fortifications held magical wards against enemies, combining practicality with superstition.
- **Queen Amina of Zaria**: A legendary figure, Amina is said to have led armies, expanded territory, and built walls around cities. That a woman could be a warrior-queen in a region often seen as patriarchal surprised some historians. Oral tales paint her as both fierce in battle and shrewd in diplomacy.
- **Trade Routes and Language**: Hausa language became a lingua franca in the region, bridging many ethnic groups. Merchants used it to sell goods from salt to gold to slaves. The city-states competed with each other yet shared cultural ties, forming a puzzle of alliances and rivalries that outsiders found complex.

---

14. The Forest Kingdom of Asante: Golden Stool and Serious Taboos

In West Africa, the **Asante (Ashanti) Kingdom** rose in the 17th century in what is now Ghana's forest region. Though it falls slightly later in our timeline, its customs illustrate the richness of African states before modern colonial rule took over.

- **The Golden Stool**: Legend says that the Golden Stool descended from the sky into the lap of the first Asante king, Osei Tutu. It symbolized the soul of the Asante people. No one was allowed to sit on it. Wars were fought over its protection. This stool's sanctity might seem strange to outsiders, but it united the entire kingdom.
- **Kumasi's Grandeur**: Kumasi, the capital, impressed visitors with large roads, markets, and a palace decorated with gold ornaments. British envoys in the early 19th century (still pre-modern times) were shocked by the abundance of gold. The Asante used gold dust as currency in daily trade.

- **Severe Taboos**: Certain days were set aside for royal ancestors, and no public work could be done. Breaking these rules was punishable by fines or worse. Asante tradition also had strict mourning customs—great displays of drumming, dancing, and firearms to honor the dead.

15. The Mande Hunters' Secret Societies

Scattered across West Africa, the **Mande** peoples (linked to Mali, Songhai, and other regions) had secret societies for hunters—sometimes called **"Donso"** or "Kamajor" in different places. These societies carried odd beliefs and used special amulets.

- **Hunter's Amulets**: Members wore vests studded with leather pouches containing herbs or charms. They believed these charms protected them from bullets or wild animals. Europeans who witnessed them in action told tales of seemingly bulletproof hunters, though it might have been skill and courage rather than magic.
- **Ritual Brotherhood**: The societies required initiations with masked dances, oaths, and knowledge of herbal medicine. They served as local "police" or guardians, punishing thieves or witches. People viewed them with respect and fear, uncertain if their powers were natural or supernatural.

- **Spirit Communication**: Hunters claimed to communicate with forest spirits, who granted success in hunts. They poured libations (drinks) on the ground to honor these spirits. Such rituals might appear odd to an outsider, but they formed the spiritual core of many Mande communities, connecting daily work (hunting) with the unseen world.

16. Art, Masks, and Secret Rituals in West and Central Africa

Beyond the large empires, many smaller kingdoms and chiefdoms also had rich cultural practices. For instance, the **Igbo**, the **Baule**, and the **Fang** peoples each created intricate masks for secret ceremonies.

- **Masquerade Societies**: In Igbo areas, masked dancers (known as **Mmuo** or other names) performed during festivals. The masks represented spirits or ancestors. Some were frightening, with bulging eyes or fierce teeth. The ceremonies often involved music, dance, and drumming, both entertaining and spiritually meaningful.
- **Ifa Divination**: Among the Yoruba, Ifa divination used sacred palm nuts and a board to communicate with the spirit Orunmila. Diviners would cast nuts and interpret patterns, giving guidance on everything from marriage to planting crops. Outsiders might see this as mere fortune-telling, but for Yoruba communities, it was a respected system of knowledge.
- **Ngil Masks of the Fang**: The Fang in Central Africa had masks called **Ngil**, used by a secret society that policed social behavior. The mask's long face and heart-shaped design looked eerie. The society traveled at night, shining torches, and punishing wrongdoers. Tales say villagers trembled upon seeing these masked figures appear out of the dark.

17. Festive Gatherings, Griots, and Storytellers

A common thread across many African societies was the role of music, dance, and oral history. **Griots** (in the Mande world) or **Praise Singers** in other cultures kept genealogies, heroic tales, and moral lessons alive through performance.

- **Griots and Oral Libraries**: Griots memorized centuries of family lines, royal successes, and local proverbs. People called them "living libraries." They also served as advisors to kings, using old tales to offer guidance. The idea of a person holding so much knowledge in memory might seem crazy to us, but it worked for societies without widespread writing.
- **Grand Drumming Ceremonies**: Celebrations for royal coronations or harvest festivals often included hours of drumming and dancing. Dancers wore elaborate costumes or body paint. Some leaps or moves looked superhuman, fueling rumors that they had hidden charms for extra energy.
- **Healing Dances**: In some regions, special dances helped cure sickness. Drummers used specific rhythms believed to chase away evil spirits. Healers called out incantations. While modern science might doubt these methods, many communities believed such dances truly restored balance to the body and spirit.

18. The Kingdom of Mutapa's Clairvoyant "Mwene"

In the region once part of Great Zimbabwe's sphere, the **Mutapa** kingdom's rulers were called Mwene Mutapa ("Lord of the Plundered Lands"). We have seen a bit about them, but let us focus on their alleged clairvoyant powers.

- **Dream-based Rule**: Some Mwene Mutapa claimed they received visions in dreams, guiding them on war or alliances. Advisors took these dreams seriously. If the king dreamed of an enemy attack, armies might mobilize at once.
- **Oracles' Advice**: Royal oracles used bone throwing or dream interpretation. They also consulted local mediums who spoke in "spirit voices." Outsiders found these sessions baffling, yet the monarchy heavily depended on such counsel for political decisions.
- **Hilltop Graves**: Certain kings were buried atop high hills to be closer to the ancestors. Oral tales say that a king's spirit watched over the land. People might climb these hills to pray for rain or for success in hunts, leaving small offerings.

19. Symbolism in African Kingship: Leopard Skins and Ostrich Feathers

Throughout many African states, kings wore **leopard skins** as a sign of power. Leopards were fierce predators, symbolizing strength and cunning. Some leaders also used **ostrich feathers** in their crowns or regalia.

- **Leopard Society**: In places like the Cross River region, secret "leopard societies" enforced laws, punishing criminals in the name of the leopard spirit. People dreaded the society's nighttime visits. Leopard imagery was carved into doorposts, drums, or staffs to show authority.
- **Ostrich Plumes**: These tall feathers were prized for ceremonial hats because of their dramatic height. Rulers in West Africa or the Sudan region might appear in public with a swirl of feathers, making them tower over the crowd. Such visual grandeur left no doubt who was in charge.
- **Royal Umbrellas**: Some societies used large umbrellas carried by attendants to shade the king or queen mother. Intricate patterns on these umbrellas told stories of the dynasty. Europeans who visited wrote that these "umbrella carriers" were essential to the royal image, a tradition that can still be seen in parts of Africa today.

---

20. Reflecting on Africa's Strange and Wonderful Past

From the gold-laden caravans of Ancient Ghana to the stone ruins of Great Zimbabwe, from the powerful Obas of Benin to the rock churches of Ethiopia, Africa's pre-modern kingdoms were as varied and intricate as any in the world. They had advanced trade networks, rich art, and systems of government that impressed (and sometimes confused) outsiders. They also had beliefs and rituals—like spirit mediums, masked dances, or the worship of mystical stools—that might seem odd to us.

Yet these so-called "strange" customs formed the backbone of societies that thrived for centuries. Some kingdoms lasted for hundreds of years, expanding and contracting, forging alliances, and waging wars—just like states elsewhere. The fact that many Europeans refused to believe Africans built structures like Great Zimbabwe reveals how entrenched stereotypes were. It took time (and archaeological proof) to acknowledge that African cultures had their own sophisticated ways of life.

By studying these odd facts and legends—from Mansa Musa's golden generosity to Luba's memory boards—we see a continent alive with creativity, trade, and tradition. The old African empires remind us that different does not mean inferior. Their uniqueness was shaped by their environment, resources, and beliefs, producing forms of power and art distinct from those in Europe or Asia. As we continue our journey, we will discover how the Americas also developed impressive states with surprising customs and beliefs, showing again that human history is full of colorful, sometimes baffling variety.

CHAPTER 14

Wild Worlds in the Americas: Surprising Facts of Aztecs, Maya, and More

When we think of the pre-Columbian Americas, certain images might come to mind: towering pyramids in the jungles, mighty stone carvings, or colorful feather headdresses. Yet, behind these famous sights, there were countless odd and remarkable facts about how societies in the Americas lived, believed, and organized themselves. Before European contact—and indeed, well before modern times—the Western Hemisphere hosted great empires and small tribes, each with its own unique culture.

In this chapter, we will journey through different parts of the Americas, from Mesoamerica's powerful city-states to the Andean highlands of South America, and beyond. We will explore the Aztecs, Maya, Inca, and lesser-known groups, uncovering crazy-sounding customs like ritual ballgames, blood offerings, and fascinating calendar systems. While some aspects may seem shocking or brutal, we must remember that these societies flourished for centuries, creating advanced systems of writing, agriculture, and architecture that still astound us today.

1. The Maya: Hieroglyphs, Star Calculations, and Lost Cities

The **Maya** civilization stretched across what is now southern Mexico, Guatemala, Belize, and parts of Honduras and El Salvador. They reached their peak during the "Classic Period" (around 250–900 CE). Though known for their pyramid temples in the jungles, they also left behind sophisticated math and writing:

- **Hieroglyphic Writing**: Maya scribes used hundreds of glyphs to record royal histories, myths, and astronomical data. They carved them on stone stelae (monuments) and painted them in folding books called **codices**. Early explorers thought they were mere pictures, but we now know it was a true writing system that encoded complex ideas.

- **Advanced Astronomy and Calendars**: The Maya had multiple calendars, including the 260-day ritual calendar and the 365-day solar calendar. They could predict eclipses and track planetary movements with impressive precision, using this knowledge for ceremonies tied to cosmic events. Outsiders found it eerie that such "primitive" people could measure time so accurately.
- **Collapsing Cities**: Many major Maya cities were abandoned around 900 CE. Historians debate why—drought, warfare, or political unrest might have played a role. Overgrown by the jungle, these once-grand centers became "lost cities" until rediscovered in later times. Tales of vines wrapped around towering temples gave them a mystical reputation.

2. The Aztecs: Eagle Warriors, Floating Gardens, and Human Sacrifice

In the Valley of Mexico, the **Aztec Empire** (14th–16th centuries) dominated until Spanish conquest. Their capital, Tenochtitlan, was built on a lake island, astonishing the Spaniards who arrived in 1519. Aztec customs have both fascinated and horrified observers:

174

- **Human Sacrifice**: Perhaps the most notorious aspect of Aztec religion was the large-scale human sacrifice performed to appease gods like Huitzilopochtli (the sun god). Prisoners of war were often sacrificed atop pyramids. While this might seem ghastly, the Aztecs believed it kept the sun rising and the world in balance.
- **Chinampas (Floating Gardens)**: To feed a massive population, the Aztecs built chinampas in Lake Texcoco—small, rectangular plots formed by piling mud and vegetation. They looked like floating gardens, producing huge crop yields of maize, beans, squash, and flowers. This farming innovation was crucial in supporting the empire's large urban centers.
- **Eagle and Jaguar Warriors**: Elite Aztec warriors belonged to orders named after fierce animals. The Eagle and Jaguar warriors wore costumes resembling those creatures, hoping to gain their power and bravery. Ceremonial battles were sometimes staged to capture sacrificial victims—referred to as "flowery wars."

---

3. Bloodletting and Royal Rituals: The Deeper Side of Mesoamerica

It was not just the Aztecs who practiced bloodletting or sacrifice. Many Mesoamerican groups believed in offering their own blood to sustain the gods. The **Maya**, for example, had kings or queens draw blood from their tongues or ears, burning the soaked paper so the rising smoke could feed the deities.

- **Auto-Sacrifice**: This self-bloodletting was not always lethal; it was a symbolic gift. However, it could still be painful, done with stingray spines or obsidian blades. Outsiders found it bizarre, but it tied to a worldview where gods demanded energy from humans.
- **Ballgame Ritual**: The famous Mesoamerican ballgame, played on stone courts, had deep ceremonial meaning. Some versions mention the losing team (or even the winners in certain local myths) might be sacrificed. Archaeologists debate how often that happened, but the strong link between sport and the sacred is definitely unique.

- **Skull Racks**: The Aztecs and other cultures erected **tzompantli**—racks displaying rows of skulls from sacrificial victims or enemies. Spanish soldiers who entered Tenochtitlan described being shocked by these displays. For the Aztecs, it proclaimed power, showing devotion to the gods and victory over foes.

4. Teotihuacan: The Mysterious City of the Gods

Long before the Aztecs, a massive city called **Teotihuacan** (around 100 BCE–550 CE) thrived near modern Mexico City. At its peak, it was among the world's largest cities, home to monumental pyramids aligned with cosmic events. Yet we do not even know the name its inhabitants called it. "Teotihuacan" is the later Aztec term meaning "place where gods were born."

- **Pyramids of the Sun and Moon**: These pyramids soared above the plains, connecting the city's cosmic layout. The Pyramid of the Sun sits on a cave, which might have been considered a sacred spot representing the underworld.
- **Apartment Compounds**: Unlike many ancient cities, Teotihuacan had vast apartment complexes, housing diverse communities of craftworkers and traders. Some compounds were decorated with murals of jaguars, serpents, and deities.
- **Mysterious Decline**: By the 6th century CE, the city began to burn in some districts, leading to a decline. We do not fully know who ruled Teotihuacan or how. The Aztecs later found it in ruins and believed it was built by giants or gods. This gave it an aura of mystery that persists today.

5. The Inca Empire: Highways, Quipus, and Llama Caravans

Further south in the Andes, the **Inca Empire** (15th–16th centuries) spread from present-day Peru across Ecuador, Bolivia, Chile, and parts of Argentina and Colombia. They ruled from their capital, **Cuzco**, employing a unique system of governance.

- **No Written Script, But Quipus**: The Inca did not develop a true writing system. Instead, they used **quipus**—strings with knots—to record numbers, tribute, and possibly historical events. Each knot's position and thread color had meaning. This "talking knot" system amazed the Spanish, who found it both impressive and baffling.
- **Massive Road Network**: The Inca built nearly 25,000 miles of roads across rugged mountains, linking all corners of the empire. They used relay runners (chasquis) to carry messages. Despite not having wheeled vehicles, they managed advanced transport with llama caravans.
- **Terrace Farming**: High in the Andes, the Inca carved terraces into steep slopes to grow potatoes, maize, and quinoa. This allowed them to farm at different elevations. Machu Picchu, the famous mountain retreat, shows how they blended architecture with natural landscapes. While many see Machu Picchu as a mystical place, it was a functioning estate for the emperor and his chosen few.

---

6. Royal Mummies and Strange Andean Rituals

The Andean region had a long tradition of preserving the dead, even before the Inca. The **Inca** continued this practice, treating royal mummies as if they were still alive.

- **Ancestor Emperors**: Inca rulers who died were mummified, kept in palaces, and given offerings of food and drink. People believed these mummies could influence events. They might be brought out during festivals or paraded in ceremonies, wearing fine clothes. To the Spanish, that looked extremely odd—talking and consulting with a corpse.
- **Capacocha Sacrifices**: The Inca performed child sacrifices, known as **capacocha**, on high mountaintops to appease mountain gods. Archaeologists have found frozen mummies of children in the Andes, so well-preserved by cold that their hair and clothes remain intact. Some children were given chicha (corn beer) to calm them before the ritual.

- **Coca Leaves and Hallucinogens**: Andean peoples chewed coca leaves to combat altitude sickness and hunger. Ritual specialists also used hallucinogenic plants during ceremonies, believing these substances allowed them to communicate with deities. Although it might appear bizarre to outsiders, coca was part of daily life in the highlands.

7. Moche and Nazca: Curious Cults and Head-Trophies

Pre-Inca cultures along the Peruvian coast had their own bizarre customs. The **Moche** (1st–8th centuries) are known for their intricate pottery, which often depicts graphic scenes of warfare or mythical creatures. Meanwhile, the **Nazca** (1st–7th centuries) created huge desert drawings visible from above.

- **Moche Sacrifice Scenes**: Moche ceramics show rituals where captives' blood is offered to warrior-priests. Archaeological sites like Huaca de la Luna contain evidence of human sacrifice, with bones showing signs of violent death. This led researchers to link the pottery scenes with real events.
- **The Nazca Lines**: The Nazca etched giant shapes—animals, plants, and geometric forms—into the desert floor. The question of why they did this remains debated. Some say they were religious pathways for ceremonies, others speculate they had astronomical significance. Early explorers once guessed aliens made them, which shows how strange they appeared to outside eyes.
- **Head-Hunting Cultures**: Both Moche and Nazca might have practiced **head-taking**, preserving enemy heads as trophies. The Nazca produced "trophy heads" with holes in the forehead to string them on cords. This gruesome practice carried spiritual importance, possibly representing control over enemies' life force.

8. Pueblo Peoples of the American Southwest

Shifting focus to North America, the **Pueblo** peoples (like the Ancestral Puebloans, also called Anasazi, and their successors) built stone or adobe dwellings in the Four Corners region (where modern Arizona, Utah, Colorado, and New Mexico meet). Places like **Chaco Canyon** and **Mesa Verde** hold ruins that reveal a once-complex society:

- **Cliff Dwellings**: At Mesa Verde, people constructed homes in alcoves high on cliff faces. These hidden villages were accessible by ladders or handholds cut into rock. Some guess they sought safety from raiders or the elements. To modern tourists, they appear almost impossible to reach, but they were everyday homes for Ancestral Puebloans.
- **Great Kivas and Ritual Spaces**: Chaco Canyon features massive circular structures called kivas, possibly used for ceremonies. The largest "great kivas" could hold hundreds of participants, suggesting large gatherings or pilgrimages. The layout of roads leading from Chaco has puzzled archaeologists—some roads go straight through difficult terrain, indicating spiritual rather than practical routes.
- **Mysterious Decline**: Like the Maya, many Pueblo sites were abandoned in the 13th century. Reasons might include drought or social upheaval. Descendants moved to new areas, forming present-day Pueblo tribes such as the Hopi, Zuni, and others, who carry forward traditions that outsiders sometimes find quite intricate or unusual—like kachina dances with masked spirit beings.

---

9. Cahokia and the Mound Builders

East of the Pueblo region, the **Mississippian** culture built earthen mounds across the Midwest and Southeast of what is now the United States (800–1600 CE). The largest urban center was **Cahokia**, near modern St. Louis.

- **Monk's Mound**: Cahokia's central feature is a huge earthen mound nearly 100 feet high. On top stood the chief's building, offering a view over the city. The mound's size rivals some Egyptian pyramids in volume, yet it is made of layered soil. Historians still wonder how thousands of workers built it without metal tools or beasts of burden.

- **Woodhenges**: Cahokia had circular arrangements of wooden posts, possibly used as solar calendars. People might stand in the center on key dates, seeing the sun align with certain posts. This advanced knowledge of astronomy was unexpected in a region often dismissed as "uncivilized" by early European settlers.
- **Human Sacrifice**: Archaeologists found mass graves near big mounds, with evidence of sacrificed individuals. The city's leaders apparently demanded tribute, labor, and even lives for ceremonies. This suggests a strong ruling class, though we do not have a written record to explain it.

10. Taino of the Caribbean: Zemis and Strange Ball Courts

Before Columbus arrived, the **Taino** populated many Caribbean islands, including Hispaniola, Puerto Rico, and parts of Cuba. They lived in villages, growing cassava, corn, and other crops. Some unusual features of Taino culture stand out:

- **Zemis**: Taino religion involved worshipping spirits called zemis. They carved zemis in wood or stone, placing them in houses or caves. Each zemi had a personality and domain—some for fertility, others for weather. Spanish explorers found these statues puzzling, labeling them "idols."
- **Ball Courts**: Like Mesoamerican groups, the Taino had ball courts (batey) surrounded by carved stones. The game might have had spiritual meaning, involving bouncing a rubber ball without using hands. However, we do not know if it included the same sacrificial element as the Aztec version.
- **Nose and Ear Adornments**: Taino men and women wore gold or shell ornaments in their noses and ears. The Spanish described these decorations with surprise. Since Taino gold was not as pure as the Spanish wanted, conflicts arose quickly, with Spaniards seizing or demanding more gold from local chiefs.

11. Mapuche Resistance in Southern Chile

The **Mapuche** in south-central Chile were known for their fierce resistance to Inca expansion and, later, Spanish colonization. Long before modern times, the Mapuche developed warrior traditions that baffled enemies.

- **Fortified Villages**: The Mapuche built **pucará**—fortified wooden structures. They positioned them strategically near rivers or hills, using their knowledge of the terrain to repel invaders. The Inca tried and failed to fully conquer them, calling them "wild men."
- **War Drums and Battle Songs**: Mapuche warriors used loud drums (kultrún) and chanting to intimidate foes. They carried **macanas** (wooden clubs) and lances. When the Spanish arrived with horses and firearms, the Mapuche adapted by capturing horses and learning to ride them, turning Spanish tactics against them.
- **Society Without a Single King**: The Mapuche did not have one supreme ruler. Instead, they had **lonkos** (chiefs) for different communities. This decentralized structure made it tough for outside empires to conquer them in one blow. Some found it odd that they had no overarching monarchy but still cooperated in defense.

---

12. Tarim Basin Mummies? Wait, That's Asia, Not the Americas!

We must be cautious not to mix up different continents' "mummy" stories. The **Tarim Basin** mummies are in Central Asia, not the Americas. This confusion highlights how global tales of mummification can be. The Andean region had its own mummy traditions, as we noted with the Inca, but let us keep on track with the Americas specifically.

(This quick note just reminds us that many cultures worldwide used mummification, but we are focusing on the Americas here, to avoid mixing continents.)

13. The Chachapoya "Cloud Warriors" of the Andes

In northern Peru's cloud forests, the **Chachapoya** (pre-Inca) built cliffside settlements and created odd burial sites.

- **Cliff Sarcophagi**: They placed large human-shaped sarcophagi (called **purunmachus**) high on cliff ledges, overlooking valleys. Each sarcophagus could hold a mummy. From a distance, these figures look like statues with eerie painted faces, perched on seemingly inaccessible spots.
- **Cloud Forest Citadels**: The Chachapoya built strongholds like **Kuelap**, a massive fortress with high stone walls. Some call it the "Machu Picchu of the north," though it predates the Inca. Mist often surrounds Kuelap, giving it a mysterious air—perfect for tales of "cloud warriors."
- **Absorbed by the Inca**: Eventually, the Inca conquered the Chachapoya region. Some Chachapoya joined Inca armies as scouts or archers. However, their distinctive cliff burials still puzzle visitors who wonder how they got coffins up those sheer drops.

---

14. The Map of the "New World" and Early Conspiracy Theories

As news of these American civilizations spread to Europe, early mapmakers tried to piece together a "New World." Some believed in bizarre myths: giant cannibals in Patagonia, the **Seven Cities of Gold** (Cibola), or even dog-headed natives.

- **Apocryphal Travel Logs**: Books like the invented "letters" of Sir John Mandeville or the hoaxes describing "Blemmyes" (headless people) in the New World led to confusion. Though obviously untrue, many Europeans read them as fact.
- **Conspiracy Myths**: Some claimed the Maya or Inca derived from lost Greek colonies or from one of the Ten Lost Tribes of Israel. Rather than accept that Americans developed advanced cultures on their own, these theories sought foreign origins. People used these conspiracies to avoid respecting local achievements.

- **Gradual Realization**: Over time, explorers realized that these myths were false. They still encountered real wonders—like huge cities on lakes, desert lines, or mountainous fortresses—yet no sign of dog-men or classical Greeks. This shift from wild speculation to actual observation shaped how the Western Hemisphere was understood.

---

15. Southeast Ceremonial Complex in North America

Aside from the Mississippian mound builders, the **Southeastern Ceremonial Complex (SECC)** encompassed various tribes across the U.S. Southeast (like the Creek, Cherokee, and others). They shared symbols of falcons, serpents, and warriors in swirling designs on shell ornaments or copper plates.

- **Falcon Dancers**: Some depictions show a "birdman" figure, possibly linked to the rising sun or war. Ceremonies might have included dancers dressed in feather capes, reenacting mythical battles.
- **Shell Gorgets**: Warriors wore carved shell gorgets around their necks. These had designs of swirling crosses or stylized animals. Foreign travelers marveled at how skilled the carving was, done with only stone tools.
- **Widespread Trade**: Copper from the Great Lakes, shells from the Gulf Coast, and other items circulated widely, indicating a broad trade network. This is surprising because many Europeans viewed North American tribes as scattered. In reality, complex exchanges and religious ideas spread across long distances.

---

16. The Tlingit and Haida: Potlatch and Totem Poles

Further north along the Pacific Northwest coast, groups like the **Tlingit** and **Haida** developed a unique culture. They used cedar trees to carve houses, canoes, and iconic **totem poles**. Their potlatch ceremonies were famously strange to outsiders.

- **Potlatch Feasts**: During a potlatch, a chief or prominent person gave away or even destroyed large quantities of goods to display wealth and status. Blankets, copper shields, and food were lavishly distributed. Europeans were puzzled: why destroy valuable items? But for these societies, it was about prestige—giving away wealth proved you had power and resources.
- **Totem Poles**: Tall wooden poles carved with clan crests—bears, eagles, ravens, whales—stood outside houses or in community areas. They told family stories, with each figure representing an ancestor or mythic event. Some visitors assumed these were "idols," but they were more like history in wood, not gods.
- **Shamanism and Animal Spirits**: Tlingit shamans wore carved masks and hide robes to interact with spirit realms. They might treat sickness using songs and spirit guides. Observers found these rituals eerie, but to the Tlingit, they were essential for balancing natural forces.

---

17. Guaraní of the Forest: Speaking to the Jaguar

In the dense forests of eastern Paraguay and nearby areas, the **Guaraní** lived in agricultural communities. They believed in strong ties to nature spirits.

- **Shaman-Jaguar Connection**: Some Guaraní shamans claimed they could communicate with jaguars, the fierce predators of the rainforest. They performed nighttime chants to keep jaguars away from villages or to harness the cat's power. Tales of shape-shifting jaguar men or women spread among certain groups.
- **Yerba Mate**: The Guaraní discovered and cultivated **yerba mate**, a leaf used to brew a caffeinated drink. It became a staple, with communal gourds passed around in a circle. Spanish colonists eventually adopted mate, finding it gave them energy. At first, many Europeans considered it an odd "jungle tea."
- **Tekoha**: The Guaraní concept of "tekoha" refers to one's place of being—land, culture, and identity combined. To them, land was not merely property but a living space of spirits and ancestors. Outsiders found it odd that Guaraní might refuse to move, even when offered trade items, because leaving tekoha meant losing part of their soul.

18. The Redwood Builders: Californians Before Missions

Along the California coast, diverse tribes thrived off abundant fish, acorns, and marine resources. They made canoes from redwood logs or planks. The **Chumash**, for example, used **tomols** (plank canoes) to travel between the Channel Islands and the mainland.

- **Shell Bead Money**: In some Californian tribes, shell beads were used as currency. Skilled artisans drilled tiny holes in shells, stringing them in exact lengths that had set values. This might seem primitive to those who rely on metal coins, but it was a sophisticated economic system within their networks.
- **Basket Weaving Arts**: Tribes like the **Pomo** made incredibly tight-woven baskets that could hold water or even cook soups by placing hot stones inside. These baskets were decorated with bright feathers or dyed fibers, sometimes telling clan stories. Early explorers prized them as exotic curiosities.
- **Medicinal Knowledge**: Californian tribes used local plants for healing, from willow bark for pain relief to sagebrush for colds. Spanish missionaries who arrived in the 18th century were surprised by how effectively the natives treated common ailments with wild herbs, in ways that seemed magical but often worked.

---

19. The Cherokee Nation's Unusual Government (Pre-Modern)

Before modern times, the **Cherokee** in the southeastern United States had a complex social structure with clan-based governance. They had peace chiefs and war chiefs, each handling different matters.

- **White and Red Chiefs**: The "white" chief presided over peace times, ceremonies, and internal affairs, while the "red" chief led during war or conflict. This rotating authority was odd to outsiders used to a single ruler. But for the Cherokee, it ensured the right leadership for each situation.

- **Green Corn Ceremony**: The annual Green Corn festival was a major event to thank the Great Spirit for the harvest. Feasting, dancing, and ritual cleaning took place. People reconciled feuds and forgave minor crimes. This social reset might appear very strange to those who rarely practiced communal forgiveness.
- **Clan Mother Influence**: Women (especially older clan mothers) had significant say in choosing chiefs or approving war. They were seen as guardians of the clan. European settlers found it odd that women held such power, contrasting with many Old World norms.

20. Connecting the Dots: A Continent of Wonders

From the Maya's towering pyramids and precise calendars to the Inca's vast mountain road networks, from the Aztecs' chinampa farms to the Pueblo cliff dwellings, pre-Columbian America was full of astonishing achievements. Yes, some customs—like large-scale human sacrifice or trophy head collections—strike us as cruel or bizarre. But these were part of complex religious beliefs that gave meaning to life and death in societies quite different from Europe or Asia.

Huge trading systems crisscrossed the continents, carrying luxury goods, crops, and ideas. Skilled artisans worked in gold, jade, feathers, or textiles to create masterpieces. Astronomers studied the stars, developing calendars and cosmic myths. Architects built cities in deserts, rainforests, and high mountains. And all of this happened long before the disruptions of European conquest and colonization.

Studying these wild worlds reminds us that human creativity is universal, taking different forms depending on environment and tradition. While some practices seem extreme, like child sacrifices on Andean peaks, they emerged from a worldview that saw mountains as living gods. So, these facts are not just "weird tales," but clues to how diverse human cultures can be.

CHAPTER 15

Ancient India's Wonders: Strange Customs and Beliefs

When we talk about the ancient world, India stands out as a land of deep spirituality, grand empires, and diverse traditions. Long before modern times, the subcontinent produced advanced cities, famous philosophies, and curious practices that might seem strange to us. From the Indus Valley Civilization to the powerful dynasties that followed, India's ancient history is filled with odd details that reveal how people understood the world.

In this chapter, we explore the unusual customs, beliefs, and achievements of ancient India. We will see how early city-builders along the Indus laid out surprising urban designs, how Vedic rituals shaped daily life, and how empires like the Maurya and Gupta introduced remarkable governance systems—and occasionally bizarre events. From sacred cows wandering city streets to mathematicians inventing the concept of zero, India's old world was both practical and mystical, blending logic with faith. Let us travel through time to discover these marvels.

1. The Enigma of the Indus Valley Civilization

One of the earliest urban cultures in the region was the **Indus Valley Civilization** (c. 3300–1300 BCE), also called the Harappan Civilization. It spread across parts of present-day Pakistan and northwest India. Archaeologists were shocked to find advanced, well-planned cities like **Mohenjo-daro** and **Harappa**.

- **Gridded Streets and Drainage**: These cities had straight, wide streets laid out in a grid pattern, with public wells and complex drainage systems. Clay pipes carried wastewater away, which is strikingly modern for such an ancient time. Such urban planning was rare in other early civilizations, making us wonder how these people organized themselves.

- **Mysterious Script**: Indus people used small seals with symbols that remain undeciphered. We do not know if it was a full language or just a series of signs representing trade goods. This script's mystery blocks us from fully understanding their beliefs.
- **No Known Big Temples or Palaces**: Unlike Mesopotamia or Egypt, Indus sites lack huge temples or grand tombs. Some historians guess that society might have been more equal, with no single king or ruling class. Or maybe their rulers left fewer traces. This puzzle fuels speculation about a possible peaceful culture—or perhaps everything was simply made of materials that did not survive.

2. Vedic Culture and the Rise of Ritual Fire

After the decline of the Indus Valley cities, new groups, often called the Indo-Aryans, brought Vedic traditions (c. 1500–600 BCE). Their practices were recorded in texts like the **Rigveda**, which shaped Indian religion and society for centuries.

- **Fire Sacrifices (Yajnas)**: In Vedic times, priests lit ritual fires to honor gods such as Agni (fire), Indra (storms), and Soma (a mysterious drink deity). They poured offerings of ghee (clarified butter) and grains into the fire, reciting Sanskrit hymns. Observers

might find it odd that these elaborate ceremonies demanded precise chanting and even specific seating for each participant. Missing a step could "anger the gods."
- **Soma Ritual**: Soma was a sacred drink from a plant that priests pressed and mixed. They believed it gave divine insight or "ecstasy." Modern researchers debate what plant Soma really was. Some think it was a hallucinogen. The fact that priests used it to reach spiritual heights sounds strange, but it was central to Vedic worship.
- **Caste Beginnings**: The Vedic era seeded the **varna** (caste) system, splitting society into four broad groups: Brahmins (priests), Kshatriyas (warriors), Vaishyas (merchants), and Shudras (laborers). Later, this system became more rigid, creating social divisions that outsiders might view as peculiar or unfair.

---

3. Epic Tales: Mahabharata and Ramayana

Alongside these rituals, ancient India produced epic stories that remain deeply influential. The **Mahabharata** and **Ramayana** are massive texts blending myth, history, and moral lessons.

- **Mahabharata's War and Magical Weapons**: This epic details a huge war between two sets of cousins, featuring gods, demigods, and mystical weapons that shoot flames or illusions. Some describe it as an ancient "superhero saga," with verses about flying chariots and cosmic illusions. Modern readers might see parallels to fantasy novels, yet for many in India, it is a sacred text offering spiritual lessons.
- **Ramayana's Monkey Army**: In the Ramayana, the hero Prince Rama enlists an army of monkeys, led by Hanuman, to rescue his wife Sita from the demon king Ravana. Hanuman's feats, like leaping across the ocean, might sound odd, but devout believers see them as symbols of devotion and faith. The story also includes building a stone bridge across the sea that floats because of divine blessings.
- **Moral and Philosophical Depth**: Though these epics contain magical elements, they explore dharma (duty), karma (action), and the complexity of right versus wrong. Western explorers who first read them were startled by both the fantasy-like themes and the profound philosophical discussions.

4. The Rise of Kingdoms: Magadha, Maurya, and the Elephant Armies

By the 6th–4th centuries BCE, the Gangetic plains saw many small kingdoms. Eventually, **Magadha** rose to prominence, leading to the **Maurya Empire** (c. 322–185 BCE) under Chandragupta Maurya. This empire is known for its vast domain and some unusual details:

- **Army with Elephants**: Maurya rulers maintained huge armies, including war elephants. These elephants wore armor and carried archers or spear-throwers on their backs. Imagine seeing a line of armored elephants thundering toward you! This gave Maurya forces a powerful advantage.
- **Chandragupta's Fears**: Legend says Chandragupta was paranoid about assassination. He used food tasters, changed bedrooms randomly, and lived in hidden quarters. Some accounts mention him eventually giving up the throne to become a Jain monk, fasting to death. If true, that is quite a life twist—from conquering king to ascetic.
- **Arthashastra and Spies**: A text called the **Arthashastra**, attributed to the strategist Kautilya (Chanakya), advised rulers on governance, espionage, and even secret assassinations. It recommended employing female spies or pretending to be ascetics to gather intel. This approach to rule might seem ruthless, but it shows how advanced political science was in ancient India.

---

5. Ashoka's Strange Turn to Peace

Chandragupta's grandson, **Emperor Ashoka** (268–232 BCE), is famous for embracing Buddhism after waging a brutal war in Kalinga. Something in that bloodshed changed him, leading to a policy of "Dharma" or righteous rule.

- **Edicts on Pillars**: Ashoka carved proclamations on pillars and rocks across his empire, urging moral living, compassion for animals, and religious tolerance. Some pillars were topped with lion capitals, now a national emblem of India. The idea of broadcasting laws on stone columns for everyone to read was quite progressive for the time.

- **Ban on Animal Sacrifice**: Ashoka gave up violence and outlawed some forms of hunting. He funded hospitals for people and animals. Outsiders might think it odd for a once-bloody conqueror to become a champion of non-violence and vegetarianism. But this transformation shaped the region's moral landscape for centuries.
- **Sending Buddhist Missions**: He sent envoys to places as far as Greece, Egypt, and Sri Lanka to spread Buddhist teachings. This global approach to religion was unusual, mixing faith with diplomacy. Some foreign courts found it strange that an emperor would push a message of peace after leading armies.

6. The Gupta Golden Age: Mathematics, Art, and Temple Carvings

After the Maurya decline, centuries later, the **Gupta Empire** (c. 320–550 CE) rose in northern India. Often called a "Golden Age," it saw advancements in math, astronomy, art, and literature. But behind these shining achievements, we find some quirky aspects:

- **Decimal System and Zero**: Scholars like **Aryabhata** and others developed the concept of zero as a number and refined the decimal system. This might not seem "strange," but it was revolutionary. Many ancient cultures hesitated to treat "nothing" as a number. The step to see zero as a placeholder and symbol of emptiness was a huge leap in math.
- **Architecture with Secret Meanings**: Gupta-era temple carvings often featured elaborate sculptures of gods, goddesses, and mythical creatures. Some had hidden messages or symmetrical designs symbolizing cosmic order. The art might show multi-headed deities or half-animal forms, startling those unfamiliar with India's symbolic iconography.
- **Couple Sculptures**: Temples sometimes displayed images of couples (mithunas) in affectionate poses, signifying fertility and harmony. Western visitors to these sites centuries later sometimes labeled them as "erotic" or "shocking," not understanding the spiritual context of celebrating life and creation.

7. Weird Ascetics: Sadhus and Extreme Practices

Beyond empires and kings, India was home to wandering ascetics who rejected normal life to seek spiritual truth. Called **sadhus**, these holy people performed intense austerities (tapas) to gain insight or spiritual power. Their behaviors could look bizarre:

- **Standing for Years**: Some ascetics stood on one leg or remained standing for extended periods, letting their limbs swell or wither. They believed this self-punishment helped them detach from worldly desires. Outsiders might view it as self-torture, but for them, it was a path to liberation.
- **Rolling from Village to Village**: A few sadhus traveled by rolling their bodies along the road instead of walking. This slow, painful act was meant as a continuous penance. Villagers often offered them food or water out of respect, seeing them as holy or insane—or both.
- **Covering with Ash**: Many ascetics smeared their skin with ash from sacred fires, symbolizing renunciation of worldly life. They might live in caves or forests, survive on alms, and recite mantras for hours. To a typical householder, these sadhus were both revered and feared for their spiritual powers.

8. Varied Schools of Thought: Charvakas to Jainism

India's philosophical scene was diverse. Alongside Vedic traditions, Buddhism, and Jainism, there were also skeptics who questioned everything. A wide range of viewpoints existed:

- **Charvaka Materialists**: This school claimed only what we sense is real. They rejected the notion of an afterlife or karma. Their motto was: "Enjoy life while you can." Others found it shocking that some Indians dared to deny the authority of the sacred texts.
- **Jain Austerity**: Jain monks practiced extreme non-violence (ahimsa). They swept the ground before walking, wore cloth masks to avoid harming insects, and in the Digambara ("sky-clad") tradition, some monks renounced clothing altogether. The idea of naked wandering monks, obsessively avoiding killing even the tiniest life, struck outsiders as very odd.
- **Debates and Public Dialogues**: Indian intellectual life included public debates. Monks and philosophers traveled from court to court, challenging each other's doctrines. Losers sometimes had to adopt the winner's faith or suffer public shame. Kings often sponsored these debates, loving the spectacle of verbal battles over the nature of reality.

---

9. The Kamasutra and Other Curious Texts

While best known in the West for its erotic content, the **Kamasutra** (written by Vatsyayana, around the 3rd century CE) is broader than many realize. It discusses social etiquette, grooming, marriage, and even personal decorum.

- **Manual of Social Behavior**: The Kamasutra includes chapters on how to dress well, conduct conversations, and maintain relationships. It even advises on how to handle suspicious spouses or how to keep a lover's interest. Many find it surprising that an ancient text dealt with such practical, everyday concerns.

- **Sensual Diagrams**: True, some sections have detailed descriptions of intimate poses. For Victorian-era European explorers who found translated copies, this was scandalous. Yet in ancient India, sexuality was not always treated as taboo; it was part of a balanced life.
- **Classes of Men and Women**: The text divides people into types depending on physical and emotional traits, giving tips for compatibility. Modern readers might see it as simplistic or stereotypical, but it shows how systematically Indians approached even personal matters.

10. Temple Erotica: Khajuraho and Konark

In medieval India (10th–13th centuries), certain temple complexes became famous for intricate sculptures depicting gods, daily life, and sometimes explicit erotic scenes. The most notable are the **Khajuraho Group of Monuments** in central India and the **Sun Temple of Konark** in eastern India.

- **Why Carve Intimate Scenes on Temples?** Scholars debate: some say it symbolizes the divine unity of male and female energies. Others suggest it was a way to celebrate life in all forms, or possibly to educate about kama (desire) as part of spiritual practice.
- **Konark's Chariot of the Sun**: The Konark temple is shaped like a giant chariot with wheels carved in stone, pulled by seven horses, representing the Sun God's vehicle. Along its walls are thousands of figures, from daily chores to cosmic dances, and some quite risqué.
- **Shock to Foreign Eyes**: When British officials first saw these temples in the 19th century, they found them "obscene" and even considered destroying them. Over time, attitudes changed, and now people appreciate them as remarkable art blending spirituality and worldly life.

11. Magical Powers of Siddhas and Alchemists

India's fascination with **alchemy** and **siddhi** (spiritual powers) led to legends of mystics who could fly, teleport, or live for centuries. Texts like the **Rasashastra** discuss alchemical processes, aiming to transform metals or prolong life.

- **Rasayana**: This branch of alchemy focused on concocting elixirs for immortality or perfect health. Practitioners experimented with mercury and plant extracts. They believed a proper mixture could rejuvenate the body. Though mainstream science discards these claims, the Rasayana tradition fueled unusual experiments.
- **Nath Yogis and Siddha Legends**: Groups like the Nath yogis told stories of gurus who could shrink to the size of an atom or fly through the sky. While these might be metaphorical, many believed them literally. Outsiders wondered if it was just yoga illusions or pure myth.
- **Tantra and Ritual Tools**: Certain Tantric sects used skull cups, bone trumpets, and symbolic diagrams (yantras) to tap cosmic energies. They might chant secret syllables, hoping to gain supernatural abilities. Such rituals, sometimes involving cremation grounds, definitely seemed eerie to observers.

---

12. Ashrams and Gurukuls: Odd Education Systems

Education in ancient India often happened in **gurukuls**—the home of a teacher (guru), where students lived and learned for years. Alternatively, ascetics formed **ashrams** in forests.

- **Living with the Guru**: Pupils, sometimes children of kings or rich merchants, would serve the guru—collecting firewood, cooking, cleaning. In exchange, they learned Vedas, grammar, philosophy, or martial arts. The notion that princes did household chores felt odd to some. But it taught humility and discipline.
- **Forest Universities**: Places like **Takshashila** and **Nalanda** later evolved into large educational centers. Students from far regions came to study grammar, medicine, logic, or Buddhism. Despite being in old times, these "universities" had thousands of pupils and multiple disciplines, which stunned travelers like the Chinese monk Xuanzang.

- **Oral Memory**: Much learning depended on memorizing huge texts. Pupils recited them daily. The teacher would correct even the slightest error in intonation. This strong oral tradition was unusual to outsiders used to writing everything down. However, it preserved knowledge for centuries even after libraries were destroyed.

---

13. The Silk Road Links and Strange Exchanges

Though called the Silk Road, it was a network of routes stretching across Asia. India played a major part, trading spices, textiles, and precious stones. This interaction brought surprising influences.

- **Greek Influence in Gandhara**: After Alexander the Great's incursions, parts of northwest India saw Greek cultural input. Art in Gandhara (in modern Pakistan) showed Buddhist subjects carved in a Greco-Roman style—Buddha statues with wavy hair and draped robes reminiscent of ancient Greece. This fusion may look odd, but it proves cultures mixed widely.
- **Roman Gold for Indian Pepper**: Ancient Roman records mention spending large sums of gold on Indian pepper and spices. They complained that Rome's wealth was draining eastward. Indian ports like **Muziris** or **Bharuch** were bustling, with Roman coins found in large numbers, shocking archaeologists centuries later.
- **Chinese Monks Visiting India**: Pilgrims like **Fa Xian** (Faxian) and **Xuanzang** traveled to India in search of authentic Buddhist teachings. They wrote about Indian cities, describing everything from hospital systems to festivals. To them, encountering naked Jain monks or cows roaming freely in markets was very peculiar.

---

14. Maritime Trade and Wacky Indian Ocean Tales

India's coastal kingdoms, like the **Chola** in the south, also engaged in sea trade. The Indian Ocean was full of ships carrying cotton, spices, gemstones, and more.

- **Chola Expeditions**: The Chola Empire (9th–13th centuries) reportedly sailed across the Bay of Bengal to attack or trade with kingdoms in Southeast Asia, establishing a presence in parts of present-day Malaysia or Indonesia. Stories say their ships carried war elephants, a terrifying sight for islanders not used to such beasts.
- **Arabian and Greek Sailors**: Foreign sailors told colorful tales of giant serpents or storms conjured by Indian wizards. While exaggerated, it highlights how the region's monsoon winds seemed magical to outsiders. The monsoon cycle allowed ships to travel outward in one season and return in another.
- **Spices and Precious Wood**: Items like sandalwood, pepper, cardamom, and black pearls were treasured globally. European merchants centuries later called the region the "Spice Lands." The fact that little seeds or bark commanded high prices led to insane voyages and sometimes piracy, reminiscent of a frenzied search for gold.

15. Ayurvedic Medicine and Odd Cures

India's traditional health system, **Ayurveda**, goes back thousands of years. It classifies people and ailments based on three doshas (vata, pitta, kapha). Some Ayurvedic cures may appear bizarre to modern eyes:

- **Panchakarma**: A cleansing therapy involving vomiting, enemas, nasal rinsing, bloodletting, and similar methods to balance the body. It might sound uncomfortable, but some people still swear by it.
- **Exotic Ingredients**: Remedies could include cow urine, snake venom, or ground pearls. The logic was that each had specific properties to correct imbalances. European travelers found these cures odd or superstitious, though Ayurvedic practitioners insisted on centuries of proven results.
- **Surgery in Ancient Texts**: The surgeon **Sushruta** (c. 6th century BCE) described rhinoplasty (nose reconstruction) using a flap of skin from the forehead. Hearing that ancient Indians performed plastic surgery was shocking to outsiders who assumed such practices were modern inventions.

---

16. Temple Elephants, Sacred Cows, and Snake Charmers

The image of India often includes docile cows wandering streets, temple elephants decorated for festivals, or snake charmers playing flutes. While these are sometimes clichés, they stem from long-standing traditions.

- **Sacred Cow Reverence**: In Hindu tradition, the cow is seen as a caretaker, symbolizing motherhood. It is not worshipped as a deity in itself (a common misunderstanding) but is protected and honored. Seeing cows roam urban roads, sipping water from taps or holding up traffic, can be puzzling to visitors.
- **Temple Elephants**: Many south Indian temples keep elephants that bless devotees with a gentle tap of the trunk. They might be painted or garlanded for festivals. Some question the ethics of keeping them captive, but historically, they were part of religious pageantry.

- **Snake Charmers**: A classic image is the charmer with a cobra in a basket, playing a flute. The snake often sways, but it is reacting to movement rather than music. While perhaps not strictly "ancient," this folk practice has old roots, symbolizing mystical control over nature.

17. The Legend of Shakuntala and Other Dramatic Works

India also had a strong theatrical tradition. Sanskrit plays, like those by the famous poet and dramatist **Kalidasa** (5th century CE), captivated royal courts.

- **Shakuntala**: Kalidasa's play "Abhijnanashakuntalam" tells of a king who falls in love with a maiden, Shakuntala, only to forget her due to a curse. Later, he recognizes her by a ring. The blending of romance, curses, and divine interference might look odd, but it shaped centuries of Indian drama.
- **Court Performances**: Plays included music, dance, and stylized gestures. Female roles could be played by men in some traditions. They used elaborate makeup and sometimes masked characters. Noble patrons or emperors might watch these performances for hours, enjoying the poetic verses.
- **Rasa Theory**: Sanskrit drama relies on rasas—emotional flavors like love, humor, pathos, anger, heroism, terror, disgust, and wonder. The goal was to evoke these feelings in the audience. A play had to balance them carefully. This emphasis on emotional "tastes" is unique, showing how seriously Indians took the art of expression.

18. Stepwells and Architectural Oddities

Ancient India's architecture extended beyond temples and palaces. **Stepwells** are large wells or water reservoirs with steps descending to the water level. They are especially common in arid regions like Gujarat or Rajasthan.

- **Geometry and Decoration**: Some stepwells, like **Rani ki Vav** in Gujarat, are incredibly ornate. As you go down each level, carved pillars and sculptures appear. Tourists today often find them hauntingly beautiful, as if descending into an inverted temple.
- **Practical Yet Artistic**: Stepwells provided water for drinking, bathing, and washing, and served as cool retreats in hot summers. People might gather there for socializing or religious rituals. The combination of utility and detailed art is striking—outsiders might marvel at how much effort went into building a fancy well.
- **Mystical Beliefs**: Locals sometimes believed spirits dwelt in the depths. Tales of ghosts or water nymphs circulated, so folks offered small prayers or coins before descending. The idea that a well could be a spiritual gateway might appear odd, but it fit the Indian perspective of sacredness in everyday life.

---

19. The Mythical Kingdom of Shambala?

While "Shambala" is often linked to Tibetan Buddhism, some Indian myths mention hidden utopian realms in the Himalayas. Legends about secret places where wise sages live in harmony are not uncommon in Indian folklore.

- **Kalachakra and the Future King**: Some stories say a future king from Shambala will appear to save the world when needed. People seeking it might wander the mountains, hoping to stumble upon this hidden paradise.
- **Tibetan-Indian Crossovers**: The Himalayas served as cultural bridges, so some Indian ascetics traveled to Tibetan monasteries, returning with new stories. Western explorers who heard about Shambala or Shangri-La included it in exotic fantasies about "mystic East."
- **Similar to Prester John Myth?**: Just as European Christians once searched for Prester John's lost Christian kingdom, some Eastern pilgrims longed to find Shambala's pure land. These parallels highlight how different cultures imagine ideal worlds hidden somewhere beyond mortal reach.

20. Reflections on India's Strange and Wonderful Legacy

Ancient India was a tapestry of dynasties, faiths, and social experiments. Kings erected pillars to spread moral teachings, astronomers mapped the skies, gurus taught students under forest canopies, and scribes penned epic stories brimming with gods and monsters. Elephant cavalry clashed in battles, while sadhus stood on one leg in silent forests. Temples displayed cosmic passion in their carvings, mathematicians invented zero, and local folklore told of shape-shifting snakes or divine monkeys.

Such variety can feel overwhelming. Yet, each facet—the Indus drainage systems, the Vedic sacrifices, Ashoka's edicts, the Kamasutra's social guidelines, the concept of zero, and those mesmerizing temple sculptures—reveals a civilization both practical and deeply spiritual. Ancient India's oddities are not just curiosities; they shaped how millions lived, prayed, and thought.

This world was not static. Over centuries, invasions, migrations, and internal reforms changed customs. Kingdoms rose and fell, forging new hybrids of culture. Even so, many of these ancient quirks endure in modern Indian life—like the reverence for cows, the quest for spiritual gurus, or the love of epic stories. As we move forward to the next chapter, we keep in mind how these ancient beliefs influenced not just the subcontinent but also travelers and thinkers across Asia.

CHAPTER 16

Shoguns and Samurai: Fascinating Feudal Japan

When people think of medieval or pre-modern Japan, images of samurai warriors, cherry blossoms, and solemn tea ceremonies come to mind. Yet, feudal Japan was far more complex and sometimes much stranger than popular myths suggest. The rise of the **shogunate**—military governments led by shoguns—shaped the archipelago's politics for centuries. Samurai followed codes of honor but also engaged in ruthless power struggles. At the same time, peasants, artisans, and merchants formed their own vibrant cultures beneath these warrior elites.

In this chapter, we will explore the peculiar side of feudal Japan: from isolationist policies that feared foreign influence to bizarre punishments and beliefs about loyalty and the afterlife. We will see how ninjas, geisha, and sumo wrestlers emerged in a society that balanced rigid traditions with moments of surprising creativity. Prepare to enter a world of sword duels, tea houses, flower arrangements, and cloak-and-dagger espionage.

1. Early Roots: Yamato Kings and Divine Lineage

Before the era of samurai, Japan's early state was led by the **Yamato** rulers (3rd–7th centuries). They claimed descent from the sun goddess **Amaterasu**, giving them a "divine right" to rule.

- **Mythical Origins**: The **Kojiki** and **Nihon Shoki**, written in the 8th century, mix myth and history. They tell how gods formed the islands, and how Emperor Jimmu, a descendant of Amaterasu, became the first ruler. Some find it strange that these texts blend genealogies with tales of giant deities and magical spears used to create land.
- **Shinto Beliefs**: Shinto, the native religion, views nature spirits (**kami**) as dwelling in mountains, trees, rivers, and even rocks. Rulers were seen as intermediaries between humans and kami. This concept of a living emperor with sacred ties continued into modern times, surprising outsiders who saw monarchy as purely political.

- **Imitating China**: Early Japan borrowed heavily from Chinese writing, bureaucracy, and Confucian ideas. Yet local traditions remained, so formal courts had Chinese-style robes and ranks while still practicing Shinto rites. This blend gave Japanese court life a unique flavor that set the stage for later developments.

2. Samurai and the Code of Bushido

From around the 10th century, the warrior class rose in power. By the 12th century, **Minamoto no Yoritomo** became the first shogun, establishing feudal rule. Samurai codes shaped Japan's identity.

- **Bushido: The Way of the Warrior**: This code emphasized loyalty, honor, and self-discipline. Samurai vowed to serve their lord (daimyo) faithfully, even unto death. If they failed, **seppuku** (ritual suicide) was an accepted way to preserve honor. Westerners found it both noble and terrifying that warriors would disembowel themselves for honor's sake.
- **Katana: The Soul of the Samurai**: Samurai prized their swords, believing them to house their very spirit. Swordsmiths were revered, forging blades folded hundreds of times. The art of testing swords on condemned criminals existed, which is grim. A sword that cut cleanly was praised.
- **Armor with Eerie Masks**: Samurai armor included elaborate helmets (kabuto) and faceplates (mempo) that could resemble demons or fierce animals. This not only protected the face but also intimidated foes. Painted mustaches or wild expressions might appear almost playful, but they were meant for psychological warfare.

3. Shogunate Power: Kamakura, Muromachi, and Tokugawa

Japan had multiple shogunates. The **Kamakura Shogunate** (1192–1333), the **Muromachi (Ashikaga) Shogunate** (1336–1573), and the **Tokugawa Shogunate** (1603–1868) each introduced oddities of governance.

- **Feudal Hierarchy**: Daimyo lords controlled domains with their samurai. Peasants farmed the land, while merchants and artisans lived in towns. A strict social order emerged, where stepping out of your class risked punishment. The rigidness might seem odd to freewheeling societies, but it was crucial for stability.
- **Zen and the Samurai**: Zen Buddhism influenced many warriors, teaching mindfulness and acceptance of death. Some samurai practiced tea ceremony, calligraphy, or poetry, balancing a lethal sword arm with refined culture. This mixture of violence and elegance puzzled observers.
- **Ashikaga's Splendor**: The Ashikaga period saw art flourish (Noh theater, ink painting). Yet behind the refined culture was near-constant warfare among rival daimyo. This paradox—elegant tea gatherings amid clan battles—defines much of Japan's medieval timeline.

---

4. Mongol Invasions and the "Divine Wind" (Kamikaze)

In the late 13th century, **Kublai Khan** tried to invade Japan twice (1274 and 1281). Both times, storms destroyed much of the Mongol fleet, an event the Japanese called **kamikaze** (divine wind).

- **Miraculous Storms**: The Japanese believed the gods sent these typhoons to protect their homeland. This boosted the idea that Japan was favored by the deities. Mongol survivors' accounts describe terrifying waves and how the storms scattered their ships.
- **New Defenses**: During the second invasion, the Japanese built a long stone wall along the coast of Hakata Bay. Samurai also changed tactics, learning from the Mongols' massed archery. Yet luck played a huge role—the typhoons wrecked the Mongol armada.
- **Legacy**: Centuries later, the term "kamikaze" would resurface in World War II for suicide pilots. But originally, it referred to these protective storms. The story further solidified Japan's sense of divine protection, making it unique among neighboring lands.

5. Ninja: Myth and Reality

Popular media loves **ninjas**—stealthy assassins dressed in black, throwing shurikens. But real ninjas (shinobi) in feudal Japan were more complicated.

- **Origins in Iga and Koga**: Regions like Iga and Koga specialized in unconventional warfare. Ninjas were basically spies or mercenaries skilled in infiltration, sabotage, and espionage. They disguised themselves as farmers or merchants to gather info.
- **Black Outfit Myth**: Stage plays popularized ninjas wearing all-black suits for dramatic effect. In actual missions, ninjas likely wore normal clothing to blend in. The iconic black garb was for kabuki theater, letting them "disappear" against the backdrop.
- **Strange Tools**: Ninjas used smoke bombs, grappling hooks, and even "poison eggs" (hollowed-out shells filled with irritants). They studied special breathing techniques to remain calm under stress. Samurai considered them dishonorable because they relied on deceit, yet daimyos often hired them anyway.

---

6. Tea Ceremony: A Quiet, Spiritual Ritual

The **chanoyu** (tea ceremony) developed under Zen influence. It is a carefully choreographed way of preparing and serving powdered green tea (matcha). For outsiders, it can appear quite formal and slow.

- **Wabi-Sabi Aesthetics**: Practitioners value simplicity, imperfections, and austere beauty. The tea hut might have rough walls, simple utensils, and a tiny entrance forcing guests to bow as they enter. This humbling approach contrasts with the luxurious tea sets in other cultures.
- **A Ceremony of Silence**: Participants observe strict etiquette—how to hold the bowl, how to bow, how to clean the utensils. Quiet mindfulness rules the atmosphere. Even whisking the tea into frothy foam must be done with a certain grace.
- **Tea Masters' Influence**: Figures like **Sen no Rikyū** (16th century) shaped the tea ceremony's strict rules. Stories say Rikyū insisted on removing any decoration that seemed excessive, aiming for a spiritual sense of emptiness. Samurai lords found it odd that a mere tea master could instruct them, but they came to respect his wisdom.

7. Seppuku (Harakiri) and Ritual Suicide

One of Japan's most dramatic customs is **seppuku**, also called **harakiri** (belly cutting). Samurai who failed in duty or committed crimes might choose suicide to preserve honor.

- **Gruesome Method**: The samurai would kneel, stab a short sword (wakizashi) into the left side of the abdomen, and draw it across to the right. An assistant (kaishakunin) might then swiftly behead him to end the agony. The entire ritual was solemn, sometimes with poetry recited beforehand.
- **Voluntary or Forced**: Sometimes daimyos ordered rebellious samurai to commit seppuku instead of executing them as common criminals. This "allowed" them an honorable death. Outsiders, from Jesuit missionaries to Dutch traders, were horrified by the practice.
- **Female Suicides**: Samurai women could commit **jigai**, slitting their throats rather than the abdomen. They would tie their knees together first so their corpse would be in a dignified position. Such acts highlight how strongly the honor code permeated all classes of the warrior family.

---

8. The Warring States Period: Chaos and Odd Alliances

From the mid-15th to late-16th century, Japan entered the **Sengoku Jidai** (Warring States Period). Local warlords (daimyos) fought endlessly, forging and breaking alliances.

- **Crescent Moon Helmets and Wild Banners**: Daimyos competed to have distinctive armor. Some wore flamboyant helmets shaped like deer antlers or demon horns. On the battlefield, each clan displayed huge flags with crests. The chaos of color made battles a spectacle.
- **Nobunaga's Ruthless Tactics**: Oda Nobunaga, a key warlord, introduced firearms (arquebuses) on a large scale after the Portuguese brought them to Tanegashima. He mercilessly crushed rivals and destroyed Buddhist warrior-monks at Mt. Hiei. For a culture praising warrior honor, his cold efficiency was both admired and feared.

- **Hostage Swaps**: Daimyos often sent their children to rival courts as "hostages" ensuring alliance loyalty. That a father would hand over a son to an enemy lord might sound insane, but it was normal. The children were treated well but lived under constant threat if treaties broke down.

9. Unifiers: Hideyoshi's Sword Hunt and the Rise of Tokugawa

After Nobunaga's death, **Toyotomi Hideyoshi** continued unification. One of his strangest policies was the **Sword Hunt** (katanagari).

- **Sword Hunt**: Hideyoshi confiscated weapons from peasants, hoping to prevent uprisings. He melted down the swords to create a statue of Buddha—symbolic, but also a way to keep the populace under control. Imagine forcibly seizing farm tools that could be weapons, leaving peasants with no defense.
- **Failed Invasions of Korea**: Hideyoshi tried to invade Korea (1592–1598), seeking further conquests. The campaigns ended in disaster, draining resources. Samurai marched across foreign lands unprepared for turtle ships and Ming Chinese reinforcements. This odd attempt at continental warfare showed how ambition could outstrip practicality.
- **Tokugawa Ieyasu**: After Hideyoshi's death, Ieyasu triumphed at the Battle of Sekigahara (1600). He became shogun, founding the **Tokugawa Shogunate** in 1603. Under Tokugawa rule, Japan enjoyed relative peace but turned inward—another strange twist for a land that once coveted expansion.

10. Sakoku: The Closed Country Policy

During the Tokugawa era (1603–1868), the shogunate enforced **sakoku**—a policy of isolating Japan from most foreign contact.

- **Only Dutch and Chinese**: Foreign trade was restricted to the port of Nagasaki, and only Dutch and Chinese ships could dock there. Other Europeans, especially Spanish and Portuguese, were banned for fear of Christian influence.
- **No One Leaves, No One Enters**: Japanese who left the country could face death if they returned. This aim was to preserve social order and prevent Western colonization or Christian revolts.
- **Catholic Persecution**: Christians faced brutal repression. There were "fumie" ceremonies where suspected Christians had to step on images of Christ or Mary to prove they were not believers. This strictness might seem harsh, but the shogunate saw foreign religion as a threat to stability.

11. Edo Culture: Pleasure Quarters and Kabuki

Despite isolation, the Tokugawa period fostered a rich cultural scene in cities like Edo (Tokyo), Osaka, and Kyoto.

- **Kabuki Theater**: Originating in the early 17th century, kabuki featured stylized acting, elaborate makeup, and dramatic plots. Initially founded by a woman named Izumo no Okuni, it eventually became an all-male domain. Actors playing female roles perfected exaggerated gestures, surprising Western visitors who expected "real" women on stage.

- **Yoshiwara Pleasure District**: Edo's licensed red-light district, Yoshiwara, boomed with courtesans, teahouses, and entertainment. It had strict rules but also refined amusements, from music to poetry. The courtesans were highly skilled in arts, not just "women for hire." This mix of fashion, flirtation, and performance was baffling to moralistic outsiders.
- **Ukiyo-e Woodblock Prints**: Artists like **Hokusai** or **Hiroshige** made famous prints of landscapes, erotica (shunga), or city life. These prints were mass-produced, marking an early form of popular art. The focus on fleeting "floating world" pleasures captured the sense that life under rigid feudal rules needed an escape.

---

12. Strange Punishments and Laws in Tokugawa Times

To maintain order, the shogunate issued many edicts regulating clothing, marriages, and even feasts. Some punishments appear severe or bizarre:

- **Crucifixion and Beheading**: Serious crimes could lead to crucifixion or public beheading. Samurai offenders had the "privilege" of seppuku instead. The idea that class determined execution method was alien to Western visitors who believed in more uniform justice (at least in theory).
- **Public Humiliation**: Minor offenders might be paraded around or have their heads shaved. Adultery could lead to "exposure," where the couple was tied together in public. These humiliations were meant to deter others.
- **Sumptuary Laws**: Ordinary people could not wear silk or lavish kimonos reserved for higher classes. Even the color combinations were regulated. Why? The shogunate worried that if peasants dressed too well, they might challenge social distinctions.

---

13. Farmer Uprisings and Strange Protests

Though peasants were considered the foundation of society, they lived under heavy taxes. Sometimes they rebelled or performed unusual protests:

- **Hyakusho Ikki (Peasant Revolts)**: Groups marched to demand tax relief, carrying banners with slogans like "We are hungry!" or "Decrease tax!" While not as large-scale as some European uprisings, these outbreaks frightened local lords.
- **Suicide as Protest**: In some cases, villagers threatened mass suicide if taxes were not eased. The thought of losing an entire labor force forced daimyos to negotiate. It is an extreme measure, highlighting the desperation peasants felt.
- **Tsujigiri**: A different phenomenon was "crossroads killing," where restless samurai tested their sword skills on random passersby at night. Though illegal, it happened often enough to sow fear among commoners. This odd, violent act shows how samurai culture could turn ugly without war to channel aggression.

---

14. Ronin: Masterless Samurai and Vengeance Tales

When a samurai's lord died or was disgraced, the samurai became **ronin**—masterless wanderers. Some turned to crime or became mercenaries. Others tried to regain honor in dramatic ways.

- **The 47 Ronin Incident**: In 1703, a group of ronin avenged their lord's forced seppuku by killing the official who had provoked him. This story, known as Chūshingura, became legendary, symbolizing ultimate loyalty. Yet after succeeding, the ronin themselves committed seppuku by shogunal command. It is an odd mix: the state punished them, but the people hailed them as heroes.
- **Ronin Gangs**: Some masterless samurai banded together, extorting peasants or acting as yojimbo (bodyguards) for hire. Their skill with swords made them dangerous. To maintain order, the shogunate tried to track them, leading to rules that restricted travel.
- **Romanticized in Theater**: Kabuki plays often featured ronin seeking revenge or redemption. Audiences loved the tension of an honorable samurai forced into dishonorable living. Western observers might see parallels to "cowboy drifters" in American lore, an interesting cultural echo.

15. Hidden Christians and Underground Faith

Despite heavy persecution, some Japanese secretly practiced Christianity (Kakure Kirishitan) after the shogunate banned it in the early 17th century.

- **Fumie Rituals**: Suspected Christians were ordered to stomp on Christian images. Those who refused faced torture or execution. Many complied out of fear, but some found subtle ways to show minimal pressure.
- **Secret Icons**: Some believers disguised Christian statues as Buddhist figures. Mary might appear as the goddess Kannon, holding a child. They read prayers disguised as Buddhist chants. This blending of imagery could look odd, but it allowed them to keep their faith in secret.
- **Discovery Centuries Later**: In the 19th century, when Japan reopened, Western missionaries were shocked to find hidden Christian communities with altered rites. Their prayers had changed over time, sounding partly Latin, partly Japanese, and partly gibberish. This survival story is both inspiring and strange.

---

16. Eccentric Daimyos and Bizarre Behavior

Feudal Japan had some daimyos known for outlandish habits:

- **Date Masamune (the One-Eyed Dragon)**: Famous for his crescent-moon helmet, he lost an eye to smallpox as a child. He was known for flamboyant style and ambitious building projects. Legends say he used golden furniture and created lavish banquets to impress guests—contrary to the typical austere samurai image.
- **Matsudaira Nobutsuna's Pet Tigers**: Some accounts say certain daimyos tried to keep exotic animals, like tigers, brought by Chinese or Korean envoys. Handling tigers in a Japanese castle must have been quite the sight, though it is uncertain how well they managed.
- **Tea Party Duels**: Occasionally, rival daimyos would host elaborate tea ceremonies but slip poison into the bowls or arrange an ambush as guests left. The courtesy and betrayal made politics in feudal Japan extremely risky. One moment, you are admiring a Zen garden; the next, you might be facing arrows.

17. Geisha, Courtesans, and the Floating World

While samurai dominated politics, the cultural side of feudal Japan included **geisha**—skilled entertainers trained in music, dance, and conversation. They often worked in pleasure districts like Kyoto's Gion or Edo's Yoshiwara.

- **Not Prostitutes**: A common misconception is that geisha sold sexual services. In reality, their role was to provide artful company and cultural performance. High-ranking geisha might choose wealthy patrons, but it was not their primary function.
- **Training from Childhood**: Young girls called maiko learned traditional instruments (shamisen), tea ceremony, and refined speech. The hours of practice were intense, and strict rules governed appearance—from white makeup to elaborate hairstyles.
- **The Floating World (Ukiyo)**: The pleasure quarters were called "floating" because they focused on fleeting enjoyment, away from strict Confucian morals. Art and literature romanticized this world, even as authorities tried to regulate it. Western visitors in the 19th century were intrigued by the refined courtesy swirling around hidden vices.

18. Sumo Wrestling: Sacred Sport with Gigantic Fighters

Sumo wrestling dates back many centuries, originally tied to Shinto rituals. By the Tokugawa period, it became popular entertainment with pro wrestlers traveling to perform.

- **Sacred Origins**: Legends say sumo was once performed to please the gods. Wrestlers throw salt into the ring to purify it. The referee's outfit resembles Shinto priests' garments. While it looks like a mere sport, it had a heavy spiritual link.
- **Massive Bodies**: Sumo wrestlers (rikishi) gain weight intentionally, following strict diets. Outsiders might be puzzled by how quickly they can move, despite their size. The ring (dohyo) is small, meaning each match can be explosive and short.
- **Rank and Ritual**: The higher-ranked wrestlers are called yokozuna. Achieving that status requires not only wins but also a dignified bearing. If a yokozuna is found lacking in behavior, it is a serious scandal. This emphasis on moral stance as well as skill is quite unique among sports.

---

19. Arrival of "Black Ships" and the End of Isolation

By the mid-19th century, Western powers forced Japan to end **sakoku**. In 1853, US Commodore Matthew Perry arrived with "black ships," demanding trade access.

- **Shock and Awe**: The huge steamships dwarfed Japanese vessels, belching black smoke. Samurai had never seen such technology. Some believed they were demon ships. The Shogunate, realizing they could not fight modern cannons, signed treaties to avoid war.
- **Samurai in Crisis**: Many samurai felt humiliated. Old ways were in jeopardy. Debates raged between those who wanted to open up and modernize vs. those who wanted to "expel the barbarians." This led to rebellions, assassinations, and turmoil.
- **The Meiji Restoration**: In 1868, the Tokugawa Shogunate fell. The emperor was "restored" to power, and Japan rushed to adopt Western technology and reforms, ending the feudal order. Swords were eventually banned in public. Samurai as a class dissolved, marking the close of a strange yet compelling chapter in Japanese history.

20. Legacy of Feudal Japan's Oddities

Feudal Japan's centuries shaped a culture that still fascinates the world. From the stoic bushido code to the delicate tea ceremony, from isolationist policies to elaborate kabuki stages, it blended severity with grace. The idea of dying for honor, training with swords as a spiritual path, or living under a shogunate that demanded strict social hierarchies might appear bizarre to outsiders. Yet these norms formed a social glue that held the archipelago together through wars and natural disasters.

The result was a distinctive civilization of well-dressed warriors, cunning ninjas, geisha artistry, and sumo spectacles. It balanced refined poetry with savage duels, philosophy with espionage. Japan's isolation ironically enriched its native traditions, letting them evolve with minimal outside influence until the 19th century. Then, with the arrival of foreign ships, everything changed.

Today, we see reflections of those old ways in modern Japan: polite bowing, the love of seasonal festivals, the respect for craftsmanship, and the continuing popularity of samurai and ninja stories. The odd customs we have explored are not just historical quirks; they shaped a national identity that, even in a modernized, globalized era, remains uniquely Japanese.

CHAPTER 17

Royal Scandals: Hidden Secrets of Kings and Queens

When people think of royalty, they often imagine grand palaces, glittering crowns, and majestic ceremonies. But behind that shiny image lurked many secrets. All over the world, long before modern times, kings and queens faced plots, betrayals, and wild affairs. Some were loving rulers who cared for their people, while others schemed ruthlessly to protect their throne. In this chapter, we will focus on the strange and scandalous side of royal life—mysteries that led to famous court gossip, hidden murders, or shocking feuds within palaces.

From the cunning queens of ancient Egypt to the sly rulers of medieval Europe, from bizarre court customs to secret lovers, we will find that royal families sometimes bent the rules they were supposed to enforce. Power struggles could tear families apart, leaving horrifying tales of poisoning, conspiracies, or exiled heirs. Outside observers often whispered about scandalous rumors, never sure if they were true. Let us open these palace doors and peer inside the hidden secrets of kings and queens across different lands—stopping well before modern times but learning how such stories shaped history's most dramatic moments.

1. The Strange Saga of Cleopatra and Her Royal Family

When we think of scandalous queens, **Cleopatra VII** of Egypt often comes to mind. She lived in the 1st century BCE, ruling as a descendant of the Greek-speaking Ptolemaic dynasty. That dynasty was already known for odd practices:

- **In-Family Marriages**: The Ptolemies often married their siblings to keep the royal bloodline "pure." Cleopatra herself married two of her younger brothers (Ptolemy XIII and Ptolemy XIV) in different periods, as required by tradition. Imagine the confusion at the palace! Outsiders found it shocking, but the Ptolemies considered it normal.

- **Alliance with Julius Caesar**: Cleopatra formed a partnership (and likely romance) with the Roman leader Julius Caesar to solidify her power. Caesar helped Cleopatra defeat her brother's forces. Later, rumors claimed Cleopatra charmed Caesar by wrapping herself in a carpet delivered to him—an odd strategy that apparently worked.

- **Love and War with Mark Antony**: After Caesar's death, Cleopatra allied with Mark Antony. They reportedly formed a lavish court life in Alexandria, holding feasts where they dressed as gods. Romans back home spread tales that Cleopatra "bewitched" Antony, calling her a temptress. Their story ended tragically at the Battle of Actium and with their famous double suicide. This mix of romance, politics, and betrayal made Cleopatra a legendary figure of scandal.

2. King Herod's Paranoia: Murder in the Family

Also in the 1st century BCE, **Herod the Great** ruled Judea under Roman influence. He was known for grand building projects like the Temple in Jerusalem. But behind the scenes, Herod's court life bristled with fear:

- **Killing His Wife and Sons**: Herod feared plots against him. He executed his favorite wife, Mariamne, suspecting she planned to overthrow him. Later, he executed two of their sons on charges of treason. Romans joked that it was safer to be Herod's pig than his son—an odd statement noting Jewish dietary laws (where pigs were not eaten), implying a pig was less likely to be killed.

- **Stormy Royal Court**: Herod's large family quarreled over inheritance. Different factions whispered rumors about heirs. Some believed Herod trusted fortune-tellers who warned of "danger from within." These endless suspicions reveal how paranoia could turn royal palaces into deadly traps.

- **Lavish Construction vs. Brutality**: Despite his cruelty, Herod erected monumental structures, like the fortress at Masada. Modern archaeologists marvel at the scale of his projects. Yet, the murders of close kin overshadow that legacy, proving how extreme a king could be in securing the throne.

3. Emperor Nero: Scandalous Feasts and Deadly Family Ties

Moving to the Roman Empire, we come across **Emperor Nero** (1st century CE). His name is nearly synonymous with scandal and cruelty:

- **Mother's Influence**: Nero's mother, Agrippina, maneuvered to place him on the throne at age 17, possibly poisoning Emperor Claudius (her husband). Once Nero ruled, he found Agrippina too controlling, so he arranged her murder—some say a ship designed to sink her, and when she survived, assassins finished the job on shore. This mother-son drama was shocking even in Roman eyes.

- **Wild Parties**: Nero held extravagant parties, where guests drank until they collapsed. At times, he forced nobles to watch his musical performances for hours. If they left early or dozed off, it could mean trouble.

- **The Great Fire and Blame**: A massive fire destroyed much of Rome in 64 CE. Rumors arose that Nero "fiddled while Rome burned," though fiddles did not exist yet; perhaps he performed on the lyre. Whether he set the fire or not, he blamed Christians for it, starting persecutions. This cruelty added to his scandalous reputation.

---

4. The Messy Affairs of Empress Wu Zetian in China

In 7th-century China, the **Tang Dynasty** reached great heights. But a fierce scandal erupted when **Wu Zetian** rose from a concubine to the position of empress—and eventually proclaimed herself Emperor of China, the only woman in Chinese history to do so.

- **Concubine to Empress**: Wu Zetian started in Emperor Taizong's harem, then entered his son Gaozong's harem after Taizong's death. She bore the emperor sons, outmaneuvering rivals. When a daughter died mysteriously, some suspected Wu blamed the emperor's wife to push her aside, though it was never proven.

- **Grasping Imperial Power**: Gaozong fell ill, letting Wu handle state affairs. She exiled or executed powerful officials, replaced them with loyal supporters, and created a secret police. Her strong tactics brought accusations of being a "dragon lady." For a woman to rule was scandalous enough—her methods made it even more shocking.

- **Reign as Emperor**: Wu Zetian declared a new dynasty (Zhou) and ruled in her own name. She promoted Buddhism, built temples, and was praised for efficient governance. Yet, stories of her punishing or killing entire clans for suspected plots persist. Some accounts might be exaggerated, but they reveal the shock many felt at her bold rule.

5. The Merovingian Kings: Hair as a Symbol of Power

In the early medieval period, the **Merovingian Dynasty** ruled the Franks (in what is now France). Known as the "long-haired kings," they had odd traditions that later European rulers mocked.

- **Sacred Hair**: Merovingian kings believed their power came partly from their uncut hair, seen as a sign of divine right. If a rival shaved a king's head, it was like stripping him of authority. Thus, tonsuring a prince could send him to a monastery, removing him from the royal line.

- **Do-Nothing Kings**: By the 7th–8th centuries, these kings barely ruled, overshadowed by powerful mayors of the palace (like Charles Martel). People joked that they lazed around, combing their hair, while mayors handled the real work. This scandal of figurehead kings ended when Pepin the Short deposed the last Merovingian, cutting his hair to show he was no longer king.

- **Strange Burials**: Some Merovingian graves included horse skulls or ornate jewelry. One tale says a Merovingian queen was buried in a barge with servants. While details vary, the theme of mixing Christian and older Germanic customs is consistent, highlighting how monarchy was enveloped in half-pagan, half-Christian rites.

---

6. Byzantine Court Intrigues: Theodora and Secret Pasts

In the Eastern Roman (Byzantine) Empire, palace intrigues were notorious. Consider **Empress Theodora** (6th century CE), wife of Emperor Justinian I:

- **Actress Turned Empress**: Theodora was rumored to have been an actress or dancer of questionable reputation before marrying Justinian. Roman elites found it scandalous that a performer could become empress. Yet Theodora proved politically savvy, helping shape empire policies.

- **Nika Riots**: During a massive uprising called the Nika riots, Justinian considered fleeing, but Theodora allegedly insisted they stand firm. She reportedly said, "Royalty is a fine burial shroud," meaning she preferred to die an empress than live in exile. Her boldness helped quell the revolt.

- **Religious Disputes**: Theodora supported Monophysitism (a Christian doctrine many in the empire saw as heretical). She used palace plots to protect Monophysites, harboring fugitive priests in secret. This drove a wedge in the imperial court, adding yet more drama to an already tense environment.

---

7. Medieval English Royals: Madness, Lovers, and Plots

Shifting to medieval England, we find kings and queens locked in epic scandals, from mental breakdowns to secret romances:

- **Eleanor of Aquitaine's Rebellion**: Eleanor married King Henry II but later joined her sons in revolt against him (1173–1174). The idea that a queen and mother would rebel was shocking. Henry imprisoned her for years. Despite this, she remained influential, guiding her sons Richard the Lionheart and John in future reigns.

- **Richard II's Tyranny and Deposition**: King Richard II faced mental instability rumors. He banished or executed those who challenged him. When he seized the estates of his dead uncle, the Duke of Gloucester, nobles rebelled. They forced him to abdicate, and he died in prison. The scandal: a king undone by his own arrogance and possibly mood swings.

- **Edward II and Favorite "Friends"**: Edward II's closeness to Piers Gaveston and later the Despenser family raised suspicions of favoritism—perhaps even romantic relationships. Nobles hated that these "favorites" had too much influence. Edward's queen, Isabella, eventually led a coup. Edward was deposed and allegedly killed with a red-hot poker. That shocking rumor suggests real disgust with his personal life.

8. The Infamous French Court: Queens, Poison, and Masked Balls

France's medieval and early renaissance eras had their share of royal drama:

- **Isabella of France (the "She-Wolf")**: We have already met her as Edward II's wife who led a rebellion. She was a French princess who claimed Edward's personal relations were improper and that he neglected her. She found an ally (and likely lover) in Roger Mortimer, overthrew her husband, and ruled as regent for their son. People in France called her wise, but in England, she was labeled a she-wolf.

- **Valois Kings and Poison Scandals**: In the later 16th century, the French court under Catherine de' Medici saw rumors of poison use. Catherine was suspected of having an Italian "flying squadron" of ladies who spied on or seduced enemies. Though partly rumor, it symbolized the paranoia in a court rocked by religious wars.

- **Bal des Ardents (The Burning Men's Ball)**: In 1393, King Charles VI hosted a masked ball. He and his companions dressed as "wild men" with flammable costumes. A torch accidentally lit them on fire. The king survived but four dancers burned to death. This bizarre mishap shocked courtiers, who saw it as a bad omen. Indeed, Charles later suffered from bouts of madness, further swirling rumors of curses.

---

9. Queen Nzinga of Ndongo and Matamba: Royal Transformations

Jumping to Africa in the 17th century, **Queen Nzinga** of Ndongo and Matamba (in present-day Angola) was a fierce leader who negotiated with the Portuguese, determined to protect her people. Yet some accounts describe odd court rituals:

- **Male Harem or "Chibados"**: Portuguese sources claim Nzinga kept a group of young men dressed as women, calling them her "wives." She might have done this to display power, reversing typical gender roles. Historians debate the accuracy of these reports—were they exaggerations by shocked foreigners?

- **Alliance Shifts**: Nzinga allied with the Portuguese, then with the Dutch, and later fought them both. She used cunning diplomacy, even converting to Christianity at one point. This shift in loyalties looked scandalous to outsiders, but it helped her survive in a region under intense colonial pressure.

- **Killing Subordinates?**: Some rumors say Nzinga tested the loyalty of her officials by ordering them to kneel as a human chair during negotiations—if they trembled or hesitated, she might have them executed. While these stories could be propaganda, they show how foreigners viewed her as both brutal and captivating.

---

10. Russian Tsars' Peculiar Court: Ivan the Terrible's Rages

In Russia, **Ivan IV (Ivan the Terrible)** (16th century) was infamous for cruelty and unpredictable behavior:

- **Oprichnina Terror**: Ivan created the Oprichnina—his personal police who wore black, rode black horses, and carried a dog's head symbolizing the sniffing out of treason. They executed boyars (nobles) suspected of disloyalty. Scenes of brutality in Novgorod or other towns became legendary.

- **Murder of His Own Son**: During a violent argument, Ivan struck his son, the Tsarevich, with a staff, killing him. This left Ivan in despair, but he never faced formal consequences. The scandal: a ruler so paranoid and rage-filled that even his heir was not safe.

- **Mood Swings and Monastic Retreats**: Ivan sometimes left Moscow, claiming to abdicate, retreating to monasteries. Then he returned to punish or pardon officials. People never knew if they were safe. Outsiders visiting Russia found his actions bizarre—like a mad tyrant toggling between religious devotion and savage killings.

11. The Mughal Empire's Royal Intrigues

In India, the **Mughal Empire** (16th–19th centuries) soared to greatness but also hosted lavish courts and hidden scandals:

- **Babur's Early Adventures**: Founder Babur wrote in his memoirs about battles and personal feelings, even referencing a boy he admired—a fact that surprised Victorian translators who found such confessions scandalous. The empire's start was thus colored by Babur's frank diaries.

- **Jahangir's Wife Nur Jahan**: Emperor Jahangir struggled with alcohol and opium. His wife, Nur Jahan, effectively ruled behind the scenes, signing imperial orders. Some nobility resented her power. Rumors said she plotted to remove potential rivals for Jahangir's attention. She also minted coins in her name, unusual for an empress.

- **Shah Jahan and the Taj Mahal**: Shah Jahan built the Taj Mahal for his beloved wife Mumtaz. Yet some claim the labor and taxes were so heavy that the empire's finances strained. Also, legends say he planned a "Black Taj" across the river for himself, though no solid evidence remains. People wondered if his grief turned into extravagance, bordering on madness.

12. Eunuchs and Palace Plots in the Ottoman Empire

The **Ottoman Empire** (13th–20th centuries) had a massive court in Istanbul. By the time it was a major power (15th–17th centuries), the sultans lived in **Topkapi Palace**, brimming with intrigues:

- **Harem Politics**: The sultan's harem included wives and concubines, each vying to have their son chosen as heir. The queen mother (valide sultan) wielded huge influence. Enemies used poison or rumors to ruin each other. European visitors spread wild tales of secret tunnels and murder at night.

- **Eunuchs' Role**: Black and white eunuchs guarded the harem. They rose to be influential officials, controlling who saw the sultan. Some eunuchs gained vast wealth. The idea of trusting eunuchs over normal guards might appear strange, but the Ottomans believed it prevented forbidden relationships in the harem.

- **Fratricide Policy**: Past sultans sometimes killed their brothers upon ascending the throne, avoiding civil war. Mehmed the Conqueror even legalized fratricide. Imagine a monarchy where a new sultan systematically executes male siblings. A terrifying but accepted rule to preserve power.

13. The Lost Princes in the Tower: England's Mysterious Disappearance

Returning to England for a famous royal mystery: In 1483, the young King Edward V and his brother Richard disappeared in the Tower of London:

- **Under Protector Richard III**: Their uncle, Richard, Duke of Gloucester, was named Lord Protector. Soon after, the princes vanished. Rumors soared that Richard III had them killed to secure his own crown.

- **Skeletons Found Later**: In 1674, workers found two small skeletons under a staircase in the tower. Many believed they were the princes. No conclusive proof existed for centuries, fueling debate: Did Richard III commit child murder? Or were they removed secretly?

- **Shakespeare's Take**: William Shakespeare's play "Richard III" portrays Richard as a scheming villain. But some historians say the Tudors (who replaced Richard's line) painted him in the worst light to legitimize their rule. The uncertainty remains one of England's enduring royal scandals.

---

14. The Blood Countess? Queen/Regent Bathory in Hungary?

Though not precisely a queen, **Elizabeth Bathory** (16th–17th centuries) was a powerful Hungarian noblewoman, rumored to have ties to the Transylvanian ruling family:

- **Tales of Torture and Vampirism**: Legends claim Bathory murdered young girls in her castle, bathing in their blood to stay youthful. This might be partly fiction or an exaggerated rumor from enemies. Still, she was eventually locked up in her own castle tower, never tried in open court due to her noble status.

- **Connection to Royal Circles**: Bathory was related to princes and high-ranking nobles. The Habsburg emperor owed her money. Some suspect the accusations were a plot to seize her lands or avoid debts. If so, it is a scandal built upon either real horror or cunning political maneuver.

- **Confined Until Death**: Officially, Bathory was walled inside a small room with minimal contact. She died years later. The scandal of a "blood countess" remains a chilling legend, reflecting how powerful aristocrats could escape normal justice procedures—and the rumors that swirl around them.

---

15. China's Forbidden City and Eunuch Politics

After Wu Zetian's era, China had other dynasties with their own palace intrigues. The **Ming Dynasty** (14th–17th centuries) built the **Forbidden City** in Beijing, a massive palace complex with thousands of rooms:

- **Eunuch Dominance**: Ming emperors often relied on eunuchs to manage daily tasks. Some eunuchs gained extraordinary power, such as the infamous Wei Zhongxian, who punished critics mercilessly. The bureaucracy tried to curb eunuch influence but often failed.

- **The Wanli Emperor's Withdrawal**: Emperor Wanli refused to attend meetings or govern actively for years, frustrated by court disputes. He stayed in his private quarters, indulging in pleasures, while eunuchs and officials ran affairs. Outsiders found it bizarre that an emperor basically "quit his job" while still on the throne.

- **Hidden Harem**: Like the Ottoman sultans, Chinese emperors had large harems. Rival consorts might bribe eunuchs to sabotage each other. If an emperor favored one concubine, the rest might conspire. Some emperors tried to keep such battles secret, but rumors spread among court watchers.

16. Goryokaku in Japan? A Late Shogunate Twist?

Though we covered Japan in the previous chapter, let us mention a lesser-known scandal from the late Edo period (mid-19th century, still not fully modern times). After Commodore Perry's arrival, internal struggles soared:

- **Assassination Craze**: Samurai loyalists, outraged at foreign intrusion, targeted officials who signed treaties. They also attacked foreign merchants. Some shogunal leaders were murdered in Edo's streets. This was scandalous: a government undone by its own warriors for "betraying" national isolation.

- **Shogun's Concubines**: Tales spread that the last few shoguns indulged in pleasures at Edo Castle while the country faced crisis. No official records confirm wild orgies, but rumor mongers insisted the shogun neglected national defense, fueling a scandal that the Tokugawa leadership had grown decadent.

- **The Fall of the Shogunate**: In 1868, the Emperor's forces overcame shogunal supporters. The final defenders retreated to Hokkaido, building a Western-style fort called Goryokaku, but lost. The scandal was that a once-mighty shogunate collapsed partly due to internal corruption and secrecy, though some blame external pressure as well.

---

17. The Romanovs in Russia? Wait, That's Modern?

We must remember we are not discussing modern times. The Romanov Dynasty's major scandals (like Rasputin or the 1917 Revolution) fall closer to modern history, so we skip those. Our focus remains on pre-modern or just borderline eras. That helps keep us within the user's request.

18. Secret Tunnels and Masked Tournaments in the Holy Roman Empire

The **Holy Roman Empire** (in Central Europe) was a patchwork of kingdoms. Some emperors and princes engaged in lavish festivals with questionable behavior:

- **Emperor Frederick II's Curiosities**: Frederick II (13th century) was known for weird experiments, like placing infants in isolation to see if they developed a "natural language." People found it cruel and scandalous. He also argued with the pope, got excommunicated, yet still claimed to be a devout Christian emperor.

- **Mask Balls in Bohemia**: Certain Bohemian and Bavarian dukes hosted "black mask" tournaments where knights jousted in disguise. Sometimes this covered romantic affairs or political deals. If a knight unhorsed a masked foe, he might discover it was his ally or even a relative, causing embarrassment.

- **Habsburg Family Feuds**: The Habsburgs, who dominated the empire, often married within their own line, leading to inbreeding. This caused physical deformities like the "Habsburg jaw." Rumors of madness or secret curses circulated. People whispered that too many cousins marrying led to mental instability—a scandalous critique of Europe's mightiest dynasty.

---

19. Mad Queens and Poison Plots: A Quick World Tour

Let us sample a few more smaller but no less bizarre royal scandals:

- **Queen Ranavalona I of Madagascar** (19th century, borderline modern but let us mention briefly): She oppressed Christian converts, used forced labor, and forced subjects to drink a poison ordeal (tangena) to prove innocence. She declared near-isolation for Madagascar. European traders described her as tyrannical but cunning, maintaining power for decades.

- **King Erik XIV of Sweden** (16th century): Struggled with mental issues, paranoia. He imprisoned his own brothers, and rumor said he put poison in their soup. He later married a commoner—a scandal for Swedish nobles. Some accounts claim he himself died from poison-laced pea soup, possibly served by guards tired of his rages.

- **Zhengde Emperor of Ming China**: Not as famous as others, but he disguised himself as a merchant, left the palace at night, and roamed the city incognito. He set up a fake "private palace" by the lake to indulge in amusements. Court officials found it scandalous for an emperor to mix with commoners so freely. But the emperor called it "adventure."

20. Lasting Lessons from Royal Scandals

These hidden secrets and scandals remind us that royal life was not always glorious. Rulers had to manage intrigue, paranoia, family rivalries, and intense public scrutiny. Some kings or queens were dethroned by their own blood relatives. Others indulged in extreme pleasures or cruelty, leaving behind outraged subjects. Court ceremonies might have looked elegant, but behind the curtains, poison, betrayal, and manipulation were common tools of survival.

Yet, many of these rulers left big marks on history. Cleopatra influenced Rome's fate, Emperor Ashoka reformed India's moral compass, Empress Wu reshaped the Tang court, and so on. Their personal dramas and questionable acts did not stop them from governing expansive empires or building wonders that still stand. The scandal itself became part of the story, passed down in legends and fueling curiosity centuries later.

CHAPTER 18

Pirate Legends: Odd Facts from the High Seas

Long before modern naval law, sailors roamed the seas under various flags—sometimes for nations, often for themselves. Piracy emerged wherever valuable cargo crossed dangerous waters. But the "pirates" we imagine, wearing eye patches and shouting "Arr!" reflect only a slice of history. In reality, pirates were a diverse lot: some were lawless rogues, others were privateers with official permission to raid enemy ships. Some formed short-lived pirate republics with codes of conduct, giving us surprising glimpses of democracy on the ocean waves.

In this chapter, we will reveal the stranger side of piracy, focusing on older times well before the 20th century. From the cunning Greek pirates of the ancient world to the fearsome buccaneers in the Caribbean, from female captains in the South China Sea to self-governing pirate havens in Madagascar, we will see how pirates defied typical rules. Their daring raids, hidden coves, and secret alliances sometimes challenged mighty empires. Prepare to weigh anchor and discover the odd realities behind the swashbuckling myths.

---

1. Ancient Pirates: Cilician Raiders and Greek Adventures

Pirates did not start in the Caribbean. Even in ancient Greece, maritime raiders attacked coastal towns. The term "pirate" comes from the Greek "peirates," meaning "one who attacks." By the 1st century BCE, **Cilician pirates** in the eastern Mediterranean caused major trouble:

- **Cicero's Complaints**: Roman statesman Cicero wrote about these pirates seizing Roman ships and even capturing important Romans for ransom. Some built mini-kingdoms along the rocky coasts of Cilicia (in modern Turkey). They minted their own coins, a sign of defiance.

- **Pompey's Swift Campaign**: Rome finally sent General Pompey, who cleared the seas in just three months (67 BCE). He offered leniency if pirates surrendered. Many accepted, but a few fled to remote areas. The speed of Pompey's victory seemed shocking, revealing how quickly an organized force could suppress piracy—if it had the will.

- **Pirate Markets**: Ancient pirates often sold loot in secret ports, trading stolen cargo for supplies. Slaves were a valuable commodity. People found it odd that entire black-market economies thrived, yet local rulers sometimes turned a blind eye if they got a cut. This cozy arrangement allowed pirates to exist openly until Rome cracked down.

---

2. Vikings: Raiders or Traders?

In northern Europe from the 8th to 11th centuries, the **Vikings** ranged far, looting monasteries or coastal towns. They might not always be called "pirates," but their hit-and-run style fits the definition:

- **Longships and Hit-and-Run Tactics**: Vikings used swift longships that navigated both open seas and shallow rivers. They raided unprotected sites, grabbing gold and slaves, then vanished. Many monks in Britain wrote terrified accounts of these "Northmen" suddenly appearing at dawn.

- **Settling Down**: Some Vikings became settlers in places like Normandy (named for "Northmen"). While they kept raiding ways initially, they blended into local culture over time. It might seem odd for "pirates" to become feudal lords, but that was their path to stability.

- **Were They All Bloodthirsty?**: Not exactly. Many Vikings were also traders and explorers. They reached Iceland, Greenland, and even North America (Vinland). Yet the image of Vikings with axes and horns on helmets (though historically horns on helmets are questionable) overshadowed their more peaceful aspects. So, we see that "piracy" and "trade" sometimes went hand in hand.

3. Chinese Pirate Queens and Coastal Empires

Asia also had maritime raiders. **Ching Shih**, a female pirate leader in the early 19th century, is famous, but we must recall there were earlier ones:

- **Madame Zheng's Predecessors**: The South China Sea has long been a hotbed of piracy. Local warlords or fisher clans turned to piracy if taxes or famine were severe. They formed fleets, controlling entire stretches of coastline. Though Ching Shih is borderline modern times, her forerunners used similar tactics, terrorizing merchant junks.

- **The Wokou in Japan-China Seas**: During medieval periods, **wokou** (Japanese pirates) raided Chinese and Korean coasts. But the term "wokou" might include mixed ethnicities—some were Chinese smugglers, Japanese ronin, or Korean outcasts. This puzzle of pirate identity is odd: a "Japanese pirate" might not be Japanese at all.

- **Trade or Piracy?**: In East Asia, lines blurred between pirate and trader. Some "pirate lords" demanded tribute from passing ships, offering "protection" in exchange for money. Foreign merchants might prefer paying them to risking an attack. Government navies tried to eradicate them but sometimes lacked resources, letting pirate networks flourish.

---

4. The Golden Age of Piracy in the Caribbean

Between the 17th and early 18th centuries, the Caribbean became known for **buccaneers** and pirates. This "Golden Age" gave rise to the classic pirate image:

- **Privateers vs. Pirates**: European powers at war gave "letters of marque" to captains, letting them attack enemy ships legally. After wars ended, many privateers lost their license but kept raiding anyway, becoming outlaws. That's how some well-known pirates started.

- **Buccaneers**: Initially, buccaneers were hunters on Caribbean islands, smoking meat (from the French "boucan"). They turned to raiding Spanish ships for extra income. Over time, they formed large fleets, capturing treasure galleons. The Spanish colonists labeled them savage criminals, while the buccaneers claimed they were just fighting Catholic Spain's monopoly in the region.

- **Port Royal: "Wickedest City on Earth"**: In Jamaica, after the English seized it from Spain (1655), Port Royal became a pirate haven. Taverns, brothels, and gambling dens lined the streets. Captain Henry Morgan famously used it as a base to raid Spanish possessions. A massive earthquake in 1692 submerged much of the city, seen by some as divine punishment for its vice.

5. Pirate Democracy and "Articles of Agreement"

One surprising fact: pirates sometimes ran ships with democratic rules. Crews agreed on "articles" defining duties, shares of loot, and punishment:

- **Electing Captains**: Many pirate crews chose their captain by vote. If a captain was cowardly or too harsh, they replaced him. This was drastically different from the strict hierarchy on merchant or navy ships. Pirates believed in equal voice because their lives depended on each other.

- **Quartermaster Power**: The quartermaster oversaw distribution of loot and discipline. Some articles specified the quartermaster could punish small offenses, while the captain commanded in battle. Each crew had its twist, but the quartermaster was often second in command.

- **Health Insurance**: Pirate codes sometimes promised compensation if a pirate lost a limb or eye in battle. For example, "an arm lost equals 600 pieces of eight." That is quite advanced for the era, showing that pirates cared about fair treatment (at least among themselves). Outsiders found it strange that criminals had benefits that normal sailors lacked.

---

6. Women Pirates: Anne Bonny, Mary Read, and Others

Though many pirate crews barred women, some women joined by disguising themselves or sailing on ships that allowed them. Famous examples from the early 18th century:

- **Anne Bonny and Mary Read**: Both served under Captain Jack Rackham (Calico Jack). Mary disguised herself as a man for much of her life. Legend says when their ship was attacked, they fought fiercely while the male pirates hid below deck. Their capture in 1720 led to a sensational trial. Bonny and Read claimed pregnancy to delay execution. Mary died in prison; Anne vanished from records—some guess her father's influence saved her.

- **Disguised Gender**: Women pirates often wore men's clothes. Crewmates might only discover the truth later. This was not purely for shock value; it was a practical necessity in a male-dominated environment. Some men admired their skill; others felt it scandalous to serve with a woman on board.

- **Historical Debate**: Historians debate how large a role female pirates played. The legends revolve around a few famous names. But even a handful is enough to show that the pirate world had room for daring women who broke social rules. That alone was odd for an era restricting women's roles on land.

7. Blackbeard's Theatrics and Fear Factor

Edward Teach, known as **Blackbeard**, roamed the Caribbean and the Atlantic coast in the early 18th century:

- **Frightening Image**: He reportedly tied slow-burning fuses under his hat, creating clouds of smoke around his face in battle. This intimidation method was as important as actual fighting skill. Sailors often surrendered without a fight.

- **Base in the Bahamas**: Blackbeard used places like Nassau in the Bahamas as a pirate base. The local English governor sometimes turned a blind eye, receiving bribes. This uneasy alliance let pirates come and go freely.

- **Short-Lived Reign**: In 1718, a British naval force cornered Blackbeard off North Carolina. After a fierce fight, he was killed, his head displayed on a ship's bow. The quick end of his career shows how ephemeral pirate fame could be. Even so, his theatrics left a lasting legacy in pirate lore.

---

8. Treasure Myths: X Marks the Spot?

Popular stories tell of pirates burying chests of gold on remote islands and marking the spot with an "X." But how true was that?

- **William Kidd's Legend**: Captain Kidd (executed 1701) is rumored to have buried treasure along the coasts of Long Island or the Caribbean. Treasure hunters have searched for centuries, rarely finding anything. It might be rumor or a small stash overblown by storytellers.

- **Burial Not Common**: Most pirates spent loot quickly on drink, gambling, or better ships. Some gave shares to family. Regular burying of treasure was less likely. Documents show few references to hidden hoards. The "X marks the spot" might be an invention of later adventure novels.

- **Coded Maps?**: The idea of cryptic maps with dotted lines, riddles, or compass directions enthralled readers of Robert Louis Stevenson's "Treasure Island" (published in 1883—still not super modern, but post-pirate golden age). Real pirates rarely used fancy maps. They navigated by memory and basic charts. The myth remains fun, though.

---

9. Pirate Havens: Tortuga and Madagascar

Some pirate crews set up communities in places with weak colonial control:

- **Tortuga (near Hispaniola)**: French buccaneers used it as a base in the 17th century. They elected "governors," minted local currency, and sold stolen goods. The Spanish tried to oust them, but the rocky terrain made it hard. Tales say the island was full of boozy taverns, duels, and secret love affairs.

- **Madagascar's "Libertalia"?**: A legend from the 17th–18th centuries mentions a pirate utopia called Libertalia on Madagascar's coast. They allegedly declared all men equal, no slavery, and minted coins reading "For God and Freedom." Historians doubt it truly existed in that form, but there was a real presence of pirates in Madagascar. They lived with local peoples, sometimes marrying into tribes. The dream of a pirate republic, free from kings, captivated many.

- **Nassau in the Bahamas**: Another major pirate hub, as mentioned earlier. Pirates like Blackbeard, Charles Vane, and Jack Rackham formed an informal alliance. British authorities eventually offered pardons if pirates surrendered. Some accepted; others fled to keep their wild independence.

---

10. Punishments and Pirate Trials

Captured pirates often faced harsh punishments. Nations wanted to make examples of them:

- **Hanged at Execution Dock**: In England, pirates were typically taken to Wapping in London, near the Thames. They were hanged, and their bodies sometimes put in gibbets (iron cages) along the river as a warning. People came to watch, turning executions into grim public events.

- **Dunking and Marooning**: Pirate crews themselves sometimes punished members by marooning them on a deserted island with minimal supplies. It was effectively a death sentence if rescue never came. Crews might also "duck" troublemakers in the sea. Oddly, these harsh methods were part of internal discipline.

- **Spectacles in Colonial Ports**: In the Caribbean or American colonies, captured pirates faced quick trials. Governors wanted to show they upheld law. Gallows near harbors reminded incoming sailors of the risk. This image of a rotting corpse in a cage was meant to deter future piracy—some found it excessively gruesome, but authorities believed it necessary.

11. Pirate Codes of Conduct: Rumors and Realities

We mentioned "articles" or "pirate codes." They sometimes included moral rules that sound surprising:

- **No Fighting On Board**: Some codes banned fighting on the ship. If two pirates had a dispute, they settled it on land with swords or pistols. This prevented damaging the ship or sails. That sense of property care was quite practical.

- **Lights Out at Eight**: A few captains demanded lights or candles be put out by a certain hour. Anyone wanting to stay up had to do so on the open deck. This rule avoided accidental fires in cramped wooden quarters.

- **Equality Among All?**: While many pirates championed equality among crew members, racism and sexism still existed. Nonetheless, compared to merchant vessels, pirates offered more chances for men of different races to share plunder. Some black pirates gained status as key crew members. This partial egalitarianism was rare in that era's society.

---

12. The Role of "Jolly Roger" Flags

The iconic black flag with a skull and crossbones (the **Jolly Roger**) is central to pirate lore:

- **Purpose of Terror**: Flying a black flag signaled no mercy if the target resisted. Some pirates flew a red flag ("bloody flag") meaning they would kill everyone if they had to. These threats made many crews surrender without a fight.

- **Different Designs**: Not all pirates used the same symbol. Some used an hourglass, skeletal figures, or swords. Blackbeard's flag allegedly had a horned skeleton stabbing a heart. Each captain tried to craft a frightening emblem. Outsiders marveled at how these criminals created "brands" for themselves.

- **Flags as Misdirection**: Pirates sometimes flew a friendly nation's flag, approaching unsuspecting ships, then hoisted the Jolly Roger at the last moment. This trickery was part of the pirate toolkit, leading to rules among navies that demanded a ship show its true flag before engaging—though pirates rarely followed such niceties.

---

13. Feared Names: Bartholomew Roberts, Henry Morgan, and More

We have references to Blackbeard, but many others attained notoriety:

- **Bartholomew Roberts ("Black Bart")**: The most successful pirate by number of captured ships—over 400. He insisted on no gambling or drinking on board. Strange for a pirate, but it kept discipline. He was eventually killed by the Royal Navy off Africa's coast in 1722.

- **Henry Morgan**: A Welsh privateer who raided Panama, Porto Bello, and Maracaibo in the mid-17th century. Knighted by King Charles II, Morgan became lieutenant governor of Jamaica. That a brutal pirate ended up as a colonial official shows how governments used pirates when convenient.

- **Samuel Bellamy ("Black Sam")**: Known for fairness to his crew. Called himself the "Robin Hood of the seas," claiming he robbed the rich to feed the poor. That might be romantic talk, but he was well-liked by his men. He died in a storm off Cape Cod (1717). People still search for his wreck, the Whydah Gally, which has yielded treasure finds.

---

14. Pirate Tactics: Grappling Hooks and Fearsome Boarding

Before cannons dominated sea battles, pirates boarded ships at close range. Even with cannons, boarding was crucial:

- **Close Combat**: Pirates threw grappling hooks to pull an enemy ship near, then rushed aboard with cutlasses, pistols, or axes. This chaotic melee often ended quickly, as merchant crews rarely matched the pirates' ferocity.

- **Psychological Warfare**: The intimidation factor was huge. The sight of a wild-looking band, some with black flags, possibly screaming curses, could break the target's morale. Many surrendered to avoid slaughter.

- **Surprise Attacks at Night**: Pirates used the cover of darkness to sneak up on anchored ships. If they captured the watch quietly, they took over with little alarm. Such cunning methods show that raw violence was not always needed; stealth could pay off.

---

15. Golden Age Collapse: Why Did Piracy Decline?

By the 1720s–1730s, the "Golden Age" fizzled out:

- **Naval Crackdowns**: Britain, Spain, and France realized pirates hurt their colonial trade. They formed stronger navies and patrolled shipping lanes more aggressively. Bounties offered for pirate captains soared.

- **Pardons**: Some governors, like Woodes Rogers in the Bahamas, offered royal pardons to pirates who surrendered. Many, tired of constant danger, accepted. This turned major pirate dens into law-abiding colonies, reducing pirate numbers drastically.

- **Changing Politics**: As European wars ended, privateers lost legal backing. The merchants they once tormented demanded safe commerce. Colonial powers began to unify policing across the seas. Pirate enclaves had nowhere left to hide, especially with new forts in strategic harbors.

16. Beyond the Caribbean: Red Sea and Indian Ocean Raiders

Piracy was not only in the New World. In the **Red Sea**, pirates targeted ships from the Middle East and India carrying spices or gold. Some European pirates also roamed off the coast of Africa, attacking Mughal or Ottoman vessels:

- **Thomas Tew and the Pirate Round**: Tew took the "Pirate Round," sailing from the Americas around Africa to the Red Sea to plunder Muslim pilgrim ships or Indian merchants. The loot could be huge, but so was the risk. Tew died in action, showing how fortune was fleeting.

- **Madagascar as a Base**: We mentioned "Libertalia," but real or not, Madagascar offered safe harbors. Pirates like Avery or England used them to rest, fix ships, or trade. The synergy between local rulers and pirates was unusual: each side gained, at least for a while.

- **Impacts on Eastern Trade**: Mughal emperors complained to British authorities about English pirates harassing pilgrim ships to Mecca. This diplomatic pressure forced the British East India Company to cooperate in hunting pirates—a factor in the decline of high-seas robbery outside the West as well.

---

17. The Strange Case of Captain Mission

A figure named **Captain Misson** (sometimes spelled Mission) is said to have founded the utopian pirate settlement of Libertalia in Madagascar. But many doubt he even existed:

- **Sources**: The main account comes from a 1728 book by Daniel Defoe (or a Defoe associate) titled "A General History of the Pyrates." It describes Misson as a French pirate influenced by a priest named Caraccioli who believed in freedom and equality.

- **Enlightenment Piracy?**: Misson's colony supposedly abolished classes, freed slaves, and welcomed local tribes as equals. The story enthralls readers: a pirate-based democracy. But historians find no direct evidence. Possibly it is an invented tale to blend Enlightenment ideals with pirate romance.

- **Popularity of the Myth**: Even if fake, Misson's story fed the dream that pirates could form a better society. Later revolutionaries sometimes cited pirate egalitarianism as proof that people could self-govern without kings. This cross between political philosophy and sea adventures remains an odd piece of pirate lore.

---

18. Myths vs. Reality: Parrots, Peg Legs, and Treasure Islands

Literature and pop culture have shaped how we see pirates, but much is exaggerated:

- **Peg Legs and Eye Patches**: Injuries were common, so some pirates indeed used wooden legs or patches. But it was not universal. Patching an eye might also help with night vision in a dim hold, though that may be more rumor than standard practice.

- **Talking Parrots**: Exotic birds were sometimes kept as pets if pirates raided tropical regions. But the image of every pirate with a chatty parrot on his shoulder is mostly from fiction, especially "Treasure Island." Still, it could happen, as parrots were valuable trading items.

- **Swashbuckling Speech**: The "Arr!" accent likely stems from West Country English, popularized by actor Robert Newton playing Long John Silver in films. Real pirates spoke many languages, from English and Spanish to Dutch, French, or African dialects. A single comedic accent in every pirate tale is purely Hollywood's doing.

19. Piracy's Impact on Nations and Trade

Though seen as criminals, pirates indirectly influenced global trade and politics:

- **Weakened Spanish Monopoly**: In the Americas, pirates battered Spanish fleets, showing other powers that the "Spanish Main" was vulnerable. This encouraged England, France, and the Netherlands to establish their own colonies.

- **Insurance and Convoy Systems**: Merchants invented maritime insurance partly to cover losses to pirates. Convoys with naval escorts became standard. In a strange way, pirate threats spurred progress in shipping security and financial instruments.

- **Social Mobility**: Some enslaved Africans escaped plantation life by joining pirate crews, finding more freedom than under colonial masters. Pirate ships could be harsh, but they offered an alternative to forced labor, especially if the crew recognized basic "articles" of fairness.

20. The Legacy of Pirate Legends

Though large-scale piracy declined by the mid-18th century in the Atlantic, the stories remain. People still dream of hidden treasure or admire the rebellious spirit of pirates who defied kings and navies. Some see them as criminals deserving no praise, while others romanticize them as early champions of a rough equality.

Their codes, trials, secret havens, and flamboyant flags all contributed to a lore that echoes in books, movies, and plays. Indeed, the reality was harsh: violence, disease, betrayal, and short life spans. But the glimpses of pirate democracy, shared loot, and flexible rules were unique for a time so bound by monarchy and strict class lines.

Now that we have sailed through these odd facts of piracy, we will continue into Chapter 19 to see how the early industrial changes reshaped societies with weird inventions and surprising shifts, still before we hit truly modern times. From steam engines to bizarre contraptions, we will find that the thirst for progress brought new forms of confusion and curiosity. Let us drop anchor on the high seas and step onto the shores of invention in the next chapter.

CHAPTER 19

The Start of Industrial Change: Crazy Inventions and Surprising Advances

After ages of knights, pirates, and royal drama, the world began to shift toward something new: machines and factories. This did not happen in an instant, but during the late 18th and early 19th centuries, certain societies—especially in Europe—saw a wave of inventions that changed everyday life. We call this the start of the "Industrial Revolution," although it was more of an evolution, step by step.

In this chapter, we will explore how people started using steam engines, water frames, and other strange devices to spin cloth, power mills, and drive trains. We will see how early factories shocked rural folk, how new ideas in science led to bizarre medical treatments and unexpected breakthroughs, and how entire landscapes changed to accommodate canals, bridges, and railroads. At the time, many found these machines frightening—some even tried to destroy them. Others believed machines would solve all problems. Through it all, the odd blend of progress and confusion gave birth to a new era. Let us walk into the noisy, steam-filled world of early industry, discovering the crazy inventions and surprising advances before truly modern times arrived.

1. The Seeds of Mechanization: Europe's Early Factories

Long before giant smoke-belching chimneys became normal, small workshops used simple machines powered by waterwheels. By the late 18th century, certain places, like Britain, saw big changes:

- **Domestic System vs. Factory System**: Previously, weaving and spinning often happened at home, with entire families working. This was called the "domestic system." But now, inventors placed large spinning machines in mills by rivers to use water power. Workers traveled there daily, marking a shift to the "factory system." Some found it exciting, others found it unnatural.

- **Cromford Mill and Richard Arkwright**: In Cromford (Derbyshire, England), Arkwright built a water-powered cotton spinning mill around 1771. Locals were awed by the loud machines, turning raw cotton into thread faster than ever. It felt almost magical to see mechanical wheels spinning day and night.

- **Social Shock**: Farmers' children might leave fields to work at the mill. Villagers worried this "mechanization" would ruin families or break social customs. While some adapted, others saw it as a threat to the old rhythm of rural life. Thus, seeds of industrialization were planted with both hope and fear.

---

2. The Oddities of Water Frames, Spinning Mules, and More

Early textile inventions often had quirky names that matched their surprising impact:

- **Water Frame**: Richard Arkwright's water frame was a huge spinning machine. People joked it was so large that it could "eat cotton faster than a hundred spinners." Because it needed a continuous water source, mills popped up near fast-flowing rivers. Some joked that rivers became the new "lords" of industry.

- **Spinning Mule**: Samuel Crompton combined two machines—the Spinning Jenny and the Water Frame—to create the "Spinning Mule" (1779). Why "mule"? It was a hybrid (like the animal) of earlier designs. It spun finer thread at greater speed, but its design looked peculiar: a long carriage moving back and forth. Visitors to mills found it mesmerizing, but also noisy and intimidating.

- **Power Loom**: Edmund Cartwright invented a loom powered by water or steam. Early models shook violently and broke threads. Mill workers laughed that it was like a "drunk loom," but improved versions gradually replaced hand weaving. Families who once wove cloth at home felt threatened, fueling resentment toward these iron contraptions.

3. Shocking Impact: Luddites and Machine Breaking

As factories grew, not everyone rejoiced. Some skilled weavers and artisans saw machines as thieves of their livelihood:

- **Who Were the Luddites?**: In the early 19th century, groups of workers in England, called "Luddites," smashed knitting frames or looms at night. Their name came from a mythical leader, "Ned Ludd." They wore masks, broke into mills, and destroyed machines they blamed for job losses.

- **Riots and Trials**: The government responded harshly. Soldiers guarded factories, and those caught breaking frames faced execution or exile. People debated whether the Luddites were criminals or desperate folks defending their craft. Newspapers printed wild stories of "Luddite mobs" terrorizing factory owners.

- **Odd Stance on Progress**: Luddites were not fully against technology; they opposed how owners used machines to lower wages or replace skilled labor without fair compensation. This conflict signaled a deeper problem: industrial progress moved fast, leaving workers unprepared. Even so, some found it bizarre that men would risk their lives to smash spinning machines in the dark.

---

4. Steam Power and the Strange Reactions

One of the biggest leaps was harnessing steam to power engines. At first, steam engines pumped water out of mines, then they branched into factories and transport:

- **Thomas Newcomen's Engine**: Early 18th century, Newcomen built a steam-driven pump. It was huge, often housed in tall wooden structures. It hissed and banged, leading local villagers to suspect the machine was "haunted by devils." Some even refused to go near it at night.

- **James Watt's Improvements**: Watt refined the steam engine, adding a separate condenser, making it more efficient (1769). This allowed factories to move away from rivers, using coal-fired steam engines. People praised Watt as a genius, but some said he "stole steam from nature's domain." Poetry and cartoons teased him, showing him harnessing a cloud with a chain.

- **Superstitions**: Early factory workers believed that if you disrespected the steam engine, it might explode in rage. Some wore talismans for protection from "boiler demons." These beliefs sound silly now, but explosions were indeed common, fueling superstition.

---

5. James Watt's Puzzling Partnerships

Despite his brilliance, **James Watt** did not act alone:

- **Matthew Boulton**: A businessman with a flair for marketing. Boulton funded Watt's experiments, turning the improved steam engine into a commercial hit. Their partnership was odd: Watt was shy and disliked direct sales, while Boulton thrived on deals. The synergy worked—one was a quiet inventor, the other a flamboyant promoter.

- **Soho Manufactory**: Boulton's factory near Birmingham was like an "industrial palace." They installed demonstration steam engines for visitors. European aristocrats and scientists toured it, gawking at mechanical wonders. Some wrote that Soho's hum sounded like "the heartbeat of a new age."

- **Letters of Grievance**: Watt fretted over patent infringers, writing angry letters about "engine thieves." He used complicated legal maneuvers to protect his patents. This drama, with lawsuits and secret investigations, felt more like a spy novel than normal business. People realized technology wars were not just modern issues.

6. Coal Mines, Child Labor, and Eccentric Reforms

The need for coal soared. Mines expanded, often employing children in grim conditions:

- **Trappers, Hurriers, and Other Strange Roles**: Kids as young as five might be "trappers," sitting in darkness to open ventilation doors. "Hurriers" dragged heavy coal wagons. Shocking? Yes, but families needed money, and laws were lax. Some described these children as "small ghosts" living underground.

- **Deadly Explosions**: Methane gas in mines caused fires or explosions. Primitive safety lamps helped, but accidents were frequent. Miners prayed to local saints or used superstitious charms. Some believed canaries in cages warned of bad air. Observers found the mixture of faith and hazard both tragic and odd.

- **Early Reformers**: By the 19th century, social activists demanded child labor restrictions. Lord Shaftesbury in Britain led investigations. Witness testimonies about kids in narrow tunnels shocked the public. Reports of children crawling with bleeding knees and stunted growth outraged society. Yet it took years to pass major reforms, revealing a twisted tolerance of cruelty for profit.

---

7. Canal Mania: Europe's Aquatic Highways

Before railways, canals were the big breakthrough in transporting heavy goods. The late 18th century saw "Canal Mania," especially in Britain:

- **Man-Made Rivers**: Engineers like James Brindley built canals connecting coal fields to industrial towns. People marveled at aqueducts crossing valleys. Some called them "water bridges," seemingly defying nature. Boaters gliding high above farmland made a surreal sight.

- **Odd Financing and Speculation**: Investors poured money into canal projects, hoping to get rich from tolls. The mania led to wild speculation. Some canals ended in the middle of nowhere or proved unprofitable. We see parallels with modern "bubbles," reminding us that hype can overshadow practicality.

- **Strange Sights**: Canal boats were drawn by horses walking along towpaths. Families often lived on these narrowboats. Observers saw children and pets on deck, laundry drying in the breeze—like floating homes. This traveling village life was unique but tough. Lock keepers controlled water levels in giant gates, and boatmen had to abide by a complicated lock schedule or risk collision.

---

8. The Quirky Growth of Iron Bridges

As iron production rose, designers built metal structures. One early masterpiece: **The Iron Bridge** (1779) over the River Severn in England:

- **A Bridge of Iron?!**: People at first found the idea bizarre. Wouldn't an iron bridge collapse under its own weight? Or crack in cold weather? The builder, Abraham Darby III, proved them wrong. Visitors traveled miles to see this "modern wonder." Some wrote that it resembled "a giant metal arch from a wizard's forge."

- **Symbol of the Age**: The Iron Bridge became a tourist spot. Painters depicted it as a sign of man's triumph over nature. Poets penned verses about crossing from old to new. Meanwhile, skeptics poked it with canes, testing for stability, half-expecting it to fail.

- **Spread of Iron Structures**: Soon, foundries churned out iron beams for factories, aqueducts, and eventually railway bridges. But early efforts had fiascos. Some designs lacked experience, leading to collapses in storms. The learning curve was steep, with tragic lessons spurring safer methods.

9. Engineer Geniuses with Strange Quirks

Many early industrial engineers were eccentric:

- **Isambard Kingdom Brunel**: A 19th-century British engineer who built massive ships, railways, and bridges. Known for wearing a top hat and smoking cigars, he once got stuck in an iron boiler during an on-site test. People teased that he tested structures "from the inside." His unwavering confidence verged on arrogance, yet his achievements were astounding.

- **John Metcalf ("Blind Jack")**: Born blind, he became a road builder in 18th-century England. He used his memory and senses to map routes, astonishing everyone. Locals saw him walking along newly laid roads, staff in hand, giving instructions. The fact that a blind man excelled in engineering defied assumptions about disability.

- **Nicholas Joseph Cugnot**: A French inventor who built a steam-powered vehicle (a sort of "car") in 1770 for hauling artillery. It was slow, often tipping forward. Rumor says he crashed it into a wall, making it one of the first motor vehicle accidents. People giggled at the "steam wagon fiasco," never guessing how important self-propelled machines would become.

---

10. Medical Oddities and the Pre-Germ Theories

Alongside engineering feats, early industrial times spurred changes in medicine. Some were helpful, others were odd or downright harmful:

- **Miasma Theory**: Many doctors believed disease spread through "bad air" or foul smells. City dwellers tried to fight cholera or typhoid by carrying flowers or burning tar. Sewers might exist, but if the smell was strong, they assumed it was still dangerous. The idea of invisible germs was not mainstream yet.

- **Quack Remedies**: Patent medicines promised to cure everything from gout to hysteria. They contained opium, mercury, or bizarre herbs. People claimed "miracle cures," ignoring side effects. Some investors grew rich marketing these tonics, while newspapers ran scandalous ads. Regulators were few, so the gullible got swindled by "snake oil."

- **Early Surgical Tools**: Surgeons in the 18th and early 19th centuries used tools not always sterilized. Blood-stained aprons were seen as badges of experience. Amputation soared in battlefield medicine, with saws that might be reused from patient to patient. One wonders how more people did not die of infection—indeed, many did, fueling slow acceptance that cleanliness mattered.

---

11. The "Miracle" of Gas Lighting

Before electricity, towns used **gas lighting** from coal gas. It was a revolution in the early 1800s:

- **Lamplighters vs. Gas Lights**: Streetlamps had been oil-based or candle-based. With gas, entire streets could glow at night. Some worried the "artificial day" would harm people's health or disrupt sleep patterns. They called it "devil's breath" because it hissed and smelled sulfuric.

- **The Gasworks**: Factories produced coal gas and piped it into buildings. Coal tar, a byproduct, was messy. Accidents caused explosions or carbon monoxide leaks. Writers described black smoke drifting from gasworks, creating eerie nighttime scenes.

- **Public Reaction**: At first, many feared gas lines might blow up half the city. Newspaper cartoons depicted buildings in flames. Over time, folks embraced well-lit streets for safer travel at night. The shift from flickering lanterns to a steady glow felt magical, if somewhat risky.

12. Balloon Craze: Daredevils in the Skies

Long before airplanes, the late 18th century saw hot-air and gas-filled balloons:

- **Montgolfier Brothers (France, 1783)**: They launched a hot-air balloon carrying a sheep, a duck, and a rooster to test high-altitude survival. Crowds cheered or fainted, thinking this a step toward heaven or madness. The animals landed safely, spurring the next step—human flights.

- **Balloon Feats**: Adventurers soared over cities, once impossible to imagine. Some performed stunts, dropping fireworks from the basket or playing music. People below either cheered or panicked that the balloon might crash onto rooftops.

- **Fashionable Fad**: Balloon prints appeared on dresses and teapots. Aristocrats hosted "balloon parties," releasing small decorative balloons. A few lunatics tried crossing entire seas; some succeeded partially, others vanished. The science was shaky, but the excitement was huge. This mania faded as more practical transport arrived, but it marked an early mania for flight.

---

13. Rise of the Railroad: Fearful Myths and Realities

By the early 19th century, steam locomotives emerged, sparking the birth of railways:

- **First Public Lines**: George Stephenson's Stockton and Darlington Railway (1825) and the Liverpool and Manchester Railway (1830) pioneered passenger trains. Spectators gawped at metal beasts chugging along tracks, belching steam. Some women fainted, believing high speeds (30 mph!) might damage the human body.

- **Public Panic**: Pamphlets warned that traveling so fast could "boil passengers' blood." Landowners worried train smoke would kill cattle or set crops ablaze. Doctors argued pregnant women might miscarry if exposed to engine vibrations. Many of these fears look silly now, but they were real concerns then.

- **Accidents and Growth**: Early trains had design flaws. The "Rocket" famously killed a politician, William Huskisson, during the opening of the Liverpool-Manchester line. Despite tragedies, railways spread. Towns fought to get a station, believing it meant prosperity. Soon, rails crisscrossed the land, ignoring initial naysayers.

14. Strange Early Locomotives: Puffing Devils and Clumsy Engines

Not all steam engines were sleek. Some were downright goofy:

- **Richard Trevithick's "Puffing Devil" (1801)**: An early road locomotive in Cornwall that repeatedly broke down. On one trial, it overheated, engine bursting into flames, forcing the driver to flee. Locals teased that the devil's puff cooked itself.

- **Salamanca and the Rack System**: The "Salamanca" locomotive (1812) used a central gear on a rack between rails. Observers said it looked like a clock's gears spinning on the track. The noise was horrendous, scaring horses. But it moved heavy coal wagons on steep lines, proving that odd solutions sometimes worked.

- **Experimental "Multi-Chimney" Engines**: Some inventors put multiple chimneys on engines to vent steam better. They resembled mechanical porcupines. Others tried vertical boilers shaped like big kettles. These prototypes often shook violently, leading passengers to jump off in fear. The trial-and-error approach yielded comedic fiascos, yet paved the way for refined designs.

15. The Great Exhibition: Showcasing Marvels

In 1851, London hosted **The Great Exhibition** in the Crystal Palace—an immense glass structure. It showcased global inventions and wonders:

- **Crystal Palace**: Architect Joseph Paxton built it from prefabricated iron and glass. Visitors likened it to a giant greenhouse. Some worried the glass roof might magnify sunlight, roasting everyone inside. When it opened, people marveled at how cool and airy it felt.

- **Bizarre Exhibits**: Companies displayed steam hammers, mechanical looms, hydraulic presses, and odd contraptions from around the world. One highlight was a giant printing press that spat out pamphlets about the exhibition. Another was a massive diamond from India, the Koh-i-Noor, displayed with special lighting. Attendees formed huge queues to see "the mountain of light."

- **International Competition**: Nations tried to outdo each other. France brought luxury silks, the US displayed reapers and telegraph machines, and India contributed exotic textiles. The variety was overwhelming. Some visitors wrote diaries complaining of exhaustion after seeing "20,000 wonders in a single day."

---

16. Early Telegraph Wires and the Skeptics

Alongside steam, communications advanced. The telegraph used electric signals over wires, sending messages in minutes:

- **Samuel Morse and Code**: By the 1840s, Morse's telegraph lines linked cities in the US. In Britain, Cooke and Wheatstone developed a similar system. People wrote that wires "carried lightning," suspecting it might be dangerous for farmland or livestock.

- **Skeptic Reactions**: Farmers said cows near telegraph poles gave sour milk. Superstitious claims abounded—some believed telegraph lines "could summon storms," since they looked like lightning conductors. Companies had to reassure the public that wires did not attract evil forces.

- **Transatlantic Cable Failure**: Early attempts to lay a cable across the Atlantic led to fiascos. The cable broke multiple times. In 1858, a cable worked briefly, but soon died. Queen Victoria managed to send a message to President Buchanan, but then signals vanished. Public saw it as a short-lived miracle, then a humiliating flop. But perseverance eventually gave us a working transatlantic link in 1866.

17. Agriculture's Surprising Mechanization

While factories grew, farms also adopted new machines:

- **Mechanical Reapers**: Men like Cyrus McCormick in the US built reaping machines that cut grain faster than manual scythes. Some European farmers refused them, calling them "contraptions from the devil." Others welcomed the chance to harvest bigger fields with fewer workers.

- **Seed Drills**: Jethro Tull's seed drill (early 18th century) placed seeds in rows at the correct depth. People teased Tull, saying nature scattered seeds randomly, so why be so precise? Yet yields increased. Over time, the weird metal machine that spat seeds in lines became normal.

- **Threshing and Ricking**: Threshing machines separated grain from stalks, replacing flails. Laborers who once did it by hand often lost seasonal wages. This fueled rural anger, leading to threats and sabotage. The conflict mirrored the Luddite story in factories—progress for some, heartbreak for others.

18. Laughable or Ingenious? Inventions That Flopped

Not every invention soared. Some were just odd or too far ahead of their time:

- **Mechanical Horse**: Various tinkerers tried building horse-like contraptions with legs powered by steam or pedals. They usually jerked and collapsed, prompting laughter from onlookers. People realized wheels were simpler than mechanical legs mimicking a real horse.

- **Steam-Powered Road Coaches**: In early 19th-century Britain, entrepreneurs launched steam carriages for roads. They faced hostility from horse-coach operators and had mechanical breakdowns on uneven roads. Parliament passed laws (like the "Red Flag Act") forcing them to have a person walk ahead with a flag. This stifled their success.

- **Automatic Beds and Chair Machines**: Some wacky creators tried to design self-rocking chairs or mechanical beds that lulled you to sleep. They used clockwork gears or small steam attachments. The idea never caught on widely; folks found them either creepy or untrustworthy at night. Perhaps a sign that not every mechanical dream was practical.

---

19. Social Shifts: Working-Class Scenes

The industrial changes did not just impact machines; they reshaped society:

- **Factory Towns**: Places like Manchester or Leeds in England exploded in population. Rows of cramped houses for workers sprang up. Chimneys spewed black smoke. Observers described "dark satanic mills," referencing the grim setting. Children roamed streets, half-clothed, while parents worked long shifts.

- **Movement to Cities**: Millions left rural areas, chasing factory jobs. Overcrowding led to disease outbreaks like cholera. Public health measures lagged behind. The stench of sewage in open gutters was normal. Some philanthropic factory owners built model villages with better housing—like the Cadburys or the Salts in later decades—but that was still rare in the earlier stage.

- **Class Tensions**: A new industrial middle class (factory owners, merchants) clashed with aristocrats who owned land. Workers formed friendly societies or unions, though early unions were sometimes illegal. Police and soldiers intervened in strikes. This swirling unrest was all part of the industrial birth pangs, as society struggled to adapt to factory life.

20. Steps Toward the Next Century

By the mid- to late-19th century, these "crazy inventions" and surprising advances had laid the foundation for further transformations. Steamships crossed oceans regularly, forging global trade networks. Railways laced continents, letting people travel hundreds of miles in a day, something unthinkable before. Telegraph lines spanned countries, shrinking distances in communication. Factories pumped out textiles, iron goods, and soon steel, ushering what we might call the second industrial wave.

Nevertheless, we must remember that not all regions industrialized at the same pace. Some stuck to old crafts, others jumped eagerly into mechanization. The tension between tradition and modernity raged. Many found the noise, smoke, and slums unbearable, longing for pastoral life. Others believed industrial progress was unstoppable, a force of nature in its own right.

Looking back, the start of industrial change was a wild time—machines improved daily, ideas came and went, and society balanced on a tightrope of wonder and worry. In the next and final chapter of our journey (Chapter 20), we will see how the nineteenth century continued to shift—politically, culturally, and technologically—still just before fully entering modern times. This will wrap our entire exploration, showing how the bizarre transformations of the past set the stage for the world that would soon arrive.

CHAPTER 20

Nineteenth Century Shifts: Strange Events Before Modern Times

The nineteenth century was a bridge between old and new. Revolutions—both political and technological—reshaped continents. While we often call it "pre-modern," this period set the final stepping stones into what we recognize as modern times. Empires expanded, nationalism rose, and new ideologies like socialism or romanticism swirled around. Scientists debated evolution, while explorers mapped remote corners of the globe. And behind these sweeping changes lay smaller, odder stories—moments of weirdness or confusion that show how big changes affect real people.

In this last chapter, we will uncover some of these strange nineteenth-century happenings that remain overshadowed by grand narratives. We will see odd medical breakthroughs, bizarre exhibitions, quack science, spiritual movements, and global influences that set the stage for the twentieth century. From wild utopian communities to hidden cults, from strange political fiascos to final glimpses of old customs, we will watch the clock tick ever closer to modern times—yet still linger in a world not fully modern in its beliefs or technology. Let us take this final leap into the nineteenth century, discovering the weird events that closed out our historical exploration.

1. Political Earthquakes and Unusual Revolutions

The Napoleonic Wars ended around 1815, but Europe kept shaking with revolutions in 1830, 1848, and beyond. People demanded constitutions, national unification, or independence from empires:

- **1848's "Springtime of the Peoples"**: Revolutions erupted in France, Germany, Italy, and Austria. Monarchs fled, then returned. The swirl of liberal and nationalist ideas was chaotic. Some revolutionaries were radical students or intellectuals with Romantic ideals. Others were workers wanting better wages. The weird alliance across classes often collapsed from internal tension.

- **Strange Slogans and Flags**: Each revolt had its own flag and motto. In some German states, revolutionaries used the black-red-gold tricolor, now Germany's flag. People pinned symbols like laurel wreaths or wore ribbons proclaiming "freedom or death." Outsiders joked that you could not keep track of who was revolting which day.

- **France's Short-Lived Republic**: In 1848, France briefly became a republic again, but soon Napoleon's nephew, Louis-Napoleon, seized power, becoming Emperor Napoleon III in 1852. The scandal: a democracy that turned imperial so fast. It proved how the century's politics often veered between radical shifts and old patterns.

2. Holy Alliances and Odd Diplomatic Pacts

After Napoleon's defeat, European powers formed alliances to maintain order:

- **The Holy Alliance**: Proposed by Tsar Alexander I (Russia), it joined Russia, Austria, and Prussia in 1815. They pledged to uphold Christian values in politics. Some diplomats found it "naïve," mocking the Tsar's mix of mysticism and power. Meanwhile, the alliance aimed to crush revolutionary movements.

- **Concert of Europe**: Britain, France, Austria, Russia, and Prussia periodically met to settle disputes. This was new—great powers negotiating in conferences, not just warring. But it also meant smaller nations had less say. The sense that a few giants carved up spheres of influence created tension, fueling conspiracies about "secret deals" in grand ballrooms.

- **Latin American Revolutions**: As Spain's colonies in the Americas broke away in the early 19th century, Europe was divided on whether to help Spain reconquer them or not. The Holy Alliance disliked revolutions, but Britain wanted trade with independent republics. This odd mismatch led to minimal European intervention, letting new nations like Gran Colombia or Mexico form. Observers marveled at how Europe's coalition ironically allowed huge political changes abroad.

3. Romanticism and the Odd Obsession with Emotion

Culturally, the 19th century saw **Romanticism** flourish. Writers, painters, and composers stressed passion, nature, and individual feelings over Enlightenment reason:

- **Gothic Revival**: People revived medieval styles in architecture, literature, and art. Castles were redesigned with fake battlements, and novels like Mary Shelley's "Frankenstein" (1818) combined science with gothic horror. That was considered scandalous: a monster made of reanimated body parts? Readers were both repelled and fascinated.

- **Nature Worship**: Romantics hiked mountains or roamed forests seeking the "sublime." They believed encountering raw nature brought spiritual insight. Poets like Wordsworth or Coleridge wandered the Lake District, rhapsodizing about lakes and daffodils. Some city folks thought them odd for praising storms and crags, rather than comfortable parlors.

- **Emotional Outbursts**: Romantic heroes in poems often raged or wept openly. Audiences found this enthralling or ridiculous. Men in frilly shirts, painting dramatic landscapes, fueled satirical cartoons. The tension: a society used to stiff manners now tolerating public expressions of tears and euphoria. Strange yet liberating.

---

4. The Great Famine in Ireland and Bizarre Reactions

Between 1845 and 1852, Ireland's potato crops failed repeatedly (the Potato Famine). It led to mass starvation and migration:

- **Dependence on Potatoes**: Many Irish peasants relied on potatoes for survival. When a fungal blight turned potatoes black, they had little else. This heavy reliance might seem odd, but potatoes yield high nutrition in small patches of land.

- **Absentee Landlords**: Many landlords, living in England, demanded rent even as tenants starved. Evictions soared. The British government's slow or limited relief seemed scandalous, with some officials advocating laissez-faire economics—letting the market "sort it out." Meanwhile, families starved or fled on "coffin ships" to North America.

- **Quack Remedies**: Some newspapers offered "cures" for potato blight, like sprinkling them with holy water or burying them in seaweed. Farmers were desperate, trying everything. The scope of tragedy was massive—over a million died, millions emigrated. It shaped Irish history, fueling resentment and diaspora communities worldwide.

---

5. The Crimean War: Mismanaged Chaos

Fought from 1853 to 1856, the **Crimean War** pitted Russia against an alliance of the Ottoman Empire, Britain, France, and Sardinia. It had bizarre elements:

- **Charge of the Light Brigade**: The British cavalry famously misunderstood orders at the Battle of Balaclava (1854), galloping into Russian artillery. This near-suicidal act became a patriotic poem by Tennyson, but also a scandal showing incompetent leadership.

- **Terrible Conditions**: Soldiers on both sides suffered disease, poor supplies, and harsh winters. Florence Nightingale's nursing efforts revealed the shocking inefficiency of the British army's medical system. Her lamp-lit rounds saved many but also exposed how unprepared the military was for modern conflict.

- **First Media War?**: Reporters like William Howard Russell sent dispatches back to British newspapers, describing real-time horrors. The public was outraged. Photographers like Roger Fenton took early battlefield photos—though often staged or sanitized. This new press coverage changed how wars were perceived, turning public opinion into a major force. People found it odd to see images of battlefront camps or wounded soldiers in newspapers.

6. Opium Wars and Unequal Treaties

In East Asia, Britain and other Western powers forced open China's markets in the mid-19th century:

- **Opium as a Trade Weapon**: Britain imported tea from China but struggled to find goods the Chinese wanted. So they exported Indian opium to China, hooking many Chinese on the drug. The Qing government tried banning opium, leading to clashes.

- **First Opium War (1839–1842)**: British gunboats easily defeated Chinese junks, capturing key coastal cities. The resulting **Treaty of Nanjing** forced China to cede Hong Kong and open ports. Chinese citizens felt humiliated. Foreigners were perplexed that an empire so large seemed militarily weak, but realized China's navy was outdated.

- **Strange Scenes**: British sailors described Chinese officials destroying crates of opium. Meanwhile, Western merchants smuggled more in. This moral scandal—profiting from addictive drugs—was rationalized as "free trade." The mismatch between Confucian moral codes and Western commerce was stark. Over time, more wars followed, deepening China's "century of humiliation."

---

7. American Frontier and the Gold Rush Oddities

Across the Atlantic, the United States expanded westward, with dramatic events in the 19th century:

- **California Gold Rush (1848–1855)**: News of gold at Sutter's Mill sparked a global rush. People from China, Europe, and Latin America flooded to California. Towns sprouted overnight. Lawlessness reigned. Strange "get rich quick" schemes multiplied, including bogus "gold magnets" or potions claiming to locate veins of gold.

- **Boomtown Chaos**: Places like San Francisco exploded from a sleepy village to a bustling city. Saloons, gambling halls, and brothels dominated. Vigilante justice replaced formal courts. The frantic pace was shocking to travelers used to stable societies.

- **Trail of Tears**: Meanwhile, the US government forcibly removed Native American tribes from their eastern lands. The Cherokee, among others, marched west under brutal conditions (1830s). This harsh policy contrasted with the glowing "Manifest Destiny" hype. Observers found the mismatch between a gold-fueled dream and the harsh reality of Native displacement unsettling.

---

8. Spiritualism and Séance Craze

In the mid-19th century, a movement called **Spiritualism** swept across Western countries. Mediums claimed to talk to the dead:

- **Fox Sisters (1848, USA)**: Margaret and Kate Fox said they heard "rappings" from a spirit in their home. They became famous, performing demonstrations. People across America and Europe held séances, eager to contact lost loved ones.

- **Table-Turning**: Séance-goers placed hands on a table, which supposedly moved or rose under spirit influence. Skeptics called it trickery, but many found it thrilling. Even respected figures like scientist William Crookes tested mediums. Some illusions were exposed, but believers persisted.

- **Fashion of the Afterlife**: Middle-class salons hosted weekly séances. Hosts served tea while mediums entered trances. "Spirit photography" emerged, with ghostly faces appearing in photos. Most were double exposures, but the curiosity soared. This mania for the supernatural matched a time of rapid change—people yearned for comfort in a shifting world.

9. Darwin's Theory: Evolution Shakes Society

In 1859, Charles Darwin published **On the Origin of Species**, proposing natural selection as the mechanism of evolution:

- **Scandal Among the Pious**: Many saw it as challenging the biblical creation story. Caricatures showed Darwin as an ape. Debates raged in newspapers and parlors. Some clergymen tried to reconcile the idea with Scripture, while others called Darwin "the devil's teacher."

- **Strange Misinterpretations**: People joked that if humans came from apes, soon we might regress into gorillas. Or that moral values would vanish. Darwin himself was shy and avoided public spats, but the swirl of controversy was unstoppable. The tension underscored how science could rock deep-rooted beliefs.

- **International Impact**: Translations appeared fast. In some places, censors banned the book as heresy. Others embraced it as proof nature was dynamic. Even so, many misunderstood the concept, mixing it with racist or eugenic ideas later on. The initial shock and confusion showed how big leaps in knowledge could spark bizarre reactions.

---

10. Unification Moves: Germany, Italy, and Odd Symbolism

The 19th century saw new nations forming. Italy and Germany, once fragmented, unified under leaders like Cavour, Garibaldi, or Bismarck:

- **Garibaldi's Redshirts**: Giuseppe Garibaldi led volunteers in red shirts to conquer southern Italy. People found it eccentric that they wore bright red in battle, making them easy targets. But it also boosted morale. Southern peasants greeted them as liberators, though many were unsure about this "Italy" concept.

- **Otto von Bismarck's "Blood and Iron"**: Prussia's prime minister orchestrated German unification through wars with Denmark, Austria, and France. His approach was ruthless but cunning. At times, Bismarck spread false telegrams to provoke enemies. People marveled at how a single statesman manipulated Europe. The "blood and iron" speech became infamous, symbolizing realpolitik over romance.

- **National Symbols**: As these new countries formed, they needed flags, anthems, and heroes. Memorial statues popped up everywhere. Some folks found the sudden wave of patriotism forced. Others embraced it wholeheartedly. The tension between local identities and the new "German" or "Italian" identity was confusing, leading to lingering regional pride.

---

11. Franco-Prussian War and the Birth of Modern Germany

In 1870–1871, tensions between France and Prussia exploded:

- **Ems Telegram Trick**: Bismarck edited a diplomatic telegram from King Wilhelm to make it seem insulting to France. Outraged, Emperor Napoleon III declared war. Bismarck got the southern German states to unite with Prussia. Observers called this manipulation brilliant but dishonest—shocking that a war started over a doctored note.

- **Siege of Paris**: Prussian armies encircled Paris. Parisians ate zoo animals and rats when food ran out, which was extremely odd to foreign correspondents. Hot air balloons carried mail out of the city, possibly a throwback to earlier balloon mania.

- **German Empire Proclaimed**: The final blow? The new German Empire was proclaimed in the Hall of Mirrors at Versailles (1871). This humiliated France. The shift from scattered German states to a mighty empire so quickly was a marvel. The political map of Europe was redrawn, overshadowing the weirdness that a faked telegram had sparked it all.

12. Colonial Scramble: Berlin Conference and Odd Boundaries

As the century advanced, European powers scrambled for colonies, especially in Africa:

- **Berlin Conference (1884–1885)**: European diplomats gathered to partition Africa among themselves, ignoring ethnic or historical lines. No African leaders were invited. The result was bizarre borders that cut through tribes or merged rival groups. Africans found themselves forced into new "countries" without choice.

- **Rubber Horrors**: In the Congo Free State, ruled personally by Belgium's King Leopold II, local people were forced to extract rubber. Brutal punishments (cutting off hands) for failing quotas became known. This scandal eventually forced Leopold to cede control to the Belgian government. People worldwide were horrified at the cruelty in pursuit of raw materials.

- **Symbolic Explorations**: Adventurers like Henry Morton Stanley or Pierre Savorgnan de Brazza "claimed" vast lands by planting flags, signing shady treaties with local chiefs who did not fully grasp European legal language. This odd practice turned entire regions into "colonies" on paper. The mismatch between local reality and foreign contracts was huge, fueling long-term conflicts.

---

13. Quack Science: Phrenology, Mesmerism, and Others

The 19th century loved grand theories, but not all were valid:

- **Phrenology**: Measuring skull bumps to judge personality or intellect. Parlors had skull models with labeled "organs" for friendship, combativeness, or cunning. People took it seriously, using it for job interviews or matchmaking. Critics said it was nonsense. Indeed, no scientific basis existed, but the fad lingered for decades.

- **Mesmerism**: Dr. Franz Mesmer believed in "animal magnetism," where invisible fluids in living beings could be balanced. He performed dramatic sessions where patients convulsed or fainted, claiming cures for illness. Society was divided: some found it miraculous, others saw it as trickery. This eventually influenced hypnosis research, but its theatrical style was quite bizarre.

- **Electrotherapy**: Inventors sold electric belts or "galvanic" devices to cure everything from arthritis to laziness. Patients felt a mild shock. Snake-oil salesmen thrived, claiming electricity was the vital force. Genuine progress in electromagnetism existed, but also an avalanche of quack gadgets. People's fascination with new "energy" overshadowed caution.

14. The American Civil War: Ironclads and Strange Reforms

From 1861 to 1865, the US was torn by civil war. While it was a major modern conflict, it had pre-modern weirdness:

- **Ironclad Ships**: The USS Monitor and CSS Virginia revolutionized naval warfare. Their strange iron hulls and turret guns baffled onlookers. The Monitor had a rotating turret that resembled a "tin can on a raft." People predicted future wars would see entire fleets of metal monsters.

- **Emancipation as a War Measure**: Abraham Lincoln's Emancipation Proclamation (1863) freed slaves in rebel states. Some considered it an odd strategy—using moral grounds as a military tactic. Over time, it became a milestone for ending slavery, but the politics behind it were complicated.

- **Medical Horrors**: Field hospitals used saws for amputations at shocking rates. Minie balls (bullets) caused devastating injuries. Thousands died from infection. The push for better sanitation started, though some doctors clung to outdated methods. Many soldiers returned with missing limbs, prompting inventions of improved prosthetics. The half-modern, half-archaic nature of the war was unsettling.

15. The Meiji Restoration in Japan: Rapid Westernization

After centuries of samurai rule (Tokugawa Shogunate), Japan abruptly modernized in 1868:

- **Emperor Restored**: The young Emperor Meiji became a symbol of new national unity. Samurai domains dissolved, feudal privileges vanished. Western experts were hired to build railways, factories, and an army. People in rural areas found it shocking to see telegraph poles or men in Western suits.

- **Samurai Discontent**: Some samurai lost their status. Rebellions like the Satsuma Rebellion (1877) broke out, led by Saigo Takamori. They wore armor against modern rifles, a tragic mismatch. Their final stand was romantic but futile, marking the end of the old ways.

- **Mixed Customs**: Court ceremonies combined old Shinto rituals with Western-style ball gowns for ladies. The government encouraged eating beef (once taboo) and short hair for men. Observers from abroad wrote about the "walking collision of East and West," seeing men in top hats but still bowing deeply in Shinto shrines. A bizarre transitional society.

16. Suez Canal and Panama Railroad: Changing Trade Routes

Large engineering projects altered global commerce:

- **Suez Canal (Opened 1869)**: French engineer Ferdinand de Lesseps led the construction across Egypt, linking the Mediterranean to the Red Sea. European ships no longer had to sail around Africa. The canal was seen as a modern marvel. But forced labor and harsh conditions for local Egyptians sparked controversy. Some said it was a "canal of blood."

- **Panama Railroad (1855)**: Before the Panama Canal, an American-funded railroad crossed the isthmus. Thousands died of tropical diseases or poor conditions. Passengers traveling from the

US East Coast to California used it, cutting months off sea voyages around Cape Horn. The idea of a railroad in a malaria-ridden jungle was quite extraordinary, yet profitable for a time.

- **French Failure at Panama Canal**: De Lesseps tried building a sea-level Panama Canal in the 1880s. Disease, corruption, and engineering challenges doomed it. Headlines in Paris labeled it a scandal. People lost investments, calling it the "Panama Affair." The fiasco showed how even heroic engineers could fail in punishing tropical climates.

---

17. Literary Oddities: Frankenstein to Sherlock Holmes

Literature in the 19th century gave us many bizarre ideas:

- **Frankenstein (1818)** by Mary Shelley introduced the concept of a scientist reanimating a corpse. Readers were shocked by the "man playing God" theme. Some insisted the novel was sinful or insane. Yet it shaped the entire genre of science fiction.

- **Edgar Allan Poe's Macabre**: Poe's horror tales and detective stories unsettled audiences. He explored madness, premature burial, and cryptic murders. Some critics called him "morbid," but fans adored the dark atmosphere. Later, detective fiction like Sherlock Holmes built on Poe's style, albeit in a more rational form.

- **Lewis Carroll's Wonderland**: "Alice's Adventures in Wonderland" (1865) seemed like a children's fantasy, but it had peculiar logic puzzles and parodies of Victorian manners. Talking animals, shape-changing potions—some said Carroll was mocking society. The bizarre dreamlike story left many readers bewildered. Over time, it became beloved.

18. Odd Social Experiments: Utopian Societies

Many 19th-century thinkers tried to form utopian communities, testing new social models:

- **Robert Owen's New Lanark**: A mill town in Scotland where Owen improved conditions, reduced working hours, and provided education. Visitors found it odd to see well-treated workers in bright, clean houses. Some labeled him a dreamer; others admired the success in raising productivity.

- **Oneida Community (America)**: Founded by John Humphrey Noyes in 1848, it practiced "complex marriage," where all adult members were married to each other. They shared property and child-rearing. Outsiders saw it as scandalous, calling them a "free-love cult." The community lasted decades, making silverware to fund their lifestyle.

- **Brook Farm (Massachusetts)**: A transcendentalist experiment (1841–1847) with shared labor and intellectual pursuits. Writers like Nathaniel Hawthorne joined briefly. They tried to blend farm chores with high-minded discussions, but finances collapsed. Some joked that too many people wanted to read poetry, not muck stables.

---

19. Final Wars and Conflicts Before Modern Times

As the century closed, conflicts hinted at the 20th century's scale:

- **Franco-Prussian War**: We discussed it. It set Germany as a new power.

- **Scramble for Africa**: Led to more colonial wars.

- **Boxer Rebellion in China (1899–1901)**: Anti-foreigner uprising. International forces crushed it. The mismatch between the Boxers' spiritual beliefs (thinking they were invulnerable to bullets) and modern guns was tragic. It signaled China's vulnerability, further pushing it toward modernization.

- **US Civil War's Aftermath**: Reconstruction in the South was chaotic. Freed slaves faced new forms of oppression. Industrial growth soared in the North. The seeds of future American power were planted, though inequality festered.

- **Russo-Japanese War (1904–1905)**: Technically in the early 20th century, but the lead-up started in the 19th. Japan's modernization let it challenge Russia. Observers found it shocking that an Asian nation defeated a European power. This signaled a major shift from the old colonial worldview.

---

20. Closing the Curtain on a Transitional Age

By the end of the 19th century, steam trains crisscrossed continents, telegraphs spread instant messages, and giant steamships navigated oceans. Empires locked horns over distant colonies, new nations formed in Europe, and revolutionary ideas like socialism or women's suffrage gained momentum. The world was on the brink of the 20th century, where automobiles, airplanes, radio, and eventually world wars would redefine everything once again.

In many ways, the 19th century was a final showcase of old styles—kings and queens still reigned in grand palaces, horse-drawn carriages clattered on cobblestones, and rural traditions endured. Yet behind the scenes, factories, public health movements, and global trade networks signaled unstoppable transformation. People lived in a swirl of excitement, anxiety, hope, and confusion. The odd events we have seen—from scientific quackery to spiritual séances, from bizarre political fiascos to utopian communes—reflect how societies struggled to adapt to rapid change.

Thus ends our exploration of Crazy History Facts across 20 chapters, spanning from ancient civilizations to the cusp of modern times. We have witnessed how every era had its share of strange beliefs, surprising inventions, and scandalous affairs. Whether it was barbarian tribes, medieval knights, Renaissance wonders, or industrial leaps, people navigated big changes with a blend of fear, creativity, and sometimes comedic misunderstanding. As we stand at the threshold of the modern age, we can look back and marvel at humanity's endless capacity for both folly and genius—always forging ahead, never quite losing the quirkiness that makes history so captivating.

Help Us Share Your Thoughts!

Dear reader,

Thank you for spending your time with this book. We hope it brought you enjoyment and a few new ideas to think about. If there was anything that didn't work for you, or if you have suggestions on how we can improve, please let us know at **kontakt@skriuwer.com**. Your feedback means a lot to us and helps us make our books even better.

If you enjoyed this book, we would be very grateful if you left a review on the site where you purchased it. Your review not only helps other readers find our books, but also encourages us to keep creating more stories and materials that you'll love.

By choosing Skriuwer, you're also supporting **Frisian**—a minority language mainly spoken in the northern Netherlands. Although **Frisian** has a rich history, the number of speakers is shrinking, and it's at risk of dying out. Your purchase helps fund resources to preserve and promote this language, such as educational programs and learning tools. If you'd like to learn more about Frisian or even start learning it yourself, please visit **www.learnfrisian.com**.

Thank you for being part of our community. We look forward to sharing more books with you in the future.

Warm regards,
The Skriuwer Team

www.ingramcontent.com/pod-product-compliance
Lightning Source LLC
LaVergne TN
LVHW012035070526
838202LV00056B/5507